AF840236

PRIVATE INTERNATIONAL LAW IN RUSSIA

This book provides the first comprehensive introduction to Russian private international law (PIL) for an international lawyer.

The book carefully examines the applicable conflict of law and jurisdictional rules on the basis of the relevant statutory provisions, case law, and doctrinal writings developed in Russia for the purposes of dealing with cross-border commercial issues. It covers topics that will be of particular interest to comparative scholars, for instance, the sources of PIL in Russia, including international conventions and treaties; party autonomy and the choice of law by the parties; determination of applicable law in the absence of choice by the parties; public policy exceptions and overriding mandatory provisions; and many more. These and other topics serve as an entry point to the hybrid system of law that Russian PIL is: modelled on European law but characterised by its Soviet past.

Volume 38 in the series Studies in Private International Law

Studies in Private International Law

Recent titles in the series

Economic Sanctions in EU Private International Law
Tamás Szabados

Clawback Law in the Context of Succession
Jayne Holliday

Place of Performance: A Comparative Analysis
Chukwuma Okoli

Private International Law in Nigeria
Chukwuma Okoli and Richard Oppong

Planning the Future of Cross Border Families: A Path Through Coordination
Edited by Ilaria Viarengo and Francesca Villata

The Private International Law of Authentic Instruments
Jonathan Fitchen

The Hague Judgments Convention and Commonwealth Model Law: A Pragmatic Perspective
Abubakri Yekini

A Guide to Global Private International Law
Edited by Paul Beaumont and Jayne Holliday

Parental Child Abduction to Islamic Law Countries
Nazia Yaqub

The Application of Foreign Law in the British and German Courts
Alex Critchley

The HCCH 2019 Judgments Convention: Cornerstones, Prospects, Outlook
Edited by Matthias Weller, João Ribeiro-Bidaoui, Moritz Brinkmann and Nina Dethloff

Jurisdiction Over Non-EU Defendants: Should the Brussels Ia Regulation be Extended?
Edited by Tobias Lutzi, Ennio Piovesani and Dora Zgrabljic Rotar

Private International Law and Competition Litigation in a Global Context
Mihail Danov

Private International Law in Russia
Edited by Anton Asoskov, Daria Levina, and Milana Karayanidi

Private International Law in Russia

Edited by
Anton Asoskov
Daria Levina
and
Milana Karayanidi

•HART•
OXFORD • LONDON • NEW YORK • NEW DELHI • SYDNEY

HART PUBLISHING

Bloomsbury Publishing Plc

Kemp House, Chawley Park, Cumnor Hill, Oxford, OX2 9PH, UK

1385 Broadway, New York, NY 10018, USA

29 Earlsfort Terrace, Dublin 2, Ireland

HART PUBLISHING, the Hart/Stag logo, BLOOMSBURY and the Diana logo are trademarks of Bloomsbury Publishing Plc

First published in Great Britain 2024

Copyright © Anton Asoskov, Daria Levina, and Milana Karayanidi and Contributors severally 2024

Anton Asoskov, Daria Levina, and Milana Karayanidi and Contributors have asserted their right under the Copyright, Designs and Patents Act 1988 to be identified as Authors of this work.

All rights reserved. No part of this publication may be reproduced or transmitted in any form or by any means, electronic or mechanical, including photocopying, recording, or any information storage or retrieval system, without prior permission in writing from the publishers.

While every care has been taken to ensure the accuracy of this work, no responsibility for loss or damage occasioned to any person acting or refraining from action as a result of any statement in it can be accepted by the authors, editors or publishers.

All UK Government legislation and other public sector information used in the work is Crown Copyright ©. All House of Lords and House of Commons information used in the work is Parliamentary Copyright ©. This information is reused under the terms of the Open Government Licence v3.0 (http://www.nationalarchives.gov.uk/doc/open-government-licence/version/3) except where otherwise stated.

All Eur-lex material used in the work is © European Union, http://eur-lex.europa.eu/, 1998–2024.

A catalogue record for this book is available from the British Library.

A catalogue record for this book is available from the Library of Congress.

Library of Congress Control Number: 2024933295

ISBN: HB: 978-1-50996-431-4
ePDF: 978-1-50996-433-8
ePub: 978-1-50996-432-1

Typeset by Compuscript Ltd, Shannon

To find out more about our authors and books visit www.hartpublishing.co.uk. Here you will find extracts, author information, details of forthcoming events and the option to sign up for our newsletters.

SERIES EDITOR'S PREFACE

This is a very readable account of Private International Law in Russia. The editors are an excellent blend of the very experienced (personal involvement in the major reforms of 2013) and the rising stars of the discipline. The individual chapters are all written by experts with impeccable English and a uniform level of clarity and economy of words. The editors are to be congratulated that the book reads as a coherent whole rather than a disparate collection of chapters by different authors.

The book gives a brief history of the subject in Russia showing its foundations in the nineteenth century. It reveals that in general it can be said that Russia follows a classically continental European approach to private international law. Multilateral conflict rules are favoured and the 21st century reforms have moved away, at least in the law of obligations, from the rigid applicable law rules favoured in the Soviet era. Many of the provisions are found in the Civil Code. In recent times the Russian Supreme Court has acted as a quasi-legislature in giving definitive guidance to lower courts as to how to interpret some provisions of Russian private international law. This guidance does not arise from having to decide specific cases.

Russian private international law has been significantly modernised in the twenty first century. The law applicable to contractual obligations is very similar to Rome I. The law applicable to non-contractual obligations has in part been inspired by Rome II but is materially different in many respects with some interesting subtleties, notably on product liability and unfair competition. Russia briefly dabbled with bringing trusts into their private international law but now appear not to recognise foreign trusts at all. It would be great if Russia were to become a party to the Hague Trusts Convention to create a clear framework for Russia to recognise foreign trusts. Russia, in my view wisely, has not followed the EU in the law of succession by abolishing scission. It takes an expansive view of what constitutes immoveables, governed by the *lex situs*, including aircraft and ships. However, the connecting factor applicable to the succession of moveables is the same as the EU, the last habitual residence of the deceased, even if habitual residence has a different meaning from that used in the Hague Conference on Private International Law or in the EU. Interestingly persons under 14 years old have the same habitual residence as their legal representatives, usually their parents, but the chapter does not make clear what happens when the parents have different habitual residences. It does make it clear that the actual residence of the child under 14 is irrelevant.

In terms of the global framework of private international law as understood in this series (ie jurisdiction, applicable law, recognition and enforcement of foreign judgments and international cooperation in relation to cross-border litigation) Russia is party to some of the core Hague Conference on Private International Law Conventions (notably Service, Evidence, Child Abduction and Child Protection). This is noted in the book but these Conventions and the practice of Russia in relation to them are not discussed. Hopefully they will be in a future edition. The book highlights that in Russia Private International Law is understood to extend to the harmonisation of substantive private law but correctly does not go into detail on any of those matters.

Recent developments in Russian private international law, linked to a number of States being classified as unfriendly by Russia, are carefully explained. In the absence of treaty relations, recognition and enforcement of foreign judgments in Russia is based on reciprocity. The book records that Russia has signed the Hague Judgments Convention 2019 but gives no insight into whether or when Russia will ratify it. One imagines that in the current climate ratification will not be pursued because the existing Parties (EU, Ukraine and Uruguay and hopefully soon the UK) might be likely to refuse to accept treaty relations with Russia under this Convention as permitted by Article 29. The book does record that reciprocity is in decline as a basis for recognition and enforcement of foreign judgments in Russia because of concerns in Russia that States which previously recognised and enforced Russian judgments will not do so in the current climate.

The book records that in response to sanctions being imposed on Russian citizens in a number of countries, Russia has created an exclusive jurisdiction for its citizens who are affected by those sanctions to litigate in Russia and the Russian courts have been empowered to grant anti-suit injunctions trying to prevent litigation in other States against Russian citizens affected by the sanctions.

We have to hope for a change in the current climate whereby the Russian government will respect the rule of law in the public international law sphere. This in turn will create a context where Russia can ratify the Hague Judgments Convention 2019 and mutual recognition and enforcement of judgments in civil or commercial matters can become the norm between Russia and the other parties to that Convention.

In the meantime, the largely technical nature of private international law allows the subject to provide a bridge between Russia and other countries even in the current climate. That narrow, technical bridge can hopefully be widened when the climate improves rather than having to be completely rebuilt. So, if parties choose a foreign law to govern their contract this is still respected in Russia and pretty much everywhere in the world. Of course, the limits on that freedom brought about by overriding mandatory norms or public policy are likely to be greater in these troubled times but the underlying principle remains.

This is an excellent book that reveals a lot about Russian private international law in an easily digestible way. It is fully up to date and written in a clear and erudite way. It is a very welcome addition to the Series.

Paul R Beaumont FRSE
Professor of Private International Law
University of Stirling

CONTENTS

LIST OF CONTRIBUTORS

Editors

Anton Asoskov is a visiting professor at the Reichman University in Haifa, Israel; until 2022, he was a full professor in the Department of Civil Law at the Faculty of Law of the Lomonosov Moscow State University. He received his doctoral and habilitation degrees from Lomonosov Moscow State University and an LLM degree with honours from the Russian School of Private Law at the Alexeev Research Centre of Private Law. He has been a member of the Working Group at the Council for the Codification of Civil Legislation responsible for preparing the amendments to the Russian Civil Code (Section 'Private International Law') and played a leading role in the 2013 reform of the Russian PIL.

Daria Levina is a PhD researcher at the European University Institute in Florence, Italy. She holds an LLM from Harvard Law School and a PhD from Lomonosov Moscow State University. She has worked for the Permanent Court of Arbitration in The Hague, The Netherlands, and for an international law firm in Moscow and Frankfurt. She has published extensively on conflict of laws in the leading Russian law journals. Her first book, devoted to the exploration of the principle of *lex propria in foro proprio* in the European and Russian private international law, came out in February 2021.

Milana Karayanidi is a managing associate at Dentons in Washington DC. She holds a PhD from Trinity College Dublin and an LLM from Harvard Law School where she reviewed articles for publication in the *Harvard International Law Journal*. Milana has published on Russian private international law and civil procedure, including with Oxford University Press and the *American Journal of Comparative Law*. Her book titled *Rethinking Jurisdiction in Private International Law* was released by Hart Publishing in 2020.

Contributors

Daria Astakhova is a dispute resolution associate at Audit-Duprey-Fekl, a boutique law firm based in Paris. She holds a PhD in law from the Moscow State Institute of International Relations (MGIMO-University) where she defended her doctoral dissertation exploring the delocalisation trends in international commercial arbitration, and an LLM from the University of Paris I: Panthéon-Sorbonne. Daria's practice focuses on commercial and investment arbitration, international commercial litigation, and recognition and enforcement of arbitral awards. She has published in Russian and French legal journals.

Egor Chilikov is a founding partner of Petrol Chilikov law firm, a boutique law firm based in Moscow. He is also a visiting lecturer at the Lomonosov Moscow State University. He has over 10 years of experience in cross-border disputes, both before state courts and in arbitration. Egor has acted as counsel and advised clients on commercial and investment arbitration matters under major arbitration rules, including ICAC (Moscow), LCIA, SCC, ICC, ICSID and UNCITRAL.[1] Prior to establishing Petrol Chilikov, Egor worked in disputes teams at international and Russian law firms and for a disputes funder.

Ivan Chuprunov is an Assistant Professor at the Russian School of Private Law, where he has been teaching corporate law since 2018. He is also a counsel at the corporate practice of Linklaters, Milan. Ivan holds a PhD in law from Lomonosov Moscow State University, where he defended his dissertation on pre-emptive rights in respect of shares in a private company, and an LLM degree from the Russian School of Private Law.

Olga Kamenskaya is an in-house dispute resolution counsel in Moscow. She holds a law degree from the Lomonosov Moscow State University and an LLM from the Russian School of Private Law in Moscow where she focused on private international law and successfully defended her master's thesis exploring the overriding mandatory norms of private international law. She has been a DAAD[2] scholar at the University of Jena, Germany and holds a certificate in the fundamentals of German law which she completed during her stay at the Humboldt University of Berlin. She has extensive experience in cross-border commercial dispute resolution.

Tatiana Lyubarskaya is the general counsel of one the largest EdTech companies in Russia. She holds a PhD in law from the Lomonosov Moscow State University where she defended the doctoral dissertation on the conflict of laws regulation of property rights, an LLM from the Russian School of Private Law in Moscow, and a first law degree from the Southern Federal University in Rostov-on-Don. She published extensively on conflict of laws in the leading Russian law journals and has participated in The Hague Academy of Private International Law.

Andrey Panov is a counsel at Allen & Overy's dispute resolution practice based in Dubai, the UAE. He holds a magister juris degree from the University of Oxford and a first law degree from the Lomonosov Moscow State University. Andrey has over 12 years of experience representing clients before Russian and foreign courts, as well as before arbitral tribunals. He regularly acts as lead counsel in his cases and has represented clients in many high-profile commercial and corporate disputes at

[1] International Commercial Arbitration Court (ICAC); London Court of International Arbitration (LCIA); Stockholm Chamber of Commerce Arbitration Institute (SCC); International Chamber of Commerce (ICC); International Centre for Settlement of Investment Disputes (ICSID); United Nations Commission on International Trade Law (UNCITRAL).

[2] Deutscher Akademische Austauschdienst (DAAD) – German Academic Exchange Service.

all levels of the Russian courts, with some of his cases becoming precedents cited in the information letters of the Presidium of the Supreme *Arbitrazh* Court of the Russian Federation.

Georgy Shashero is a managing associate at ELWI, a law firm based in Moscow (formerly Latham & Watkins). Prior to that, he was a dispute resolution associate for the A1 investment fund and the Akin Gump Strauss Hauer & Feld office in Moscow. He holds an LLM degree from the National Research University – Higher School of Economics, and a first law degree from the Moscow State Institute of International Relations (MGIMO-University). He is an active member of the LCIA – YIAG and Young ICCA[3] and a regular contributor to the *Global Arbitration Review* and Russian legal journals.

Andrey Shirvindt is a senior research fellow at the Max Planck Institute for Comparative and International Private Law in Hamburg. He holds a PhD from the Institute of State and Law of the Russian Academy of Sciences and two master's degrees, one from the University of Manchester and another from the Russian School of Private Law. Until 2022, Andrey was an associate professor in the Department of Civil Law at the Faculty of Law of the Lomonosov Moscow State University.

Gleb Sudarev is a PhD student at Lomonosov Moscow State University, Russia. His doctoral research concerns contributory negligence in tort law. He holds a first law degree and an LLM degree from the Lomonosov Moscow State University. He has published on non-contractual obligations in the leading Russian law journals and, together with Egor Chilikov, co-wrote a report on Russia for *Civil Liability for Human Rights Violations: A Handbook for Practitioners* for the Bonavero Institute of Human Rights at the University of Oxford.

[3] Young International Arbitration Group (YIAG); International Council for Commercial Arbitration (ICCA).

TABLE OF CASES

TABLE OF CASES

TABLE OF LEGISLATION

Acts of International Law

EU Legislation

Russian Legislation

Other National Legislation

Introduction

ANTON ASOSKOV, DARIA LEVINA AND MILANA KARAYANIDI

In turbulent times, the role of private international law becomes ever more important. International relations between states may deteriorate; one state may characterise certain other states as 'unfriendly'[1] or even hostile, but still, private-law relations between individuals and legal entities from those states continue to arise and demand adequate legal regulation. Private international law rules remain the basis for cultural and economic interchange among people and businesses even in the dark times of history, which determines their relevance for continued study and analysis.

Russian private international law has a long and exciting history. In the late nineteenth – the beginning of the twentieth century, the Russian Empire was one of the architects of the Hague Conferences on Private International Law, which opened the modern page of history of this field of law and gave impetus to its rapid development. At that time, the Russian conflict-of-laws doctrine was largely influenced by the writings of German authors.[2]

During the Soviet era, private international law in Russia had many peculiarities. Yet, notwithstanding the offensive public rhetoric in respect of the foreign 'capitalist' world, Soviet courts and arbitral tribunals routinely applied the foreign law of Western countries based on the Soviet conflict-of-laws provisions. Developments in foreign legislation, case law and doctrine remained under the focus of Soviet scholars on private international law,[3] whose works, in turn, were translated and published in Europe. Even in the times of irreconcilable antagonism of the Cold War, the exchange of academic ideas in the field of conflict of laws was not interrupted.

Modern Russian private international law was shaped in the beginning of the twenty-first century. It employed a number of concepts developed in the European private international law, including the concepts of overriding mandatory provisions,[4] characteristic performance for determining the *lex contractus*,[5] and the directed activity for consumer contracts.[6] Simultaneously, it developed

[1] Pursuant to the Order of the Russian Government No 430-r dated 5 March 2022, the EU Member States, USA, Canada, Australia, Switzerland and other states implementing economic sanctions against Russia and Russian persons are characterised as 'unfriendly' states.

[2] For example, academic works of the most famous Russian PIL scholar, Michail Brun, used a lot of concepts and ideas from the writings of the German author Franz Kahn.

[3] See, eg, L Lunts, *Kurs mezhdunarodnogo tchastnogo prava* (*Course of Private International Law*) In 3 vols (Moscow, Spark, 2002).

[4] Literally called 'rules of direct application' in Article 1192 of the Civil Code.

[5] Article 1211(1) and (2) of the Civil Code.

[6] Article 1212(1) of the Civil Code.

unique original statutory provisions, which will be of interest to foreign academics and practitioners. To name a few, these are the specific rules about the protection of 'active' consumers who find a professional party outside the place of the consumer's residence;[7] statutory provisions on the law applicable to contracts on formation of legal entities and shareholders' agreements;[8] rules on the scope of application of party autonomy for determining the governing law of rights *in rem* and non-contractual obligations.[9] Some of these rules represent a unique mixture of approaches taken from Soviet history and modern Western codifications (eg, rules on the law applicable to the form of transactions[10]). The legislative provisions of Russian private international law were further significantly modernised during the 2013 reform of the Civil Code.[11] In particular, new provisions were adopted on the law applicable to subrogation,[12] agency,[13] set-off,[14] and pre-contractual liability (*culpa in contrahendo*).[15]

The peculiar feature of the Russian legal system is the power of the Plenary Session of the Russian Supreme Court to adopt binding interpretations of statutory provisions, which are formulated in an abstract manner and are not directly connected to the resolution of particular disputes. Such interpretations look like a more detailed version of the existing statutory provisions. In 2019, the Russian Supreme Court adopted the Resolution on the application of rules of private international law,[16] which is very important for understanding the way the conflict-of-laws rules are applied in practice by Russian courts. All the above-mentioned instruments are addressed in detail in this book.

This book follows the classic structure for textbooks on private international law. It starts with a description of the history, sources and fundamental concepts of Russian private international law (Chapters one to three) which are followed by the analysis of the specific fields of conflict of laws (Chapters four to nine). The final chapters are devoted to procedural issues – such as international jurisdiction, recognition and enforcement of foreign judgments, as well as international commercial arbitration (Chapters ten to twelve).

We hope that this book will help to maintain bridges between Russia and foreign countries. It will show how the country with a unique history and peculiar legal constructs may adapt its private international rules to the surrounding rapidly changing reality.

[7] Article 1212(4) of the Civil Code.
[8] Article 1214 of the Civil Code.
[9] Articles 1206(3), 1219(3) and 1223.1 of the Civil Code.
[10] Article 1209 of the Civil Code.
[11] Federal Law No 260-FZ dated 30 September 2013, which came into force on 1 November 2013.
[12] Article 1216.1 of the Civil Code.
[13] Article 1217.1 of the Civil Code.
[14] Article 1217.2 of the Civil Code.
[15] Article 1222.1 of the Civil Code.
[16] Resolution of the Plenum of the Supreme Court dated 9 July 2019 No 24 'On the Application of Rules of International Private Law by the Courts of the Russian Federation'.

1

Introduction to Russian Private International Law

DARIA ASTAKHOVA

This chapter provides a historical and conceptual background to the Russian private international law (PIL). It highlights the major points of its development, outlining the Soviet heritage and its influence on the modern Russian PIL. It investigates the defining characteristic of PIL as a field dealing with private law relations involving a foreign element and explores various dimensions of foreign elements in a private law context. It further specifies the scope of regulation and the methods of PIL. The chapter concludes with the current development trends of the Russian PIL.

I. Historical Background of the Concept of PIL in Russia

Since the second half of the nineteenth century, Russian scholars have reflected on the notion, characteristics, and nature of PIL. While the first works were largely inspired by the foreign doctrine of PIL, the subsequent contributions of Russian scholars permitted an original concept of PIL to develop. The evolution of the Russian doctrine of PIL is characterised by a debate on the nature of PIL, centred around the relationship between PIL and international law.

At the same time, despite their divergent views on the nature of PIL, all scholars studying PIL have been conscious of the fact that the evolution of PIL is conditioned by the strengthening of contacts between private persons and legal entities from different states in various fields, in particular in the context of international trade, and that the purpose of PIL lies in the facilitation of cross-border legal relationships by offering their participants the means of regulation and protection of their rights.

According to Mikhail Brun, a famous Russian scholar of the twentieth century who taught PIL at the Moscow Commercial Institute, this ultimate purpose of PIL justifies, together with other reasons, the interest of Russian scholars in PIL:

> For the very fact that this discipline [PIL] is full of puzzling questions, for the very fact that the process of seeking the truth is more valuable than the attained level of knowledge, which is always only relative, but also because its ultimate goal is the recognition and defence of subjective rights all over the world, regardless of mere local conditions in which they are claimed, and because its sparkle is humanity standing beyond national boundaries, for all these reasons it attracts and engages everyone who became familiar with it.[1]

The modern Russian concept of PIL evolved due to the legal heritage composed of the works of the Russian PIL scholars, which can be classified into three key periods: the nineteenth-century Russian Empire, the twentieth-century pre-Revolutionary Russia, and the Soviet period.

A. The Emergence and Development of the PIL Concept in the Nineteenth-century Russian Empire

According to some Russian scholars,[2] the first works in the field of PIL in Russia belong to two young scholars who in 1850 defended their Master's theses at the Saint-Petersburg University: Blagoveshchensky (whose first name is not known to legal historians) ('On the Effects of Public and Civil Laws in International Law') and Faddey Bobrovsky ('On the Effects of Civil and Criminal Laws of One State in Another'). These manuscripts did not become well known, but they reflect the rising interest in PIL issues at that time.

The early period of development of the Russian PIL is associated with academic works of two scholars from the Kazan University, namely Dmitry Meier and Nikolay Ivanov.[3] Dmitry Meier, who was the head of the department of civil law and in addition gave lectures on international law at the same university, was the first to address the problem of conflict-of-laws rules, namely, the question of the effects of domestic law outside the borders of the state in which such law was

[1] M Brun, 'Mezhdunarodnoe Chastnoe Pravo, Lektsii, Chitannye v Moskovskom Kommercheskom Institute v 1908–09 Akadmicheskom Godu' ('Private International Law, Courses Given at the Moscow Commercial Institute in 1908–09 Academic Year') in A Kolodkin and V Ershov (eds), *Zolotoy Fond Rossiiskoy Nauki Mezhdunarodnogo Prava* (*Golden Heritage of the Russian Science of Private International Law*) (Moscow, Mezhdunarodnye otnosheniya, 2009) 107 (translation from Russian).

[2] See S Lebedev and E Kabatova (eds), *Mezhdunarodnoe Chastnoe Pravo: Uchebnik v Dvuh Tomah, Tom 1: Obchshaya Chast* (*Private International Law: Coursebook, in 2 volumes, Volume 1: General Part*) (Moscow, Statut, 2011) 39; A Abdullin, 'Zarozhdenie i Razvitie Nauki Mezhdunarodnogo Chastnogo Prava v Dorevolyutsionnoy Rossii' ('Emergence and Development of the Science of Private International Law in the Pre-Revolutionary Russia') in *Zolotoy Fond Rossiiskoy Nauki Mezhdunarodnogo Prava* (*Golden Heritage of the Russian Science of Private International Law*) (Moscow, Mezhdunarodnye otnosheniya, 2009) 9; S Bakhin, 'K Voprosu ob Istokhakh Izucheniya Mezhdunarodnogo Chastnogo Prava Rossii' ('On the Origins of the Study of Private International Law in Russia') (2022) 4 *Russian Law Journal* 56.

[3] Lebedev and Kabatova (eds), *Mezhdunarodnoe Chastnoe Pravo* (*Private International Law*) (n 2 above) 40–46; A Krivenky, *Zarozhdenie i Razvitie Mezhdunarodnogo Chastnogo Prava (XII–XX veka)* (*Emergence and Development of Private International Law (Twelfth–Twentieth centuries)*) (Moscow, INFRA-M, 2022) 74–88.

enacted. His lectures were first published in 1858.[4] In particular, Dmitry Meier considered that three connections are important to determine the law applicable to a cross-border relationship: the place of residence of a relevant natural person, the place where the property involved is situated, and the place where the legally significant act is performed.[5]

It is generally admitted within contemporary Russian doctrine that the first specialised work on PIL in the Russian language belongs to Nikolay Ivanov, who was Dmitry Meier's student and disciple.[6] Nikolay Ivanov in 1864 defended and in 1865 published his thesis on the topic 'The Grounds of Private International Jurisdiction',[7] which largely contributed to further development of the PIL doctrine in Russia.

Nikolay Ivanov introduced the term 'private international law' into Russian legal science.[8] He also suggested a systematic approach to PIL. He analysed, in distinct chapters, both the historical background and foundations of 'private international jurisdiction', and explained how it applies to specific legal concepts, such as the legal status of persons, rights *in rem*, legal obligations, and the form of legal acts.[9] Besides, Nikolay Ivanov affirmed that, in some circumstances, the legislator could and should recognise the effect of foreign laws on its territory.[10] The author believed that there are two pillars of a cross-border legal relationship: the principle of state sovereignty and the principle of reciprocal interaction between nations.[11] Finally, Nikolay Ivanov emphasised the need to harmonise private law in Europe.[12]

[4] A Abdullin, *Ocherki Istorii Nauki Mezhdunarodnogo Chastnogo Prava v Rossii: Problemy Ponimaniya Prirody Mezhdunarodnogo Chastnogo Prava v Trudakh Otechestvennykh Pravovedov XIX–Nachala XX Vekov* (*Essays on the History of Science of Private International Law in Russia: Problems of Understanding of the Nature of Private International Law in the Works of Russian Legal Scholars of the Nineteenth–the beginning of the Twentieth Century*) (Kazan, Kazansky Gosudarstvennyi Universitet, 2004) 11.

[5] Krivenky, *Zarozhdenie i Razvitie Mezhdunarodnogo Chastnogo Prava (XII–XX veka)* (*Emergence and Development of Private International Law (Twelfth–Twentieth centuries)*) (n 3 above) 75–76.

[6] Lebedev and Kabatova (eds), *Mezhdunarodnoe Chastnoe Pravo* (*Private International Law*) (n 2 above) 42; Krivenky, *Zarozhdenie i Razvitie Mezhdunarodnogo Chastnogo Prava (XII–XX veka)* (*Emergence and Development of Private International Law (Twelfth–Twentieth centuries)*) (n 3 above) 80; G Dmitrieva (ed), *Mezhdunarodnoe Chastnoe Pravo: Uchebnik* (*Private international law: Coursebook*), 4th edn (Moscow, Prospekt, 2017) 41.

[7] Lebedev and Kabatova (eds), *Mezhdunarodnoe Chastnoe Pravo* (*Private International Law*) (n 2 above) 43.

[8] I Getman-Pavlova, *Mezhdunarodnoe Chastnoe Pravo*: *Uchebnik* (*Private International Law: Coursebook*), 3rd edn (Moscow, Eksmo, 2011) 13; Abdullin, *Ocherki Istorii Nauki Mezhdunarodnogo Chastnogo Prava* (*Essays on the History of Science of Private International Law in Russia*) (n 4 above) 16.

[9] Lebedev and Kabatova (eds), *Mezhdunarodnoe Chastnoe Pravo* (*Private International Law*) (n 2 above) 43.

[10] Lebedev and Kabatova (eds), *Mezhdunarodnoe Chastnoe Pravo* (*Private International Law*) (n 2 above) 44.

[11] Lebedev and Kabatova (eds), *Mezhdunarodnoe Chastnoe Pravo* (*Private International Law*) (n 2 above) 44; N Ivanov, 'Osnovaniya Chastnoy Mezhdunarodnoy Jurisdiktsii' ('The Grounds of Private International Jurisdiction') in *Zolotoy Fond Rossiiskoy Nauki Mezhdunarodnogo Prava* (*Golden Heritage of the Russian Science of Private International Law*) (Moscow, Mezhdunarodnye otnosheniya, 2009) 73.

[12] Lebedev, and Kabatova (eds), *Mezhdunarodnoe Chastnoe Pravo* (*Private International Law*) (n 2 above) 45.

Subsequently, the Russian doctrine of PIL was represented by two main schools of thought, having divergent views on the nature of PIL. The first academic school was formed by the works of such Russian authors as Piotr Kazansky, Mikhail Kapustin, Fiodor Martens and Andrey Stoyanov, who believed that PIL forms part of international law, the latter being a broad concept covering both public international law and PIL.[13] The origins of the second academic school were associated with the works of a famous Russian specialist in private law, Kronid Malyshev, who laid down the bases of the civil law concept of PIL, meaning that PIL is a part of the domestic civil law, while at the same time, it takes into account comparative law and international instruments.[14]

The ideas of the Russian scholars of the second half of the nineteenth century set up a scientific framework for further evolution of the Russian doctrine of PIL, the field which then attracted the interest of Russian scholars throughout the twentieth century.

B. The Concept of PIL in the Works of the Russian Scholars of the Twentieth Century: Pre-Revolutionary Russia

The beginning of the twentieth century offered favourable conditions for the evolution of the PIL doctrine in Russia. This was notably due to the rapid growth of international trade and the increasing foreign investment in Russia.[15] During this period, such Russian authors as Piotr Kazansky, Aleksander Pilenko, Boris Nolde and Mikhail Brun, extensively published their works on different topics of PIL.[16]

The development of the concept of PIL in Russia at the beginning of the twentieth century was characterised by a heated debate on the nature of PIL. In the continuation of the exchange of divergent views on this topic in the nineteenth century, Russian authors further discussed whether PIL formed part of private or public law. Thus, in 1916, in a publication called 'Two Sketches', Alexey Rozhdestvensky, a Russian lawyer and Professor at the Moscow State University and the Demidov Law Lyceum in Yaroslavl, expressed a novel view, according to which the conflict of laws belonged neither to the sphere of private nor of public law, because the rules of PIL do not regulate social relations or public-private relations and are therefore not legal rules, but technical norms.[17]

[13] Dmitrieva (ed), *Mezhdunarodnoe Chastnoe Pravo* (*Private International Law*) (n 6 above) 42.

[14] Dmitrieva (ed), *Mezhdunarodnoe Chastnoe Pravo* (*Private International Law*) (n 6 above) 44.

[15] Lebedev and Kabatova (eds), *Mezhdunarodnoe Chastnoe Pravo* (Private International Law) (n 2 above) 51.

[16] Lebedev and Kabatova (eds), *Mezhdunarodnoe Chastnoe Pravo* (*Private International Law*) (n 2 above) 51–55.

[17] A Rozhdestvensky, *Dva Etyuda* (*Two Sketches*) (Moscow, Snegireva Publishing House, 1916) 21–23.

In 1908, another Russian author, Mikhail Brun, famous for his works on conflict of laws and PIL, stated that 'private international law is neither international nor private law within the meaning of civil or trade law.'[18] For Mikhail Brun, PIL was a part of domestic law having a public nature, because, through conflict-of-laws rules, the state indicated to its judges and public officials in what circumstances they should apply a foreign law.[19] Analysing the nature of PIL, Mikhail Brun used the terms which later became central to the definition of PIL in the Russian doctrine. Mikhail Brun explained that PIL applies to 'legal relationships, in which one or some of the elements are linked to a foreign state', for example, one party to the legal relationship is a foreigner, or the legal relationship occurred abroad, or the relevant property is situated abroad, or the legally significant act is performed abroad.[20]

Consequently, at the beginning of the twentieth century, Russian scholars writing about PIL tried to justify a *sui generis* nature of PIL. They went beyond the approach of their predecessors, who classified PIL either as a part of international law or as a part of domestic law. This step was essential for the future genesis of the modern Russian concept of PIL.

Overall, as stated by a contemporary Russian author, Adel Abdullin, the works of the Russian scholars at the beginning of the twentieth century made it possible for the Russian doctrine of PIL to become an independent branch of legal doctrine. The author explains that, at that time, Russian scholars extensively discussed various topics of PIL; they created its conceptual, terminological, and methodological framework; and further discussed the nature of PIL. They also advocated in favour of codification of PIL and the inclusion of international instruments within its scope.[21]

C. The Role of Soviet Legal Heritage in the Development of the Russian PIL

The modern concept of PIL is also influenced by Soviet legal heritage, as, during the Soviet period, PIL continued to attract the attention of many legal scholars who analysed and conceptualised it.

[18] Brun, 'Mezhdunarodnoe Chastnoe Pravo, Lektsii, 1908–09' ('Private International Law, Courses, 1908–09') (n 1 above) 109 (translation from Russian).

[19] Brun, 'Mezhdunarodnoe Chastnoe Pravo, Lektsii, 1908–09' ('Private International Law, Courses, 1908–09') (n 1 above) 116–17.

[20] M Brun, *Mezhdunarodnoe Chastnoe Pravo, Kurs, Chitannyi v Moskovskom Kommercheskom Institute 1910–11* (*Private International Law, Course Given at the Moscow Commercial Institute in 1910–11*) (Moscow, Publishing House of Prokhorov and Yashkin, 1911) 6–7.

[21] Abdullin, 'Zarozhdenie i Razvitie Nauki Mezhdunarodnogo Chastnogo Prava v Dorevolyutsionnoy Rossii' ('Emergence and Development of the Science of Private International Law in the Pre-Revolutionary Russia') (n 2 above) 25.

According to the Russian doctrine, the Soviet period in the development of PIL comprised three key stages: first, from 1917 to 1930, Soviet authors published their first research works on PIL; second, from 1930 to 1940, the Soviet science of PIL was characterised by the elaboration of the structure and fundamental provisions of the Soviet theory of PIL; and third, from 1940 to 1991, Soviet scholars examined a large variety of theoretical and practical aspects of PIL.[22] During these three stages of evolution of the Soviet doctrine of PIL, Soviet scholars offered a more detailed analysis of PIL issues as compared to the previously published works. They also highlighted the key elements of PIL which strongly influenced further development of the doctrine of PIL in Russia.

In the early stages of the development of the Soviet doctrine of PIL, the issues related to PIL were often discussed in coursebooks on international law. However, that situation later changed because most Soviet authors took the position that PIL was not a branch of international law, but rather an independent branch of domestic law.[23]

Notably, the classical concept of PIL, which was later endorsed by the majority of Russian scholars, was formulated during this period by a famous Soviet and Russian scholar, Lazar Lunts, Professor at the Moscow State University. He further developed the original conceptual position of another Soviet scholar, Ivan Peretersky, according to whom 'private international law is a sphere of international civil relations, i.e., relations of a civil law nature arising from international life.'[24] The Soviet doctrine considered that the international nature of civil law relations governed by PIL is determined by the presence of a 'foreign element'. Such element would be present in one of the following circumstances: (i) a foreign citizen or a foreign legal entity participated in the legal relationship; (ii) the subject-matter of the legal relationship was situated abroad; or (iii) the legally significant facts which triggered the creation, change or termination of the legal relationship occurred within a foreign state.[25]

Based on these key features of PIL, a famous Russian specialist in PIL, Sergey Lebedev, Professor at the Moscow State Institute of International Relations (MGIMO-University) concluded that 'it is necessary to consider private international law as a special branch of law which is of civil nature as to its content' and 'not as a part, subsystem, etc. of international law which represents a special system different from the national law system.'[26]

Due to the high value of the scientific findings of the Soviet authors on the nature and essential characteristics of PIL, they remained topical after the fall of

[22] Dmitrieva (ed), *Mezhdunarodnoe Chastnoe Pravo* (*Private International Law*) (n 6 above) 57.

[23] Dmitrieva (ed), *Mezhdunarodnoe Chastnoe Pravo* (*Private International Law*) (n 6 above) 65.

[24] S Lebedev, 'On the Nature of Private International Law' (1980) *Soviet Yearbook of International Law* 61, 78. See also L Lunts, *Kurs mezhdunarodnogo chastnogo prava: v 3 t.* (*Course of Private International Law in 3 Volumes*) (Moscow, Spark, 2002) 21.

[25] Lebedev, 'On the Nature of Private International Law' (n 24 above) 61, 78; Lunts, *Kurs mezhdunarodnogo chastnogo prava: v 3 t.* (*Course of Private International Law in 3 Volumes*) (n 24 above) 26–27.

[26] Lebedev, 'On the Nature of Private International Law' (n 24 above) 61, 79.

the Soviet Union. At the same time, when writing and publishing their scientific works, the Soviet scholars had to take into consideration Soviet socialist ideology.

For instance, Ivan Peretersky – who has the credit of publishing in 1924 'Essays on Private International Law of the RSFSR', a first comprehensive study on PIL in Soviet Russia – believed that Soviet PIL was an integral part of socialist law, reflecting a compromise between capitalism and socialism.[27]

Moreover, for Soviet authors like Lazar Lunts, the use of the word 'private' in the term 'private international law' was questionable, since the Soviet law did not distinguish between public and private law.[28] Also, according to Lazar Lunts, Soviet PIL preferred more rigid conflict-of-laws rules as compared to more flexible conflict-of-laws rules used in PIL of some foreign countries.[29]

The characteristic features of the Soviet law, such as the denial of the distinction between private and public law, the belief that the legal system reflects a compromise between capitalism and socialism, and a cautious attitude towards flexible conflict-of-laws rules, did not survive after the fall of the Soviet Union. However, they did not prevent the key concepts of the Soviet doctrine of PIL from forming a solid basis for the modern Russian concept of PIL. This proves the quality of the works of the Soviet authors and the value of their contribution to the Russian doctrine of PIL.

II. The Concept of PIL in the Modern Russian Doctrine

The modern concept of PIL, formulated by scholars in post-Soviet Russia, relies on several key ideas developed by the Soviet authors. The prevailing approach to the nature of PIL, which considers that it is a separate branch of domestic law governing private law relations involving a foreign element, was designated as a 'civil law concept' in the doctrine.[30]

A. The Civil Law Concept of PIL Prevailing in the Russian Doctrine

Throughout the years of development of the Russian doctrine of PIL, the so-called 'civil law concept' of PIL, whose pioneer was Lazar Lunts, became the leading

[27] Dmitrieva (ed), *Mezhdunarodnoe Chastnoe Pravo* (*Private International Law*) (n 6 above) 59.

[28] Lunts, *Kurs Mezhdunarodnogo Chastnogo Prava: v 3 t.* (*Course of Private International Law in 3 Volumes*) (n 24 above) 47.

[29] Lunts, *Kurs Mezhdunarodnogo Chastnogo Prava: v 3 t.* (*Course of Private International Law in 3 Volumes*) (n 24 above) 53.

[30] L Lunts, *Voprosy Mezhdunarodnogo Chastnogo Prava* (*Private International Law Issues*) (Moscow, Gosudarstvennoe Izdatelstvo Youridicheskoy Literatury, 1956) 5.

school of PIL in Russia as it was endorsed by other renowned Russian scholars such as Mikhail Boguslavsky, Galina Dmitrieva, Sergey Lebedev, Aleksander Makovsky, Natalia Marysheva, Oleg Sadikov, Viktor Zvekov, and others.[31]

The modern doctrine defines PIL as a field dealing with private law relations 'involving a foreign element'.[32] The key characteristics of PIL as described by the followers of the civil law concept can be summarised as follows:

- PIL is a separate branch of domestic private law.[33]
- The private nature of PIL stems from the scope of regulation of PIL, which covers private law relations: civil law relations (for example, arising from cross-border trade contracts, rights *in rem*, intellectual property, torts, or inheritance), as well as family and employment relations if they contain a foreign element (for example, they involve a foreign national or a foreign legal entity).[34]
- The main methods of PIL are the conflict method and the substantive method, the former being based on conflict-of-laws rules, and the latter on substantive law rules.[35]
- The international nature of PIL is derived from the core feature of the legal relationships regulated by PIL, that is, the foreign element, which takes the legal relationship beyond the borders of one country's legal system.[36]

According to Russian authors, the foreign element usually emerges in one of the following circumstances:

(i) one of the parties to the legal relationship is a foreign person or a foreign legal entity (for example, where a contract is concluded between a Russian and a foreign company);
(ii) the subject-matter of the legal relationship (for example, movable or immovable property) is situated abroad; or

[31] N Marysheva, T Lazareva and N Vlasova, 'Tsivilisticheskaya Kontsentsiya Mezhdunarodnogo Chastnogo Prava' ('Civil Concept of the International Private Law') (2015) 9 *Russian Law Journal* 57, 59.

[32] Dmitrieva (ed), *Mezhdunarodnoe Chastnoe Pravo (Private International Law)* (n 6 above) 7; V Kanashevsky, *Mezhdunarodnoe Chastnoe Pravo: Uchebnik (Private International Law: Coursebook)* (Moscow, Mezhdunarodnye Otnosheniya, 2019) 16; A Abashidze, K Gasanova and D Strigunova (eds), *Mezhdunarodnoe Chastnoe Pravo: Uchebnik dlya Studentov Vuzov, Obuchayoushikhsya po Napravleniyu Podgotovki Yourisprudentsiya (Private International Law: Coursebook for Students of Universities Pursuing Legal Studies)*, 2nd edn (Moscow, UNITY-DANA: Zakon i Pravo, 2022) 11; Getman-Pavlova, *Mezhdunarodnoe Chastnoe Pravo (Private International Law)* (n 8 above) 13–14; N Erpyleva, *Mezhdunarodnoe Chastnoe Pravo: Uchebnik dlya Vuzov (Private International Law: Coursebook for Universities)* (Moscow, Higher School of Economics Publishing House, 2015) 20.

[33] Marysheva, Lazareva, Vlasova, 'Tsivilisticheskaya Kontsentsiya' ('Civil Concept') (n 31 above) 57, 58; Lunts, *Kurs Mezhdunarodnogo Chastnogo Prava: v 3 t. (Course of Private International Law in 3 Volumes)* (n 24 above) 21.

[34] Marysheva, Lazareva and Vlasova, 'Tsivilisticheskaya Kontsentsiya' ('Civil Concept') (n 31 above) 57, 58.

[35] Marysheva, Lazareva and Vlasova, 'Tsivilisticheskaya Kontsentsiya' ('Civil Concept') (n 31 above) 57, 58.

[36] Lebedev and Kabatova (eds), *Mezhdunarodnoe Chastnoe Pravo (Private International Law)* (n 2 above) 9.

(iii) the legally significant fact which triggers the creation, change or termination of the legal relationship occurs abroad (for example, conclusion of a marriage, performance of works).[37]

These are the most common elements, the presence of one of which is sufficient to establish the international character of the legal relationship in a private law context. This list of foreign elements is nevertheless not exhaustive.[38]

B. The Concept of PIL in the Russian Legislation

The dominant concept of PIL in Russia is also enshrined in the Russian legislation.

Article 1186 of the Civil Code essentially repeats the elements of the definition of PIL expressed in the Russian doctrine. As follows from its text, the PIL rules are applicable to 'civil law relations, with the participation of foreign persons or foreign legal entities, or civil law relations involving other foreign element, including where the subject-matter of the legal relationship is situated abroad.'

As explained in the Russian doctrine, while Article 1186 of the Civil Code does not expressly specify the 'legally significant fact' arising abroad as one of the types of foreign elements, the use of the words 'including where' to introduce the examples of foreign elements cited in this article suggests that their enumeration is not exhaustive and therefore civil law relations can include other types of foreign elements not specified in Article 1186.[39]

Remarkably, the very fact that the rules on PIL are enshrined in the Russian Civil Code, and not in a separate legal act on PIL, contributes to the understanding of PIL as a field governing civil law relations.

C. The Scope of Regulation and Methods of PIL

The way PIL is perceived in the doctrine is intrinsically related to the approach taken to the scope of regulation and the methods of PIL in the doctrine.

According to the contemporary Russian doctrine, the two classical methods of PIL are the conflict method and the substantive method.[40] The Russian authors agree that the conflict method regulates the legal relationship through

[37] M Boguslavsky, *Mezhdunarodnoe Chastnoe Pravo: Uchebnik* (*Private International Law: Coursebook*), 7th edn (Mocow, Norma: INFRA-M, 2016) 18; Dmitrieva (ed), *Mezhdunarodnoe Chastnoe Pravo* (*Private International Law*) (n 6 above) 8–9.

[38] Dmitrieva (ed), *Mezhdunarodnoe Chastnoe Pravo* (*Private International Law*) (n 6 above) 9.

[39] Lebedev, Kabatova (eds), *Mezhdunarodnoe Chastnoe Pravo* (Private International Law) (n 2 above) 10.

[40] Erpyleva, *Mezhdunarodnoe Chastnoe Pravo: Uchebnik dlya Vuzov* (*Private International Law Coursebook for Universities*) (n 32 above) 26.

conflict-of-laws rules, both domestic and those harmonised in international instruments, aiming to determine the applicable law.[41]

However, there is a debate in the Russian doctrine as to the exact scope of the substantive method, which offers regulation of the legal relationship through substantive rules.[42] Depending on what is understood by substantive rules governing PIL, the scope of regulation of PIL can be considered in a broader or a narrower way. According to some Russian authors, only harmonised substantive rules contained in international instruments relate to the scope of PIL, to the exclusion of the substantive domestic rules.[43] In contrast, others consider that domestic substantive rules governing private law relations involving a foreign element also form part of the substantive method.[44]

The authors advocating for the exclusion of domestic substantive rules from the scope of regulation of PIL argue that if such rules have a public law nature (for example, rules governing foreign investment), they apply as mandatory provisions and do not fall within the scope of PIL, which has a private law nature.[45] As far as the domestic substantive rules of a private nature governing legal relationships involving a foreign element are concerned (for example, the prohibition on foreign nationals acquiring certain land plots, existing in Russian law), such rules do not prevent the conflict-of-laws issues from arising and apply only after Russian law is determined to be applicable on the basis of the conflict-of-laws rules.[46]

In contrast, the proponents of the inclusion of domestic substantive rules in the scope of regulation of PIL maintain that the domestic rules aimed at governing private law relations involving a foreign element imply the existence of a certain 'hypothetical (or hidden) conflict-of-laws rule', which chooses substantive rules of Russian law as the law applicable to such relations. Such rules thus fall within the scope of PIL.[47]

The latter approach results in a broader understanding of the scope of PIL. PIL gains an even broader meaning due to the inclusion in its scope by some Russian

[41] See Lebedev and Kabatova (eds), *Mezhdunarodnoe Chastnoe Pravo* (*Private International Law*) (n 2 above) 30; Marysheva, Lazareva and Vlasova, 'Tsivilisticheskaya Kontsentsiya' ('Civil Concept') (n 31 above) 57, 58; Dmitrieva (ed), *Mezhdunarodnoe Chastnoe Pravo* (*Private International Law*) (n 6 above) 15–19; Abashidze, Gasanova and Strigunova (eds), *Mezhdunarodnoe Chastnoe Pravo* (*Private International Law*) (n 32 above) 19; Getman-Pavlova, *Mezhdunarodnoe Chastnoe Pravo* (*Private International Law*) (n 8 above) 44.

[42] See Lebedev and Kabatova (eds), *Mezhdunarodnoe Chastnoe Pravo* (*Private International Law*) (n 2 above) 33; Erpyleva, *Mezhdunarodnoe Chastnoe Pravo: Uchebnik dlya Vuzov* (*Private International Law Coursebook for Universities*) (n 32 above) 26; Dmitrieva (ed), *Mezhdunarodnoe Chastnoe Pravo* (*Private International Law*) (n 6 above) 26.

[43] Lebedev, Kabatova (eds), *Mezhdunarodnoe Chastnoe Pravo* (*Private International Law*) (n 2 above) 35; Dmitrieva (ed), *Mezhdunarodnoe Chastnoe Pravo* (*Private International Law*) (n 6 above) 27.

[44] Erpyleva, *Mezhdunarodnoe Chastnoe Pravo: Uchebnik dlya Vuzov* (*Private International Law Coursebook for Universities*) (n 32 above) 26; Getman-Pavlova, *Mezhdunarodnoe Chastnoe Pravo* (*Private International Law*) (n 8 above) 46.

[45] Dmitrieva (ed), *Mezhdunarodnoe Chastnoe Pravo* (*Private International Law*) (n 6 above) 27.

[46] Dmitrieva (ed), *Mezhdunarodnoe Chastnoe Pravo* (*Private International Law*) (n 6 above) 28.

[47] Erpyleva, *Mezhdunarodnoe Chastnoe Pravo: Uchebnik dlya Vuzov* (*Private International Law Coursebook for Universities*) (n 32 above) 56.

scholars of the rules governing international civil procedure and the rules on international commercial arbitration.[48]

Consequently, all modern scholars essentially agree that the main methods of PIL are the conflict method and the substantive method, but they do not share the same view as to the scope of the substantive method. The discussion on the methods of PIL thus allows for justification of a broader or a narrower understanding of the notion of PIL in the Russian doctrine.

D. The Current Development Trends of the Russian PIL

The history of the development of the Russian concept of PIL shows that it was conditioned by the progressive opening of the Russian state to cooperation with other states, the expansion of international trade, and the increasing involvement of Russian nationals in legal relationships with their foreign counterparts.

According to Mikhail Boguslavsky, the interest in PIL in Russia is explained in particular by the access of Russian companies to the international market, the expansion of labour migration processes, the expansion of various contacts between Russian and foreign citizens, the accession of Russia to a number of international organisations, and an increasing number of cases involving foreign parties examined in the courts and by way of arbitration.[49]

In this context, PIL has been perceived as a legal field whose purpose is to facilitate links between nationals from different countries. While the original purpose of PIL consisted in determining state jurisdiction and preventing and solving sovereignty conflicts, its purpose is currently more oriented towards a search for a legal system which can regulate the legal relationship in the most efficient and fair way.[50] This purpose is notably achieved through a wider use of flexible rather than rigid connecting factors in the conflict-of-laws rules.[51]

Furthermore, the development of the Russian PIL is currently characterised by broadening of the scope of the legal relationships which are covered by PIL. For example, PIL recently faced a need to offer regulation for legal relationships arising from electronic commerce.[52]

[48] See Erpyleva, *Mezhdunarodnoe Chastnoe Pravo: Uchebnik dlya Vuzov* (*Private International Law Coursebook for Universities*) (n 32 above) 56–57.

[49] Boguslavsky, *Mezhdunarodnoe Chastnoe Pravo* (*Private International Law*) (n 37 above) 21–22.

[50] N Bogdanova-Pataud, 'Emergence d'un nouveau droit international privé en Russie et en CEI' (Doctor of Law thesis, Université Paris 1 Panthéon Sorbonne 2005) 87–88.

[51] See Erpyleva, *Mezhdunarodnoe Chastnoe Pravo: Uchebnik dlya Vuzov* (*Private International Law Coursebook for Universities*) (n 32 above) 27–29.

[52] V Popondopulo, 'Mezhdunarodnoe Chastnoe Pravo: Priroda i Tendentsii Razvitiya' ('Private International Law: Its Nature and Trends of Development') (2018) 2 *Russian Law Journal* 91, 96; O Zasemkova, 'Mezhdunarodnoe Chastnoe Pravo v XXI Veke: Sovremennye Vyzovy I Perspektivy Razvitiya' ('Private International Law in the 21st Century: Contemporary Challenges and Development Prospects') (2019) 11 *Lex Russica* 30, 31.

In addition, we also witness an increasing role of international instruments as sources of PIL. On the one hand, they offer harmonised substantive rules to govern cross-border legal relationships, but on the other hand, they permit certain conflict-of-laws rules to be coordinated.[53]

PIL, just like any branch of domestic law, is likely to bear the effects of political and social changes in the modern Russian state. However, unlike domestic public law, which is more directly impacted by the political agenda of the state, domestic private law, and PIL as its composite part, are more likely to preserve their core values and goals, which, as far as PIL is concerned, undoubtedly consist in creating an efficient legal framework for interaction between private actors coming from different states. Indeed, as stated by Nikolay Ivanov, whose works triggered the development of PIL in Russia and remain still relevant today, '[c]ommunication between nations, which is expressed in their mutual relations, constitutes a vital need for the effective existence of mankind.'[54]

Notwithstanding the context, the Russian PIL will have to evolve and serve the interests of the nationals from different states participating in cross-border legal relationships.

[53] Popondopulo, 'Mezhdunarodnoe Chastnoe Pravo' ('Private International Law') (n 52 above) 91, 96–97.

[54] Ivanov, 'Osnovaniya Chastnoy Mezhdunarodnoy Jurisdiktsii' ('The Grounds of Private International Jurisdiction') (n 11 above) 74.

2

Sources of Private International Law in Russia

OLGA KAMENSKAIA AND ANDREY SHIRVINDT

This chapter examines the legal framework of Russian private international law (PIL). It first describes the role public international law plays in the formation of Russian PIL, including international conventions that contain conflict-of-laws rules and treaties on mutual legal assistance in civil and commercial matters that Russia is a party to. The most prominent among them are the Kiev Convention on Settling Disputes Related to Commercial Activities of 20 March 1992 and the Minsk Convention on Legal Assistance and Legal Relations in Civil, Family and Criminal Law Matters of 22 January 1993. The chapter further outlines regional treaty networks that Russia participates in as a Member State of political and economic unions formed by the former Soviet republics, in particular the Commonwealth of Independent States and the Eurasian Economic Community. It further explains the national PIL laws, primarily the Civil Code and the procedural codes, in particular discussing the legislator's decision not to consolidate conflict-of-laws rules in a single codification. The chapter concludes with an introduction to the role of case law, doctrinal writings, and customary rules in Russian PIL.

OLGA KAMENSKAIA

I. Public International Law

A. Introduction

Public international law is an integral part of the Russian legal system. Under the Constitution, 'the universally recognised norms of international law and international treaties in force on the territory of the Russian Federation are a component of Russian law'.[1] If an international treaty in force in the Russian Federation specifies rules that conflict with national legislation, the rules of the international treaty prevail.[2]

If the Russian Federation accedes to an international treaty, such treaty automatically becomes a part of the Russian legal system and does not require the adoption of additional statutory or administrative acts for its entry into force.[3] The provisions of international treaties can be integrated into the Russian legal system in two ways: by direct application or by a special statutory act that amends the existing national law if so required by the treaty. Provisions of international treaties that do not require the laws of a Member State to be amended apply directly if officially published. Treaties requiring the adoption of relevant legal acts and amendments to the domestic legislation cannot apply directly.[4] For their application state authorities must pass the corresponding legal acts. The official media for publication of international law acts are the 'Legislation Bulletin of the Russian Federation', the 'Bulletin of International Treaties', and a designated webpage.[5]

Depending on the type of a treaty (interstate, intergovernmental, or interagency treaties), the Russian Federation can join international treaties on its own behalf, on behalf of its government, or of federal executive authorities. All international treaties of the Russian Federation are an integral part of its legal system,

[1] Article 15(4) of Konstitutsiya Rossiyskoy Federatsii (Constitution of the Russian Federation), adopted by the national vote on 12 December 1993.

[2] Ibid. See also: V Zor'kyn (ed), *Kommentarij k Konstitutsii Rossiyskoy Federatsii* (*Commentary to the Constitution of the Russian Federation*), 2nd edn (Moscow, Norma, 2011); S Sinitsyn, 'Mezhdunarodnye Dogovory i Rossiiskoye Grazhdanskoe Zakonodatel'stvo: k Structure i Sisteme Sovremennogo Prava (chast' 1)' ('International Agreements and Russian Civil Laws: on the Modern Law Structure and System (Part 1)') (2021) 2 *Mezhdunarodnoe Publichnoe i Chastsnoye Pravo* 23; B Shakhnazarov, 'Neposredstvennoye Primenenie Pravil Mezhdunarodnykh Dogovorov pri Osyschestvlenii Zaschity Prav Subjektov Vnutrigosudarstvennykh i Transgranichnykh Otnoshenii' ('Direct Application of the Rules of International Agreements in the Implementation of the Protection of the Rights of Subjects of Domestic and Cross-Border Relations') (2020) 8 *Aktualnye Problemy Rossiiskogo Prava* 174; V Zhuikov, 'Rossiyskoe Zakonodatel'stvo i Mezhdunarodnoe Pravo: Problemy Vzaimodeystviya na Osnove Konstitutsii Rossiyskoy Federatsii' ('Russian Legislation and International Law: Interaction on the Basis of the Russian Constitution') (2020) 3 *Zakon* 115.

[3] N Marysheva (ed), *Mezhdunarodnoye Chastnoye Pravo*: *Uchebnik* (*Private International Law: Textbook*), 4th edn (Moscow, Contract, 2018); V Zhuikov, LB Alekseeva and II Lukashuk (eds), *Mezhdunarodnye Normy o Pravakh Cheloveka i Primenenie ikh Sudami Rossiyskoy Federatsii* (*International Norms on Human Rights and their Application by Russian Courts*) (Moscow, Prava cheloveka, 1996) 11 et seq.; B Osminin, *Prinyatie i Realizatsiya Gosudarstvami Mezdunarodnykh Dogovornykh Obyazatelstv* (*Undertaking and Performance of International Contractual Obligations by the States*) (Moscow, Wolters Kluwer, 2006); S Bakhin, 'Mezhdunarodnaya Sostavlayschaya Pravovoi Sistemy Rossii' ('International Element of Russian Legal System') (2007) 6 *Pravovedenie* 126–37; V Kanashevkiy, 'O Neposredstvonnom Deystvii Mezhdunarodnykh Dogovorov v RF' ('On Direct Application of International Treaties in the RF') (2002) 4 *Rossijskij Yuridicheskiy Zhurnal*.

[4] Article 5 of Federal'niy Zakon ot 15.07.1995 No 101-FZ 'O Mezhdunarodnykh Dogovorakh Rossiyskoy Federatssii' (Federal Law of the Russian Federation 'On the International Treaties of the Russian Federation' dated 15 July 1995 No 101-FZ); I Lukashuk, *Sovremennoye Pravo Mezhdunarodnykh Dogovorov* (*Modern Law of International Treaties*) vol 1 (Moscow, Wolters Kluwer Russia, 2004).

[5] Currently, it is www.pravo.gov.ru.

regardless of the level at which a decision to participate in the treaty was made and the means of expressing governmental consent to be a party to the treaty (signing, ratification, approval, accession, etc).[6]

The Russian Federation's Constitution provides that international treaties apply alongside domestic laws. If domestic laws set forth a rule that contradicts a rule under an international treaty, the provisions of the treaty prevail. At the same time, *not all* treaties overrule national laws. A difficult situation arises where the provisions of a Russian federal act enacted by the Parliament conflict with the provisions of an international treaty, especially if the consent to accede to such treaty has been given not by the Parliament but by a different authority (for example, by the Russian government). On this matter, the Russian Supreme Court takes the view that only international treaties ratified by the Russian Parliament and duly promulgated through publication in the official media prevail over national federal laws.[7]

Although international treaties in principle supersede national legislation, the interpretation of provisions of international conventions produced by interstate authorities cannot contradict the Constitution of the Russian Federation. Decisions of such interstate authorities (for instance, courts, and specifically the European Court of Human Rights[8]) interpreting specific provisions of international treaties that the Russian Federation is party to, must pass the constitutional review of the Constitutional Court.[9]

B. International Conventions

Russia acts as a successor to the Union of Soviet Socialist Republics (USSR). In January 1992 Russia issued a diplomatic note according to which it continued to exercise rights and duties arising out of international treaties formerly in force on

[6] N Ageshkina, *Nauchno-Praktichenskyi Kommentariy k Federal'nomu Zakonu ot 15 iula 1995 g. No. 101-FZ 'O Mezhdunarodnykh Dogovorakh Rossiyskoy Federatssii'* (*Scientific Practical Commentary to the Federal Law of the Russian Federation 'On the International Treaties of the Russian Federation' dated 15 July 1995 No. 101-FZ*) (ConsultantPlus, 2013); B Osminin, *Zaklucheniye i Implementatsiya Mezhdunarodnykh Dogovorov i Vnutrigosudarstvennoye Pravo* (*Conclusion and Implementation of International Treaties and Internal Legislation*) (Moscow, Infotropic, 2010); Lukashuk (n 4 above).

[7] Postanovlenie Plenuma Verkhovnogo Suda Rossiyskoy Federatsii ot 10 oktyabrya 2003 g. No 5 'O Primenenii Sudami Obscheiy Iurisdiktsii Obschepriznannykh Printsypov i Norm Mezhdunarodnogo Prava i Mezhdunarodnykh Dogovorov Rossiyskoy Federatsii' (The Supreme Court Resolution No 5 dated 10 October 2003 'On Application by Courts of General Jurisdiction of Universally Recognised Principles and Norms of International Law and International Treaties of the Russian Federation').

[8] In 2022 Russia ceased to be party to the Convention for the Protection of Human Rights and Fundamental Freedoms of 4 November 1950 (European Convention on Human Rights), thus the decisions of the European Court of Human Rights passed after the denunciation of the Convention are no longer applicable in Russia.

[9] Article 5 of Federal'niy Zakon ot 15.07.1995 No 101-FZ 'O Mezhdunarodnykh Dogovorakh Rossiyskoy Federatssii' (Federal Law of the Russian Federation 'On the International Treaties of the Russian Federation' dated 15 July 1995 No 101-FZ).

the USSR's territory.[10] Thus, a number of international treaties that were ratified or acceded to by the USSR continue to apply on Russian territory.

In particular, being the USSR's successor, Russia was party to the New York Convention of 10 June 1958 on the recognition and enforcement of foreign arbitral awards (330 UNTS 3) and the United Nations Convention of 11 April 1980 on Contracts for the International Sale of Goods (1489 UNTS 3). Russia also acceded to the United Nations Convention of 23 November 2005 on the Use of Electronic Communications in International Contracts (2898 UNTS 3).

Russia participates in the activities of the main intergovernmental international organisations aimed at the unification of private international law, in particular, the International Institute for the Unification of Private Law (UNIDROIT). The following UNIDROIT Conventions are in force in Russia: the UNIDROIT Convention of 28 May 1988 on International Financial Leasing (2312 UNTS 195), the UNIDROIT Convention on International Factoring of 28 May 1988 (2323 UNTS 373; 27 ILM 943), the Convention of 16 November 2001 on international interests in mobile equipment (2307 UNTS 285), and the Protocol of 16 November 2001 to the Convention on international interests in mobile equipment on matters specific to aircraft equipment (2307 UNTS 615).

Regarding the legal instruments developed by the Hague Conference on Private International Law, Russia has ratified or acceded to a number of Hague Conventions related to civil procedure and child protection. Among them are the Hague Civil Procedure Convention (Hague Convention of 1 March 1954 on civil procedure, 286 UNTS 265), the Hague Legalisation Convention (Hague Convention of 5 October 1961 abolishing the requirement of legalisation for foreign public documents, 527 UNTS 189), the Hague Service Convention (Hague Convention of 15 November 1965 on the service abroad of judicial and extrajudicial documents in civil or commercial matters, 658 UNTS 163), the Hague Evidence Convention (Hague Convention of 18 March 1970 on the taking of evidence abroad in civil or commercial matters, 847 UNTS 241), the Hague Child Abduction Convention (Hague Convention of 25 October 1980 on the civil aspects of international child abduction, 1343 UNTS 89) and the Hague Child Protection Convention (Hague Convention of 19 October 1996 on jurisdiction, applicable law, recognition, enforcement and co-operation in respect of parental responsibility and measures for the protection of children, 35 ILM 1391).

Russia is a party to the European Convention of 21 April 1961 on International Commercial Arbitration (484 UNTS 349) and the European Convention of 7 June 1968 on information on foreign law (720 UNTS 147).

[10] Nota Ministerstva Inostrannykh Del RF of 13.01.1991 No 11/Ugp 'O Prodolzhenii Osuschestvleniya Prav i Vypolnenii Obyazatel'stv Vytekauschikh iz Mezhdunarodnykh Dogovorov i Soglasheniy Zakluchennykh SSSR' (Diplomatic Note of Foreign Affairs Ministry of the Russian Federation dated 13 January 1992 No 11/Ugp 'On Continuation of Exercising Rights and Performing Obligations Arising out of International Treaties and Agreements Signed by USSR') (1992) 2 *Diplomaticheskiy Vestnik* 34.

In the sphere of payment instruments, Russia is party to the Convention of 7 June 1930 for the Settlement of Certain Conflicts of Laws in Connection with Bills of Exchange and Promissory Notes (143 UNTS 317), the Convention of 7 June 1930 Providing a Uniform Law for Bills of Exchange and Promissory Notes (143 UNTS 257), and the Convention of 19 March 1931 on the Stamp Laws in Connection with Bills of Exchange (143 UNTS 7).

In addition, Russia is a party to a number of conventions in the sphere of transport law, in particular the Warsaw Convention (Convention of 12 October 1929 for the unification of certain rules relating to international carriage by air, 137 LNTS 11), the Hague Rules (International Convention of 25 August 1924 for the unification of certain rules relating to bills of lading, 120 LNTS 155), the Athens Convention 1974 (Athens Convention of 13 December 1974 relating to the carriage of passengers and their luggage by sea, 1463 UNTS 20), the CMR (Convention of 19 May 1956 on the contract for the international carriage of goods by road, 399 UNTS 189), the TIR Convention (Geneva 14 November 1975 UN Customs Convention on the international transport of goods under cover of TIR Carnets, 1079 UNTS 89), the COTIF (Convention of 9 May 1980 concerning international carriage by rail, 1396 UNTS 2, as amended by the Protocol of Modification of 3 June 1999), and a number of others.

Russia participates in a number of the World Intellectual Property Organization (WIPO) treaties and as of 2012 is a Member State of the World Trade Organization.

C. Regional Multilateral Treaties

Russia participates in political and economic unions formed by the former Soviet republics. These unions have produced a number of international treaties and other legal instruments, some of which include rules on private international law.

Among these unions is the Commonwealth of Independent States (the CIS) which was founded in December 1991 by 11 out of 15 former Soviet republics, with the exception of Estonia, Latvia, Lithuania, and Georgia.[11] The CIS aims to achieve political and economic cooperation among its Member States.

[11] Treaty on the Creation of the Commonwealth of Independent States dated 8 December 1991; Postanovlenie Plenuma Verkhovnogo Suda Rossiyskoy Federatsii ot 12 dekabrya 1991 g. No 2014-1 'O Ratifikatsii Soglasheniya o Sozdanii Sodruzhestva Nezavisimykh Gosudarstv' (The Supreme Court Resolution No 2014-1 dated 12 December 1991 'On Ratification of the Treaty On Creation of the Commonwealth of Independent States'); M Boguslavskiy (ed), *Sovremennoye Mezhdunarodnoye Chastnoye Pravo v Rossii i Evrosoyuze* (*Modern Private International Law in Russia and European Union*) Book 1 (Moscow, Norma, 2013) chapter 6; S Kashkin, *Integratsionniye Pravo v Sovremennom Mire: Sravnitel'no-Pravovoye Issledovaniye* (*Integrated Law in the Modern World: a Comparative Legal Study*) (Moscow, Prospekt, 2015).

The CIS conventions in the field of private international law include, among others, the Kiev Agreement on Settling Disputes Related to Commercial Activities of 20 March 1992,[12] the Minsk Convention on Legal Assistance and Legal Relations in Civil, Family and Criminal Law Matters of 22 January 1993,[13] as amended by the Protocol of 28 March 1997, and the Chisinau Convention on Legal Assistance and Legal Relations in Civil, Family and Criminal Matters of 7 October 2002.[14] These conventions contain provisions on international jurisdiction, the applicable law, and the recognition and the enforcement of foreign judgments.

The 2002 Chisinau Convention serves as the replacement for the 1993 Minsk Convention; in particular, Article 120 of the 2002 Chisinau Convention states that the 1993 Minsk Convention terminates for the states parties of the 2002 Chisinau Convention.[15] The 1993 Minsk Convention remains in effect with respect to the participating Member States that have not yet acceded to the 2002 Chisinau Convention. On 26 June 2022, the 2002 Chisinau Convention entered into force for Russia.[16] The 1993 Minsk Convention continues to apply to relations involving parties from Russia, Georgia and Moldova.

The provisions of the above CIS conventions do not enjoy universal application or fully replace the corresponding national rules on private international law. This creates a patchwork of rules where the applicability of conventions or national private international law rules depends on the parties' nationality and their place of residence.

[12] Parties to the Kiev Agreement are Azerbaijan, Armenia, Belarus, Kazakhstan, Kyrgyzstan, Russia, Tajikistan, Turkmenistan, Uzbekistan, and Ukraine.

[13] The Minsk Convention is in force for Azerbaijan, Armenia, Belarus, Georgia, Kazakhstan, Kyrgyzstan, Moldova, Russia, Tajikistan, Turkmenistan, Uzbekistan, and Ukraine.

[14] The Chisinau Convention is in force for Azerbaijan, Armenia, Belarus, Kazakhstan, Kyrgyzstan, Russia, Tajikistan, and Uzbekistan.

[15] See, generally, A Zhiltsov, 'K Voprosy o Tselesoobraznosti Ratifikatsii Konventsii o Pravovoi Pomoschi i Pravovykh Otnosheniyakh po Grazhdankim, Semeinym i Ugolovnym Delam ot 7 October 2002 (Kishinevskoi Konventsii)' ('On the Issue of Practicability of Ratification of the Convention on Legal Assistance and Legal Relations in Civil, Family and Criminal Matters of 7 October 2002 (the Kishinev Convention)') (2021) 8 *Jurist* 52–56; E Bykova, 'O Ratifikatsii Konventsii o Pravovoi Pomoschi i Pravovykh Otnosheniyakh po Grazhdankim, Semeinym i Ugolovnym Delam' ('On Ratification of the Convention on Legal Assistance and Legal Relationship in Civil, Family and Criminal Matters') (2013) 9 *Rossijskij Sud'ya* 39–42; S Lebedev, *Mezhdunarodnoye Chastnoye Pravo: Uchebnik* (*Private International Law: Textbook*) vol 1 2011 para 3.2.2; O Grigoryeva, 'Razvitiye Pravovykh Osnov Mezhdunarodnoi Pomoschi po Grazhdanskim Delam v Ramkakh Souyza Nezavisimykh Gosudarstv' ('Development of Legal Grounds of International Assistance on Civil Matters Within the Commonwealth of Independent States') (2011) 1 *Pravo i Ekomonika* 72–75; S Bakhin, A Ignatiev, 'Pravovaya pomoshch' i pravovye otnosheniya po grazhdanskim i semeynym delam: korrektirovka reglamentatsii v ramkah SNG (Kishinyovskaya konventsiya 2002)' ('Legal Assistance and Legal Relations in Civil and Family Matters: Amendments to the Regulation within the CIS (2002 Kishinev Convention)') (2005) 4 *Zhurnal mezhdunarodnogo chastnogo prava* 3–20.

[16] Federal'niy Zakon ot 30.12.2021 No 452-FZ 'O Ratifikatsii Konventsii o Pravovoi Pomoschi i Pravovykh Otnosheniyakh po Grazhdankim, Semeinym i Ugolovnym Delam' (Federal Law of the Russian Federation 'On ratification of the Convention on Legal Assistance and Legal Relations in Civil, Family and Criminal Matters' dated 30 December 2021 No 452-FZ).

Another economic union which Russia had been a part of was the Eurasian Economic Community (EurAsEc). It existed from 2000–14 and was formed by Russia, Belarus, Kazakhstan, Tajikistan, and Kyrgyzstan. After 2014, the EurAsEc became the basis of the currently existing Eurasian Economic Union (the EAEU) formed on 1 January 2015. The Member States of the EAEU are Russia, Belarus, Kazakhstan, Kyrgyzstan, and Armenia, and its principal aim is to intensify the economic cooperation between the Member States. Therefore, most legal instruments of the EAEU relate to public law fields such as customs regulations (eg the unified Customs Code of EAEU which is in force in the Member States as of 1 January 2018) and technical standards.

In 1999, Russia and Belarus formed a Union State by signing the Treaty of 8 December 1999 on the Creation of the Union State between the Russian Federation and the Republic of Belarus. Within this framework, the 2001 Agreement between Russia and Belarus on the procedure of mutual enforcement of court judgments provides that judgments of the Russian *arbitrazh* (commercial) courts and judgments of the Belarusian commercial courts are automatically recognised and enforced on each other's territory without additional formalities and without the need to receive *exequatur* in the local courts. The action plan for the implementation of the Union State Treaty introduces the creation of unified legislation such as the Tax Code and the Principles of Civil Law.

D. Bilateral Treaties

Russia is a party to over 40 bilateral treaties addressing the issues of legal assistance in civil, family, civil procedure, and criminal law matters. The majority of these treaties have been signed by the USSR and include provisions on the recognition and enforcement of court judgments. Some of them include choice of law rules as well, such as the treaties with Hungary (1958), Bulgaria (1975), Vietnam (1981), Czech Republic (1982), Slovakia (1982), Cuba (1984), Lithuania (1992), Kyrgyzstan (1992), Azerbaijan (1992), Estonia (1993), Latvia (1993), Moldova (1993), Iran (1996), Poland (1996), Egypt (1997), Mongolia (1999), and India (2000).

Russia is a party to a number of bilateral agreements for the encouragement and protection of investments, most of which contain clauses on the resolution of disputes arising between private investors and the Contracting State by means of arbitration. Bilateral investment agreements have been concluded with, among others, Austria, Argentina, Canada, Finland, France, Germany, Indonesia, Italy, Japan, Luxembourg, Norway, Qatar, Switzerland, UAE, the United Kingdom, the United States.[17]

[17] The full list of bilateral treaties that Russia is a party to can be found on the official website of the Ministry of Foreign Affairs, https://www.mid.ru/ru/foreign_policy/international_contracts/international_contracts/2_contract/.

II. National Law

Under the Constitution, conflict-of-laws rules fall within the exclusive competence of the federal legislation, as opposed to the laws of the divisions of the federation, ie administrative parts of the federation with legislative powers that include republics, territories, regions, autonomous areas, and cities of federal significance. This means that private international law rules can be enacted only by the Russian Parliament in the form of federal laws.[18]

Russia is a civil law jurisdiction, and the statutory laws enacted by the Parliament are a major source of law. There is no Private International Law Code or Act in Russia similar to that in some other countries, such as Switzerland or Serbia, or any other special Act comprising conflict-of-laws rules. Instead, private international law rules are contained in Section VI of Part III of the Russian Civil Code, titled 'Private International Law',[19] as well as some other federal laws. The Supreme Court clarified[20] that in addition to the Civil Code the sources of private international law in Russia include, among others, the Family Code[21] (Section VII 'Application of the family law to family relations with foreigners and stateless persons') and the Maritime Code[22] (Chapter XXVI 'Applicable Law' containing conflict-of-laws provisions regarding vessel property, shipping contracts, tort obligations arising out of 'marine adventure', and other maritime matters).

The most important source of Russian private international law is Section VI of Part III of the Russian Civil Code. Part III of the Civil Code was adopted in 2002 and underwent a substantial reform in 2013. Current conflict-of-laws rules contained in the Russian Civil Code take into account the latest developments in private international law of the EU and Switzerland. Section VI of the Civil Code consists of three chapters. Chapter 66 'General provisions' contains general rules on private international law, such as concepts of reciprocity, *renvoi*, public policy, and the norms of direct application (overriding mandatory provisions). Chapter 67 'Law Applicable to Determination of the Legal Status of Persons' covers the rules concerning the law applicable to individuals and corporations. Chapter 68 'Law Applicable to Property and Personal Non-Property Relations' contains the rules on determining the law applicable to property rights, contractual obligations, and

[18] Article 71 of the Constitution.

[19] Federalniy Zakon ot 26.11.2001 No 146-FZ, Grazhdankiy Kodeks Rossiyskoy Federatsii, Chast' Tretiya (Federal Law dated 26 November 2001 No 146-FZ, Civil Code of the Russian Federation, Part three).

[20] Postanovlenie Plenuma Verkhovnogo Suda RF ot 9.07.2019 No 24 'O Primenenii Norm Mezhdunarodnogo Chastnogo Prava Sudami Rossiyskoy Federatsii' (Resolution of the Plenum of the Russian Supreme Court 'On the Application of Private International Law Rules by the Courts of the Russian Federation' dated 9 July 2019 No 24).

[21] Semeiniy Kodeks Rossiyskoy Federatsii ot 29.12.1995 No 223-FZ (Family Code of the Russian Federation dated 29 December 1995 No 223-FZ).

[22] Kodeks Torgovogo Moreplavaniya Rossiyskoy Federatsii ot 30.04.1999 No 81-FZ (Maritime Code of the Russian Federation dated 30 April 1999 No 81-FZ).

conflict-of-laws provisions for certain groups of relationships such as unilateral contracts, assignment, agency, tort liability, unjust enrichment, and inheritance.[23]

The rules concerning international jurisdiction in civil and commercial matters and the recognition and enforcement of foreign judgments are contained in procedural codes. The Russian state court system consists of two separate sub-systems and includes courts of general jurisdiction, which hear civil disputes involving at least one natural person who is not registered as an entrepreneur, and state *arbitrazh* (commercial) courts, which hear commercial disputes involving business parties (ie legal entities and natural persons registered as entrepreneurs). The supreme judicial authority for both court sub-systems is the Supreme Court of the Russian Federation.[24]

The procedure in courts of general jurisdiction follows the Russian Civil Procedural Code,[25] which sets forth the rules on international jurisdiction in Chapter 44, rules on the recognition and enforcement of foreign judgments and foreign arbitral awards in Chapter 45, and the rules governing cases where a party is a foreign state in Chapter 45.1. Simultaneously, the procedure in *arbitrazh* courts follows the Russian *Arbitrazh* Procedure Code,[26] which includes inter alia Chapter 31 on the recognition and enforcement of foreign judgments and foreign arbitral awards, Chapter 32 on international jurisdiction, Chapter 33 on the rules governing cases with the participation of foreigners, and Chapter 31.1 on the rules governing the cases where a party is a foreign state.

A number of laws govern the status of foreign persons on the territory of the Russian Federation,[27] the treatment of international investments,[28] and

[23] A Makovskiy, *O Kodifikatsii Grazhdanskogo Prava (1922–2006)* (*On Codification of Civil Law (1922–2006)*) (Moscow, Statut, 2010); O Sadikov,'Die Kodifikation Des Internationalen Privatrechts Rußlands' (2003) 67(2) *Rabels Zeitschrift Für Ausländisches Und Internationales Privatrecht* 318–40, www.jstor.org/stable/27878374; S Lebedev, A Muranov, R Khodykin and E Rabatov, 'New Russian Legislation on Private International Law' (2002) 4 *Yearbook of Private International Law* 118; N Marysheva and V Zvekov, 'Novaya Kodifikatsiya Norm Mezhdunarodnogo Chastnogo Prava' ('New Codification of Private International Law Norms') (2002) 4 *Khozyaistvo i Pravo* 3–16; N Marysheva and V Zvekov, 'Novaya Kodifikatsiya Norm Mezhdunarodnogo Chastnogo Prava' ('New Codification of Private International Law Norms') (2002) 5 *Khozyaistvo i Pravo* 3–10.

[24] A Vereschagin, 'O Proiskhozdenii Rossiiskoi Sudebnoi Sistemy i ee Persepktivakh' ('Russian Judicial System: Roots and Prospects') (2019) 4 *Zakon* 54–66; N Yurova, *Mezhdunarodnoye Grazhdanskoye Protsessual'noye Pravo: Teoreticheskiye Osnovy Implementatsii Norm v Pravovoy Sisteme Rossiiskoy Federatsii* (*International Civil Procedure Law: Theoretical Grounds of Implementation of Norms in the Legal System of the Russian Federation*) (Moscow, Wolters Kluwer, 2008); N Marysheva, 'Voprosy Kodifikatsii Norm Mezhdunarodnogo Grazhdanskogo Protsessa v Rossii' ('On Codification of International Civil Procedure Norms in Russia') (2004) 6 *Zhurnal Rossijskogo Prava*.

[25] Grazhdanskiy Protsessualniy Kodeks Rossiyskoy Federatsii ot 14.11.2002 No 138-FZ (Civil Procedural Code of the Russian Federation dated 14 November 2002 No 138-FZ).

[26] Arbitrazhniy Protsessuakniy Kodeks Rossiskoy Federatsii ot 24.07.2002 No 95-FZ (*Arbitrazh* Procedure Code of the Russian Federation dated 24 July 2002 No 95-FZ).

[27] Federalniy Zakon Rossiyskoy Federatsii 'O Pravovom Polozhenii Inostrannykh Grazhdan v Rossiyskoy Federatsii' ot 25.07.2002 No 115-FZ (Federal Law of the Russian Federation 'On Legal Status of Foreign Citizens in the Russian Federation' dated 25 July 2002 No 115-FZ).

[28] Federalniy Zakon Rossiyskoy Federatsii 'Ob Inostrannykh Investitsiyakh v Rossiyskoy Federatsii' ot 9.07.1999 No 160-FZ (Federal Law of the Russian Federation 'On International Investments in the Russian Federation' dated 9 July 1999 No 160-FZ).

international commercial arbitration.[29] The Russian Labour Code provides for conflict-of-laws provisions governing the employment of foreign persons on Russian territory.[30]

III. Case Law

Russia has historically been a civil law jurisdiction.[31] Accordingly, case law and judicial precedent are not officially recognised as sources of law.[32] However, rulings and legal reasoning of the highest judicial authorities, ie the Constitutional Court, the Supreme Court, and the former Highest *Arbitrazh* (Commercial) Court,[33] are all important sources of guidance for the lower courts.

The Constitutional Court in particular has contributed to the increasing role of judicial practice in the Russian legal system.[34] The Constitutional Court has the power to assess the constitutionality of a normative act of any state or other body, including the President, the Parliament, the government, federal and regional ministries, local authorities, etc,[35] and, among other things, reviews the constitutionality of federal laws and other normative acts upon requests from lower courts.[36] Laws or their specific provisions recognised as unconstitutional do not have legal force, and the international treaties of the Russian Federation that do not comply with the Constitution may not enter into force and apply in Russia.[37] The Constitutional Court has the authority to modify the law by recognising its legal norms as unconstitutional ('negative law-making').[38]

[29] Zakon RF 'O Mezhdunarodnom Kommercheskom Arbitrazhe' ot 7.07.1993 No 5338-1 (Law of the Russian Federation 'On International Commercial Arbitration' dated 7 July 1993 No 5338-1).

[30] Trudovoy Kodeks Rossiyskoy Federatsii ot 30.12.2001 No 197-FZ (Labour Code of the Russian Federation dated 31 December 2001 No 197-FZ).

[31] See, eg, D Maleshin, 'The Russian Style of Civil Procedure' (2007) 21 *Emory International Law Review* 543.

[32] M Karayanidi, 'Adjudicative Jurisdiction in Civil and Commercial Matters in Russia: Analysis and Commentary' (2016) 64 *The American Journal of Comparative Law* 981, 983.

[33] The Highest *Arbitrazh* Court, which was the highest judicial authority for commercial disputes, was abolished during the constitutional reform of August 2014, and its powers transferred to the Supreme Court.

[34] E Taribo, *Sudebnyj Konstitutsionnyi Normokontrol': Osmysleniye Rossiiskogo Opyta* (*Normative Control of the Constitutional Court: Understanding the Russian Experience*) (Moscow, Norma, 2018); A Malyushin, *Konstitutsionno-sudenboye Pravotvorchestvo v Rossiiskoy Federatsii: Problemy Teorii i Praktiki* (*Lawmaking of Constitutional Court in the Russian Federation: Theoretical and Practical Problems*) (Moscow, Yurist, 2013).

[35] Paragraph 7 of Postanovlenie Plenuma Verkhovnogo Suda RF ot 31.10.1995 No 8 'O Nekotorykh Voprosakh Primeneniya Sudami Konstitutsii Rosskiyskoy Federatssi Pri Osuschestvlenii Pravodudiya' (the Resolution of the Plenum of the Supreme Court dated 31 October 1995 No 8 'On Certain Issues of the Application by Courts of the Constitution of the Russian Federation').

[36] Article 125(4)(b) of the Constitution.

[37] Article 125(6) of the Constitution.

[38] See, eg, I Ostapovich, 'Osobennosti Zakonotvorcheskikh Polnomochiy Konstitutsionnogo Suda Rossiyskoy Federatsii' ('Features of Legislative Powers of the Constitutional Court of the Russian Federation') (2014) 4 *Vestnik Omskogo Universiteta* 100, 104.

Since 2016,[39] the Constitutional Court has also been empowered to recognise a norm as constitutional but only under the interpretation given to it by the Constitutional Court ('positive law-making'), and such interpretation has to lead to a corresponding amendment of the law.[40] The application of such legal norms in a manner diverging from the interpretation given to them by the Constitutional Court is thus not allowed. The Constitutional Court's rulings are an important source of guidance on PIL matters as well. For example, in 2011 the Constitutional Court clarified the issue of arbitrability of real estate disputes. Previously, there had been a consistent practice of *arbitrazh* (commercial) courts that considered real estate disputes to be non-arbitrable on the grounds that they involved a public element, ie registration of legally relevant actions concerning a land plot in the state register.[41] On this basis, a conclusion was made that real estate disputes fall within the exclusive jurisdiction of the Russian *arbitrazh* courts under Article 248 of the Russian *Arbitrazh* Procedure Code and cannot be arbitrated. The Constitutional Court assessed the constitutionality of relevant provisions and concluded that a mere requirement of state registration did not confer a public nature upon real estate disputes, and the latter were therefore capable of adjudication by arbitral tribunals.[42]

The Supreme Court of the Russian Federation plays an important role in the formation of law as well. Article 126 of the Constitution grants the Supreme Court the power to provide clarifications of the court practice, and such clarifications are binding for the lower courts. Up until 2014, the Highest *Arbitrazh* Court had the same function, sometimes doing this jointly with the Supreme Court.[43] Clarifications can be given by means of resolutions of the Plenum of the

[39] Federal'niy Konstitutsionniy Zakon ot 21.07.1994 No 1-FKZ 'O Konstitutsionnom Sude Rossiyskoy Federatssii' (Federal Constitutional Law of the Russian Federation 'On the Constitutional Court of the Russian Federation' dated 21 July 1994 No 1-FKZ).

[40] Ostapovich (n 38 above) 101.

[41] See, in particular, para 27 of Informatsionnoe Pismo Presidiuma VAS RF ot 22.12.2005 No 96 'Obzor Praktiki Rassmotreniya Arbitrazhnymi Sudami Del o Priznanii i Privedenii v Ispolnenie Resheniy Treteiskikh Sudov i o Vudache Ispolnitel'nykh Listov na Prinuditel'noe Ispolnenie Resheniy Treteyskikh Sudov' (Information Letter of the Presidium of the Highest *Arbitrazh* Court dated 22 December 2005 No 96 'The Overview of the Practice of Consideration by *Arbitrazh* Courts of Cases Concerning the Recognition and Enforcement of Foreign Court Judgments, Appeal of Arbitral Awards, and Enforcement of Arbitral Awards').

[42] Postanovlenie Konstitutsionnogo Suda ot 25.05.2011 No 10-P 'Po Dely o Proverke Konstitutsionnosti Polozheniy Punkta 1 Statii 11 Grazhdanskogo Kodeksa Rossiyskoy Federatsii, Punkta 2 Statii 1 Federal'nogo Zakona "O Treteyskikh Sudakh v Rossiyskoy Federatsii", Statii 28 Federalnogo Zakona "O Gosudarstvennoy Registratsii Prav na Nedvizhimoe Imuschestvo i Sdelok s Nimi", Punkta 1 Statii 33 i Statii 51 Federalnogo Zakona "Ob Ipoteke (Zaloge Imuschestva)" v Svayzi s Zaprosom Vysshego Arbitrazhnogo Suda Rossiyskoy Federatsii' (Resolution of the Constitutional Court of the Russian Federation dated 26 May 2011 No 10-P 'In the Case Concerning the Assessment of the Constitutionality of Article 11(1) of the Civil Code of the Russian Federation, Article 1(2) of the Federal Law "On Arbitration Courts in the Russian Federation", Article 28 of the Federal Law "On State Registration of Rights to Immovable Property and Transactions with Such Property", Articles 33(1) and 51 of the Federal Law "On Mortgage (Pledge of Immovable Property)" in Connection with the Request by the Highest *Arbitrazh* Court').

[43] Karayanidi (n 32 above) 983–84.

Supreme Court, which consists of all the Supreme Court judges; resolutions of the Presidium of the Supreme Court, which consists of the 13 members, including the Court President, its deputies, and approved judges of the Supreme Court; and court practice reviews approved by the Presidium of the Supreme Court. Most resolutions that were issued by the Highest *Arbitrazh* Court during the time of its functioning currently remain in force unless revised later by the Supreme Court and are applied by the *arbitrazh* courts. Under Russian law, references to the legal positions of the Supreme Court and the Highest *Arbitrazh* Court can be made in the statement of reasons of a court judgment. Abstract clarifications of the highest judicial authorities have become such an integral part of the Russian law that they are considered to be de facto sources of law in the academic doctrine.[44]

Regarding PIL matters, the most important rulings in this respect are the Resolutions of the Plenum of the Supreme Court 'On the Application of Private International Law Rules by the Courts of the Russian Federation' dated 9 July 2019 No 24[45] – that gives guidance on the application of the post-reform provisions of Russian PIL – and 'On the Consideration by *Arbitrazh* Courts of Economic Disputes Arising out of Relationships Involving a Foreign Element' dated 27 June 2017 No 23,[46] as well as the Review of the *Arbitrazh* Court Practice on Certain Matters Related to the Proceedings Involving Foreign Persons dated 9 July 2013 No 158.[47]

IV. Doctrine

As a rule, academic writings are not a formal source of law in Russia. It is therefore quite uncommon for a Russian judge to refer to academic literature in a court judgment. Nonetheless, legal doctrine has significantly influenced recent

[44] G Esakov, 'The Russian Criminal Jury: Recent Developments, Practice, and Current Problems' (2012) 60 *The American Journal of Comparative. Law* 665, 672 fn 21; see also: T Neshataeva, 'K Voprosy ob Istochnikakh Prava – Sudebnom Pretsedente i Doktrine' ('On the Sources of Law – Court Precedent and Doctrinal Writings') (2000) 5 *Vestnik VAS RF* 105–7; see discussion in: V Zvekov, 'Sources of Private International Law' in N Marysheva (ed), *Mezhdunarodnoe Chastnoe Pravo: Uchebnik* (*Private international Law: Textbook*), 4th edn (Moscow, Contract, 2018) 15.

[45] Postanovlenie Plenuma Verkhovnogo Suda RF ot 9.07.2019 No 24 'O Primenenii Norm Mezhdunarodnogo Chastnogo Prava Sudami Rossiyskoy Federatsii' (Resolution of the Plenum of the Russian Supreme Court 'On the Application of Private International Law Rules by the Courts of the Russian Federation' dated 9 July 2019 No 24).

[46] Postanovlenie Plenuma Verkhovnogo Suda RF ot 27.06.2017 No 23 'O rassmotrenii arbitrazhnymi sudami del po ekonomicheskim sporam, voznikajuschim iz otnoshenii, oslozhnennykh inostrannym elementom' (Resolution of the Plenum of the Russian Supreme Court 'On the Resolution by *Arbitrazh* Courts of Economic Disputes Arising out of Relationships Involving a Foreign Element' dated 27 July 2017 No 23).

[47] Informatsionnoe Pismo Presidiuma VAS RF ot 9.07.2013 No 158 'Obzor Praktiki Rassmotreniya Arbitrazhnymi Sudami Del s Uchastiem Inostrannykh Lits' (the Information Letter of the Presidium of the Highest *Arbitrazh* Court of the Russian Federation No 158 dated 9 July 2013 'Overview of the Practice of Consideration by *Arbitrazh* Courts of Cases Involving Foreign Persons').

developments of PIL in the country.[48] The members of the working group responsible for the reform of private international law analysed deeply Russian and foreign legal doctrine in the search of the best theoretical and practical solutions.[49]

Furthermore, until January 2021, the Constitutional Court officially accepted amicus briefs, ie opinions of legal institutions and scholars, on cases under consideration in the Constitutional Court.[50] Such legal opinions could contain information highly relevant to the legal issue, its historical background, comparative law research, and an analysis of public attitudes. The parties to a dispute in the *arbitrazh* courts and courts of general jurisdiction can obtain legal opinions from scholars and refer to the doctrinal writings in their briefs. The resulting legal opinions are attached to the case file as evidence and, though they do not constitute a source of law and are not officially binding, can be taken into account by a judge.

V. Customary Law

Customary rules are an official source of Russian law, including PIL, both according to national laws[51] and international treaties that Russia is a party to. For instance, references to customary rules can be found in the 1980 UN Convention on the International Sale of Goods (CISG) and the 1961 European Convention on International Commercial Arbitration. It should be noted, however, that these rules are predominantly of a substantive rather than a conflict-of-laws character.[52] As a matter of illustration, the Russian Maritime Code provides that customary

[48] I Khuzhokova, *Doktrina Dobrykh Nravov i Publichnogo Poryadka v Dogovornom Prave: Sravnitel'noye Issledovaniye* (*The Doctrine of Bona Fides and Public Policy in the Contract Law: a Comparative Study*) (Moscow, Norma, 2011); I Getman-Pavlova and N Yerpyleva, 'Rossiiskoye Zakonodatel'stvo po Mezhdunarodnomu Chastnomu Pravu: Problemy Sovershenstvovaniya' ('Russian Legislation on Private International Law: Improvement Problems') (2009) 1 *Mezhdunarodnoye Publichnoye i Chastnoye Pravo*; I Shugurova, 'Mezhdunarodnoye Chastnoye Pravo: Vzaimodeystviye Nauki i Praktiki' ('Private International Law: Interaction of Science and Practice') (2008) 5 *Mezhdunarodnoye Publichnoye i Chastnoye Pravo*; Neshataeva (n 44 above).

[49] 'Obobscheniya Diskussij Rabochei Gruppy po Podgotovke Izmenenyi i Dopolnenyi v Razdel VI "Mezhdunarodnoye Chastnoye Pravo" GK RF' ('Overviews of the Discussions of the Working Group on the Preparation of Amendments to the Division VI "Private International Law" of the Civil Code of the Russian Federation') (2019) 19(2) *Vestnik Grazhdanskogo Prava*.

[50] Reshenie Konstitutsionnog Suda Rossiyskoy Federatsii ot 28.01.2021 (Decision by the Constitutional Court of the Russian Federation dated 28 January 2021).

[51] Articles 5 and 1186 of the Civil Code. The provision of Article 5 used to cover only customary rules applicable to business relations and trade matters but was amended in 2013 with a view to giving it a wider scope (see Federalniy Zakon 'O Vnesenii Ismeneniy v Glavy 1, 2, 3 i 4 Chasti Pervoy Grazhdanskogo Kodeksa Rossiyskoy Federatsii' ot 30.12.2012 No 302-FZ (Federal Law of the Russian Federation 'On the Amendment of Chapters 1, 2, 3 and 4 of Part One of the Civil Code of the Russian Federation' dated 30 December 2012 No 302-FZ)).

[52] Zvekov (n 44 above) 37; L Lunts, *Kurs mezhdunarodnogo chastnogo prava* (*Course of Private International Law*) (Moscow, Spark, 2002) 103.

rules recognised on the Russian territory are a source of law governing the relationships arising out of commercial maritime matters involving foreign persons or otherwise complicated by a foreign element.[53] It further establishes that, if agreed upon by the parties or in case of lacunae in the applicable law, the York Antwerp rules or other customary rules apply to rights and duties of the ship and cargo owners if the cargo must be jettisoned to save the ship.[54]

Reference to customary rules in commercial arbitration is explicitly sanctioned by Russian law, which provides that an arbitral tribunal renders an award on the basis of the terms of the contract and taking into account applicable customary trade.[55] Arbitral practice shows that such codifications of customary rules as Incoterms and various ICC codifications (eg, ICC Uniform Rules for Demand Guarantees, the ICC Uniform Customs and Practice for Documentary Credits, and the ICC Uniform Rules for Collections) are applied by arbitral tribunals constituted under the rules of the International Commercial Arbitration Court at the Chamber of Commerce and Industry of the Russian Federation.[56]

In the hierarchy of sources of law, customary rules follow applicable laws and contractual terms. The Civil Code, in particular, envisages that if a contractual term is not determined by the parties or a dispositive norm of applicable law, it is to be defined by customary rules.[57] If the parties to a cross-border contract use the trade terms accepted in international commerce in their contract, then in the absence of other indications in the contract, it is considered that the parties have agreed to the application to their relationships of the customs designated by the relevant trade terms.[58]

The definition of a customary rule is not set out by the laws. A customary rule is usually defined by scholars as an existing rule of conduct that can be objectively verified and widely applies in civil and commercial relations.[59] The Plenum of the Supreme Court confirmed that customary rules in trade law, as well as customary

[53] Article 414 of the Maritime Code.

[54] Article 285(2) of the Maritime Code. The York Antwerp Rules codify maritime rules that have existed since 1890 and can be accessed via the official website of the Comité Maritime International: https://comitemaritime.org/work/york-antwerp-rules-yar/.

[55] Article 28(3) of Zakon RF 'O Mezhdunarodnom Kommercheskom Arbitrazhe' ot 7.07.1993 No 5338-1 (Law of the Russian Federation 'On International Commercial Arbitration' dated 7 July 1993 No 5338-1).

[56] I Zykin, *Vneshneekonomicheskie Operatsii: Pravo i Praktika* (*Foreign Economic Operation: Law and Practice*) (Moscow, International Relations Publishers, 1994) 241; see also: M Karayanidi, 'Russian Perspectives on the Hague Principles' in D Girsberger, T Kadner Graziano and JL Neels (eds), *Choice of Law in International Commercial Contracts* (Oxford, Oxford University Press, 2021).

[57] Article 421(5) of the Civil Code.

[58] Article 1211(11) of the Civil Code.

[59] Marysheva (n 3 above) chapter 2 para 4; K Ananyeva and A Ananyev, 'Obychaj i Iego Znacheniye kak Istochnika Grazhdanskogo Prava' ('Customary Rule and its Meaning as a Source of Civil Law') (2015) 15 *Yurist* 35–39; I Novitskiy, *Obychaj Grazhdanskogo Oborota v Projekte Obyazatel'stvennogo Prava* (*Customary Rule in Civil Commerce in the Draft Law of Obligations*) vol 1 (Moscow, Statut, 2006); V Laptev, 'Lokal'niy Pravovoy Obychay kak Istochnik Regulirovaniya Pradprinimatel'skikh Otnosheniy' ('A Local Custom As A Source of Regulation of Business Relations') (2017) 4 *Lex russica* 110–19.

rules in other areas, eg customary rules for determination of the procedure of using common property and performing contractual obligations, fall within the scope of Article 5 of the Civil Code. According to Article 5(2) of the Civil Code, customary rules do not apply if they contravene the basic principles of civil law, legislative provisions, or an agreement that is binding upon the parties.[60]

A customary rule does not require to be recorded in a specific form to apply, although there can exist a written record of it.[61] For instance, the customary rule can be published in the press, or set out in a court judgment rendered in a specific case with similar factual circumstances, or attested by the Chamber of Commerce and Industry of the Russian Federation. The existence of the record, however, is not necessary. The burden of proof of the existence of a customary rule is on the party who refers to it.[62] Under the Civil Code the parties to a contract can also refer to the standard contractual terms published in the press.[63] It has been clarified by the Highest *Arbitrazh* Court that if not provided otherwise, standard contractual terms can apply as customary rules.[64] That being said, customary rules are not widely used in court practice. Mainly, courts refer to them in the context of disputes arising out of maritime and rail transportation matters.

ANDREY SHIRVINDT

VI. Non-State Rules of Law

Various kinds of rules developed or 'restated' by non-state actors and not backed by a sovereign's power – typically referred to as 'soft law', 'non-state law', '*lex mercatoria*', or the like – have been warmly received by the Russian legislature, judiciary, and academia. Thus, the UNIDROIT Principles of International Commercial

[60] Postanovlenie Plenuma Verkhovnogo Suda Rossiyskoy Federatsii ot 23.06.2015 No 25 'O Primenenii Sudami Nekotorykh Polozheniy Razdela I Chasti Pervoy Grazhdanskogo Kodeksa Rossiyskoy Federatsii' (Resolution of the Plenum of the Supreme Court of the Russian Federation dated 23 June 2015 No 25 'On the Application of Certain Provisions of Section I Part I of the Civil Code of the Russian Federation').

[61] N Samsonov, 'K Voprosy o Sudebnykh Obychayakh i Obyknoveniyakh' ('On Judicial Customs and Usages') (2020) 3 *Vestnik Grazhdanskogo Protsessa* 261–80.

[62] See generally A Sukhanov (ed), *Rossiyskoe Grazhdanskoe Pravo: Uchebnik (Russian Civil Law: Textbook)*, Vol I (Moscow, Statut, 2011) 89 et seq; M Panarina, 'Rol' Pravovykh Obychaev v Sovremennoi Sudebnoi Praktike: Pravovoye Issledovaniye' ('The Role of Customary Rules in the Modern Judicial Practice: Legal Review') (2018) 3 *Advokatskaya Praktika* 18–24; N Shtykova, 'Pravovaya Priroda Obychaev Delovogo Oborota v Grazhdanskom Oborote Rossii' ('Legal Nature of Business Customary Rules in Russian Civil Commerce') (2013) 4 *Rossijskaya Yustitsiya* 7–10.

[63] Article 427 of the Civil Code.

[64] Postanovlenie Plenuma Vysshego Arbitrazhnogo Suda Rossiyskoy Federatsii ot 14.03.2014 No 16 'O Svobode Dogovora i Ee Predelakh' (Resolution of the Plenum of the Highest Arbitrazh Court dated 14 March 2014 No 16 'On the Freedom of Contract and its Limits').

Contracts (UPICC),[65] the Principles of European Contract Law (PECL), and the Draft Common Frame of Reference (DCFR) as well as multiple publications of the International Chamber of Commerce (Incoterms, uniform rules for collections, demand guarantees, and letters of credit) have inspired the drafters of the Civil Code as well as those working on its large-scale reform launched in 2008;[66] these instruments, further, have frequently been cited by courts and arbitral tribunals[67] and are among standard reference works in legal literature.[68]

Non-state rules may, under certain conditions, become the applicable law. As far as international commercial arbitration is concerned – which is subject to specific choice of law rules[69] – the parties' freedom to choose the applicable law encompasses the possibility of picking non-state sets of rules. This approach has been long entrenched in Article 28(1) of the Law 'On International Commercial Arbitration' 1993, which, being a verbatim reproduction of Article 28(1) of the UNCITRAL Model Law on International Commercial Arbitration, stipulates that 'the arbitral tribunal shall decide the dispute in accordance with such rules of law ['*normy prava*'] as are chosen by the parties as applicable to the substance of the dispute' (first sentence). In a number of reported arbitral awards, the parties' choice

[65] Alexander Komarov, a prominent Russian scholar and arbitrator, involved, inter alia, in the drafting of the Civil Code and its reform, was a member of the working groups that prepared the first three editions of the UPICC (of 1994, 2004, and 2010). His personal commitment to promoting the Principles, including his translations of them into Russian, seems to have contributed to the rise of soft law and to the eminent role of the UPICC among comparable instruments.

[66] A Shirvindt, 'The Effectiveness of International Legal Harmonization through Soft Law (with a Focus on the UCP 600): Russian Report' in A Brandão, L Gama and G Saumier (eds), *The effectiveness of international legal harmonization through soft law (with a focus on the UCP 600)* General Report presented at the XXI Congress of the International Academy of Comparative Law (Intersentia, forthcoming 2024); A Shirvindt, 'Reforming the Russian Civil Code – A Search for Better Law-Making' in J Basedow, H Fleischer and R Zimmermann (eds), *Legislators, Judges, and Professors* (Tübingen, Mohr Siebeck, 2016) 58–59.

[67] The total number of state court judgments explicitly citing the UPICC, PECL, or DCFR (the UPICC being an absolute leader) amounts to several hundred, including six relevant decisions of the highest courts (resolution of the Presidium of the Highest *Arbitrazh* Court No 17984/13, dated 8 April 2014 (UPICC and DCFR); four rulings of the Chamber for Commercial Disputes of the Supreme Court, No 306-ES14-1977, dated 22 January 2015 (DCFR), No 307-ES14-4641, dated 20 May 2015 (UPICC), No 305-ES19-11815, dated 10 September 2019 (UPICC), No 305-ES19-25839, dated 11 June 2020 (UPICC, PECL and DCFR); ruling of the Chamber for Civil Disputes of the Supreme Court No 5-KG20-143-K2, dated 16 February 2021 (UPICC)). For more or less comprehensive accounts of the case law, see V Koval, 'Primenenie negosudarstvennyh svodov chastnogo prava rossijskimi sudami' ('Application of Non-State Restatements of Private Law by Russian Courts') in A Shirvindt and N Scherbakov (eds), *Opyty civilisticheskogo issledovanija* (*Essays in Civil Law*), 5th edn (Moscow, Statut, 2023); A Shirvindt, 'The UNIDROIT Principles as Reference for the Uniform Interpretation of National Laws: National Report for Russian Federation' in AM Garro and JA Moreno Rodríguez (eds), *Use of the UNIDROIT Principles to Interpret and Supplement Domestic Contract Law* (Cham, Springer, 2021); O Malkin and V Domrachev, 'Primenenie principov mezhdunarodnyh kommercheskih kontraktov UNIDRUA dlja tolkovanija i vospolnenija nacional'nogo zakonodatel'stva' ('The Use of the UNIDROIT Principles of International Commercial Contracts to Interpret and Supplement Domestic Law') (2016) 94(4) *Zhurnal mezhdunarodnogo chastnogo prava* (*Journal of International Private Law*) 3.

[68] For an overview, see Shirvindt, 'The Effectiveness of International Legal Harmonization' (n 66 above).

[69] See paragraph 2 of Article 1186(1) of the Civil Code.

of non-state laws has been given effect. The UPICC have been applied as explicitly chosen by the parties[70] or as reflecting 'general principles of *lex mercatoria*'[71] or 'legal principles generally recognised in international trade'[72] based on a party agreement that such principles shall apply.

By contrast, as regards choice of the law to be applied in litigation before state courts, the stance of the legislature has remained conservative. Notwithstanding voices calling for reform,[73] the drafters of the reform of the Civil Code have deliberately left unchanged Article 1210(1), which provides for the parties' freedom to choose the 'law' – meaning only state law and not soft-law instruments – that is applicable to their contractual rights and duties.[74] In 2019, however, a paradigm shift was brought about by factually binding interpretative guidelines issued by the Plenum of the Supreme Court. These guidelines explained that '[t]he parties may also choose documents containing rules recommended … by international organisations or unions of states (e.g. UNIDROIT Principles of International Commercial Contracts, Principles of European Contract Law, Model Rules of European Private Law)'.[75] Under a fair interpretation, the Supreme Court has thus acknowledged the choice of non-state instruments as a genuine choice of law.[76]

Nevertheless, the language of the guidelines reveals a cautious attitude of the Supreme Court towards this novelty. Unlike the Hague Principles on Choice of Law in International Commercial Contracts (Article 3), the guidelines speak only

[70] Award of the ICAC in case No 166/2012, dated 24 May 2013; Award of the ICAC in case No 116/1996, dated 20 January 1997.

[71] Award of the ICAC in case No 11/2002, dated 5 June 2002. See also the award of the ICAC in case No 302/1996, dated 27 July 1999, where the UPICC were invoked by the tribunal as an expression of the *lex mercatoria* that served to supplement the applicable law (CISG, Russian law).

[72] Award of the ICAC in case No M-170/2019, dated 19 February 2020.

[73] See eg A Asoskov, *Kollizionnoe regulirovanie dogovornyh objazatel'stv* (*Contractual Obligations in the Conflict of Laws*) (Moscow, Infotropik Media, 2012) 339–40.

[74] I Zykin in I Zykin, A Asoskov and A Zhiltsov (eds), *Kommentarij k razdelu VI 'Mezhdunarodnoe chastnoe pravo' chasti tret'ej Grazhdanskogo kodeksa Rossijskoj Federacii (postatejnyj)* (*Article-by-Article Commentary on Division VI 'Private International Law' of Part Three of the Civil Code of the Russian Federation*) (Moscow, Statut, 2021) 297.

[75] Paragraph 32, second sub-paragraph of the Postanovlenie Plenuma Verkhovnogo Suda RF ot 09.07.2019 'O Primenenii Norm Mezhdunarodnogo Chastnogo Prava Sudami Rossiyskoy Federatsii' (Resolution of the Plenum of the Russian Supreme Court 'On the Application of Private International Law Rules by the Courts of the Russian Federation' dated 9 July 2019 No 24), https://vsrf.ru/en/files/28804/.

[76] A Asoskov, 'Novoe Postanovlenie Plenuma Verhovnogo Suda RF o primenenii norm mezhdunarodnogo chastnogo prava: kljuchevye raz'jasnenija' ('New Resolution of the Plenum of the Supreme Court of the Russian Federation on the Application of Rules of Private International Law: Key Explanations') (2019) 11 *Sud'ja* (*The Judge*) 12 (Anton Asoskov was a member of the Supreme Court's working group set up to prepare the draft guidelines); O Malkin, 'Vybor principov UNIDRUA v kachestve primenimogo prava: ispol'zovanie gosudarstvennymi sudami podhodov MKAS pri TPP RF' ('Choice of the UNIDROIT Principles as Applicable Law: The Use by State Courts of the Approaches of the International Commercial Arbitration Court at the Chamber of Commerce and Industry of the Russian Federation') (2022) 1 *Tretejskij sud* (*The Arbitral Tribunal*) 79. See, however, Zykin (n 74 above), 296–302, who is still reluctant to admit that Russian PIL allows for the choice of non-state laws, even after the issuance of the guidelines of the Supreme Court.

of 'documents', and hence only of written rules, which means, for instance, that a choice of '*lex mercatoria*' would appear problematic. Further, the guidelines require that rules chosen by the parties have been 'recommended' by international organisations or associations of states. Obviously, this latter prerequisite, vague in itself, becomes even less clear if one considers the examples explicitly mentioned by the Supreme Court.[77] Unlike the general rule on the choice of law by the parties, pursuant to which '[t]he parties' agreement on the choice of the applicable law shall be express or shall clearly follow from the terms of the contract or the entire circumstances of the case' (Article 1210(2) of the Civil Code), the guidelines require that there be an express agreement.[78]

Strictly speaking, if not chosen by the parties as the applicable law, non-state sets of rules cannot be applied except in cases where they are recognised as restatements of (trade) customs, and the custom applies. Thus, Article 28(2) of the Law 'On International Commercial Arbitration', here again following the UNCITRAL Model Law, stipulates that '[f]ailing any designation by the parties, the arbitral tribunal shall apply the law determined by the conflict of laws rules which it considers applicable'. In contrast to Article 28(1), the provision does not refer to 'rules of law'. Yet the UPICC have been applied pursuant to paragraph 4 of the instrument's preamble: 'They may be applied when the parties have not chosen any law to govern their contract'.[79]

Customs belong to the official catalogue of sources of Russian civil law (Articles 5, 6(1), 421(5) of the Civil Code, and others). They are supposed to play a particularly important role in international commercial arbitration since the arbitral tribunal 'shall take into account the usages of the trade applicable to the transaction' 'in all cases' (Article 28(3) of the Law 'On International Commercial Arbitration', reproducing Article 28(4) of the UNCITRAL Model Law). In an array of reported arbitral awards, non-state sets of rules have been considered reliable restatements of international trade customs.[80] Obviously, in such cases the weight of non-state instruments depends on the position of customs in the relevant hierarchy of the sources of law. For instance, the UPICC – seen as a restatement of

[77] On the peculiar status of the UPICC, which were not formally approved by the Governing Council of UNIDROIT but simply published with its authorisation, see S Vogenauer in S Vogenauer (ed), *Commentary on the UNIDROIT Principles of International Commercial Contracts (PICC)*, 2nd edn (Oxford, Oxford University Press, 2015) 9–10.

[78] For criticisms, see Malkin, 'Choice of the UNIDROIT Principles as Applicable Law' (n 76 above).

[79] UPICC, Preamble. Awards of the ICAC in case No M-140/2019, dated 13 January 2020; case No M-17/2017, dated 9 October 2017.

[80] UPICC: award of the ICAC in case No 224/2009, dated 30 June 2010 (through Article 28(3) of the Law 'On International Commercial Arbitration'); awards in case No 83/2008, dated 22 December 2008, and in case No. 217/2001, dated 6 September 2002 (taking customs into account while construing the contract in accordance with Article 431 of the Civil Code); award of the ICAC in case No 229/1996, dated 5 June 1997 (through Article 9(2) of the CISG); awards of the ICAC in case No 302/1996, dated 27 July 1999, and case No 33/2014, dated 5 September 2014. On a tendency to consider the ICC Uniform Customs and Practice for Documentary Credits (UCP 600) as a restatement of trade usages or customs applicable to international transactions, see Shirvindt, 'The Effectiveness of International Legal Harmonization through Soft Law' (n 66 above).

customs – must yield to statutory provisions as far as domestic Russian law applies (Articles 5(2) and 421(5) of the Civil Code), but they will prevail over the CISG if it is applicable (Articles 6 and 9(2) of the CISG).

The UPICC have been used to interpret or supplement international uniform law instruments, mainly the CISG,[81] as well as Russian domestic law.[82] But despite being a relatively widespread practice, such a use of non-state sets of rules is not based on a clearly established doctrine.[83]

[81] Awards of the ICAC in case No 246/2016, dated 14 May 2018 (ambiguous reasoning, may be subsidiary law); case No 11/2009, dated 30 June 2009; case No 23/2006, dated 1 February 2007; case No 97/2002, dated 6 June 2003; case No 302/1996, dated 27 July 1999; case No 152/1998, dated 16 April 1999; case No 229/1996, dated 5 June 1997. See also A Komarov, 'Reference to the UNIDROIT Principles in International Commercial Arbitration Practice in the Russian Federation' (2011) 16(3) *Uniform Law Review* 657, 661–64.

[82] In particular, thus far all the relevant judgments of the Supreme Court and the Highest *Arbitrazh* Court citing the UPICC, the DCFR, and the PECL have concerned purely domestic disputes (see n 67 above). For use of the UPICC as a gap-filler in respect of Russian law in an international context, see the award of the ICAC in case No 218/2012, dated 1 July 2013.

[83] As revealed by surveys of the case law, in an overwhelming majority of cases the courts refer to the UPICC without offering any justification at all, while the patterns of reasoning employed in other judgments tend to be fairly exotic (see Shirvindt, 'The UNIDROIT Principles as Reference for the Uniform Interpretation of National Laws' (n 67 above) 310–12).

3

Fundamental Concepts of Private International Law

ANTON ASOSKOV

I. Types of Conflict Rules and Connecting Factors

Most Russian conflict rules have a structure, which is typical for European private international law. The conflict rule consists of a legal category and a connecting factor (or a combination of several of them). The legal category describes the field of law in which the rule operates, while the connecting factor indicates the applicable law.

Russian private international law uses different types of conflict rules.

A. Bilateral (Multilateral) vs Unilateral Conflict Rules

Typically, conflict rules are formulated as bilateral (multilateral), ie they use a neutral connecting factor, which can lead to the application of either the *lex fori* or foreign law. For example, the conflict rule about the application to rights *in rem* of the law where the thing (asset) is located[1] is a bilateral one, as it can lead to the application of either Russian law (if the asset is in the territory of Russia), or foreign law (if the asset is located abroad). The general tendency is the increase in the number of bilateral conflict rules.

However, there are still some unilateral conflict rules that have various origins. First, several unilateral conflict rules apply in conjunction with rules on international jurisdiction of Russian courts. Russian courts would otherwise lack jurisdiction in cases where there is no basis for the application of domestic law. In other words, the connecting factor that establishes the international jurisdiction of Russian courts is indirectly adopted for the determination of applicable law via the reference to the *lex fori*. For example, the Russian courts have jurisdiction

[1] Article 1205 of the Civil Code.

to declare an individual as missing or deceased if the relevant individual had Russian citizenship or his/her last place of residence was in Russia.[2] Taking this into account, the Russian conflict rule provides that the *lex fori* applies to issues related to the declaration of an individual as missing or deceased.[3]

Another type of unilateral conflict rule is the one which creates an exception from the application of a general multilateral rule in view of significant public interest or third-party interest in application of the *lex fori*. Such rules are known as 'exclusive rules' (*Exklusivnormen*) in the German doctrine of private international law.[4] For example, the general multilateral rule sets forth that the law of the closest connection is applicable to contracts in respect of immovables – introducing also a presumption in favour of the law of the country where the respective immovable property is located.[5] However, the unilateral conflict rule creates an exception and prescribes that the *lex fori* applies for immovables located in Russia.[6] This exception was introduced due to the desire of the Russian legislator to maintain the public reliability of the Russian register of rights to immovable property and taking into account the practical difficulties for Russian registrars to check the contracts' validity based on foreign law.[7]

At the same time, there are no conflict rules in Russian law that would demand the court to assess the scope of application of foreign substantive law provisions (other than foreign overriding mandatory provisions discussed below), ie rules which would follow the concepts of unilateralism in its strict sense.[8]

B. Mandatory vs Facultative (Non-Mandatory) Conflict Rules

This division between mandatory and facultative rules depends on the ability of private parties to choose the applicable law, deviating from objective conflict rules formulated by the legislator (principle of party autonomy in private international law).

Detailed rules on the principle of party autonomy are established in the context of contractual obligations.[9] The parties can choose applicable law by their agreement not only at the moment of entering into a main contract, but also at a later stage.[10] The choice-of-law agreement may be either expressed or implied, ie

[2] Article 403(2)(3) of the Civil Procedure Code.
[3] Article 1200 of the Civil Code.
[4] J Nojack, *Exklusivnormen im IPR* (Tübingen, Mohr Siebeck, 2005).
[5] Article 1213(1) of the Civil Code.
[6] Article 1213(2) of the Civil Code.
[7] AV Asoskov, *Osnovy kollizionnogo prava* (*Basics of Conflict of Laws*) (Moscow, Infotropic Media, 2012) 98–103.
[8] See S Francq, 'Unilateralism' in J Basedow, G. Ruehl, F Ferrari and PM Asensio (eds), *Encyclopedia of Private International Law* Vol 2 (Cheltenham, Edward Elgar Publishing, 2017) 1779–91.
[9] Article 1210 of the Civil Code. See Chapter 5 of this volume for more details.
[10] Article 1210(3) of the Civil Code.

may follow from the terms of the contract or the totality of the circumstances of the case.[11] The parties can split the applicable law, agreeing to apply different law systems to various parts of the contract.[12]

At the same time, the principle of party autonomy applies far beyond the sphere of contractual obligations, making the respective conflict rules from other fields also facultative (non-mandatory). Spouses may choose the applicable law for marriage contracts and maintenance agreements provided that the spouses are citizens of different states and do not have a common place of residence at the date of agreement's conclusion.[13] Parties to the obligation arising from tort or unjust enrichment may choose any applicable law provided that their agreement is concluded after the occurrence of tort or unjust enrichment.[14] Before reform of the Civil Code in 2013, such a choice was limited to *lex fori* only.[15]

Even the law applicable to transfer of ownership and other rights *in rem* in respect of movables may be chosen by the parties' agreement, but this choice is limited to the *lex contractus* applicable to contractual obligations arising out of the same contract, and this choice has *inter partes* effect only (it does not affect the ability of third parties to rely on objective conflict rules).[16] Thus, Russia joins a rather small pool of countries that allow the limited use of party autonomy in the sphere of rights *in rem*.[17]

Russian law also knows optional rules, when the choice of applicable law depends on the will of one party only. For example, for claims arising out of product liability (defects in goods, works or services), the victim can choose between the law of the country where the seller or the manufacturer resides, the law where the victim resides, and the law of the country where the work was performed, the services were rendered, or the goods were acquired.[18]

C. Hard-and-Fast vs Flexible Conflict Rules

Unlike a number of other states,[19] Russian private international law does not have a general universal exception clause which would allow a court to deviate from

[11] Article 1210(2) of the Civil Code.

[12] Article 1210(4) of the Civil Code.

[13] Article 161(2) of the Family Code.

[14] Article 1223.1 of the Civil Code.

[15] See Articles 1219 and 1223 of the Civil Code in the version applicable before 1 November 2013.

[16] Article 1206(3) of the Civil Code.

[17] See, eg, Article 104 of the Swiss Federal Act on Private International Law, which allows the parties to choose not only the *lex contractus*, but also the law of the place of dispatch or destination of movable goods.

[18] Article 1221(1) of the Civil Code. The last two options are not available for choice if the tortfeasor proves that he neither foresaw nor should have foreseen the distribution of goods in the relevant country.

[19] See, eg, Article 15 of the Swiss Federal Act on Private International Law and Article 19 of the Belgian Code on Private International Law.

conflict rules in any field. This was the conscious choice of the Russian legislator, who preferred predictability and certainty in conflict of laws.[20]

The area of flexible conflict rules is limited to contractual obligations. If it clearly follows from the terms or nature of a contract or the totality of circumstances of the case that the contract is more closely connected with the law of some other country, then the law of the country with which the contract is more closely connected shall be applied.[21] In this legislative formula, the term 'clearly' was added by the 2013 legislative reform following the suit of Article 4 of the Rome I Regulation. This indicates the desire of the Russian legislator to strengthen the presumption contained in conflict rules on contractual obligations.[22]

The Supreme Court, in a resolution, provides illustrations of the application of such an 'escape clause'. For example, if a contract is concluded and, according to its terms, is performed via a branch or establishment in another country, the court may apply not the law of the principal place of business,[23] but the law of the country where such branch or establishment is located.[24] The same instrument clarifies that the court, when evaluating the totality of circumstances of the case, should take into account only those circumstances that have already materialised by the date of the contract's conclusion.[25]

D. Conflict Rules with Combinations of Connecting Factors

The remarkable tendency of recent years is the increase of conflict rules with a multiplicity of connecting factors. On many occasions, such a multiplicity helps to give effect to the substantive law result already at the stage of choice of applicable law (eg *favor negotia*, *favor testamenti*, etc).

Alternative connections give the court several options among which the court should choose depending on the optimal substantive result. For example, the conflict rule about the form of transactions contains three various connecting factors – the law applicable to the substance of a transaction (*lex contractus*), the

[20] IS Zykin, 'Razvitie mezhdunarodnogo chastnogo prava v svete prinjatija chasti tret'ej Grazhdanskogo kodeksa Rossijskoj Federacii' ('Development of Private International Law in the Light of Enactment of Part Three of the Civil Code of the Russian Federation') (2002) 12 *State and Law* 60.

[21] Article 1211(9) of the Civil Code.

[22] 'Obobscheniya diskussiy rabochei gruppy po podgotovke dopolneniy i izmeneniy v razdel VI "Mezhdunarodnoe chastnoe pravo" GK RF' ('Summary of the Discussions of the Working Group for Preparing Amendments to Section VI "Private International Law" of the Russian Civil Code') (2019) 2 *Civil Law Review* 133, 151–52.

[23] Which is a default rule under Article 1211(1) of the Civil Code.

[24] Paragraph 36 of the Resolution of the Plenum of the Supreme Court dated 9 July 2019 No 24 'On the Application of Private International Law Rules by the Courts of the Russian Federation'.

[25] Ibid.

law of the place where a transaction was made, and the *lex fori* (Russian law).[26] The optimal substantive result here is the preservation of the formal validity of a transaction. If the application of any of the above-mentioned three legal systems allows the achievement of this optimal substantive result, the court shall apply the respective law and recognise the transaction as formally valid.

Cumulative connections can be characterised as the opposite of alternative connections. Cumulative connections demand the *simultaneous* application of substantive rules of several legal systems in order to achieve a certain substantive-law result. Such a combination makes the respective substantive result more stable and prevents so-called limping relationships or statuses, which are recognised in one state but not in other states. For example, the adoption of a minor having Russian citizenship by a foreign citizen is subject to both the law of nationality of the adoptive person and mandatory rules of Russian family law.[27] This minimises the risk of non-recognition of adoption in both countries.

Distributive connections have the effect of applying different legal systems to separate conditions of the same legal event. Usually, this is also aimed at the prevention of limping relationships. For example, requirements for marriage validity are checked separately for the spouses based on the law of nationality of each of them; certain mandatory provisions of Russian law must also be complied with if the marriage is registered in Russia.[28]

Combined connections safeguard the application of mandatory rules of a certain legal system, which has an important role in protecting a weak party, third party or public interest. For example, a consumer cannot be deprived of his/her right to refer to the mandatory rules of the country of his/her residence provided that a professional party runs its business activities in this country or has otherwise targeted this jurisdiction.[29] Another example is the incorporation contract or shareholders' agreement: the choice-of-law clause shall not affect the effectiveness of the mandatory rules of the country in which a legal entity was incorporated.[30]

'Accessory connections' refers to conflict provisions devoted to distinct but connected legal issues. This helps to avoid unnecessary splitting of applicable law on such closely connected issues (*dépeçage*). For example, no self-standing connecting factor is formulated for the limitation of actions – these issues shall be determined according to the law of the country which is applicable to the respective principal relationship (eg in contract or in tort).[31] The same accessory connection is used for issues related to interest on monetary obligations.[32]

[26] Article 1209(1) of the Civil Code. The last option is available if at least one of the parties has a Russian 'personal statute' (nationality) – see Chapter 4 of this volume.
[27] Article 165(1) of the Civil Code.
[28] Article 156(2) of the Family Code.
[29] Article 1212(1) of the Civil Code.
[30] Article 1214(1) of the Civil Code.
[31] Article 1208 of the Civil Code.
[32] Article 1218 of the Civil Code.

II. Characterisation (Classification)

Characterisation (classification) is the process of interpreting legal concepts and categories contained in conflict rules in order to determine the one that is applicable to a particular issue.[33] This process is an inseparable element of the modern European private international law, which divides all private relationships into a number of groups using broad legal categories (eg contract, tort, unjust enrichment, inheritance, etc), which may have divergent interpretations and scopes of application under various legal systems.

Unlike most other countries, Russia has special statutory provisions on characterisation. As a general rule, the characterisation is made on the basis of the *lex fori* (Russian law).[34] It is natural that the Russian legislator proceeds from the basic legal concepts of Russian substantive law when it formulates legal categories in Russian conflict rules. This solution also helps to avoid a vicious logical circle, which arises in case of the adoption of foreign legal classifications, ie it is impossible to choose a conflict rule until the characterisation is made, but in order to make such a characterisation we need to know what foreign substantive law will be applicable.

If the characterisation was successfully made on the basis of the *lex fori*, and the selected conflict rule points out to a foreign law, this foreign law cannot be disapplied even if it views the same issue as having a different legal nature. The Russian Supreme Court gives an important example: according to Russian law, the limitation of actions is characterised as a substantive-law concept, to which foreign law may apply.[35] Even if the applicable foreign law (eg the law of some common-law jurisdiction) gives another classification (ie views the limitation of actions as a procedural concept subject to the *lex fori*), this shall not prevent Russian courts from applying such foreign law according to the reference in the Russian conflict rule.[36]

However, some foreign legal concepts may be unknown to Russian substantive law (eg the Islamic concept of *mahr*, which must be paid by a groom to a bride under certain circumstances) or known with differing content (eg the Russian concept of fiduciary management is a concept from contract law, which is very different from the Anglo-American trust). In such situations, the court should analyse the specific features of the relevant legal relationship under foreign law[37]

[33] See a similar definition, eg, in S Bariatti 'Classification (Characterization)' in J Basedow, G Ruehl, F Ferrari and PM Asensio (eds), *Encyclopedia of Private International Law* Vol 1 (Cheltenham, Edward Elgar Publishing, 2017) 357.

[34] Article 1187(1) of the Civil Code.

[35] Article 1208 of the Civil Code.

[36] Paragraph 7 of the Resolution of the Plenum of the Supreme Court dated 9 July 2019 No 24.

[37] Article 1187(2) of the Civil Code.

and then look for the closest category of domestic law that performs a similar function (so-called functional characterisation).[38]

An exception is also expressly made for classifying property as movable or immovable. This process must be carried out based on the law where the property is located (*lex rei sitae*).[39] The rationale is that the law of the place of the property's location may contain mandatory provisions in respect of certain assets, which are classified as immovables there. It would be unwise to ignore such provisions by insisting on the concepts of the *lex fori*.

Characterisation on the basis of the lex *lex fori* or *lex causae* is also unsuitable for conflict rules arising from international treaties, as this would undermine their uniform interpretation in various contracting states. In view of that, the Supreme Court emphasises that the interpretation of legal concepts and categories from the conflict rules of international treaties must be conducted using the generally recognised rules from section 3 of the 1969 Vienna Convention on the Law of Treaties.[40]

Once the appropriate conflict rule is selected, provisions on the process of characterisation are no longer applicable. The interpretation of foreign substantive law (which the conflict rule of *lex fori* indicates) must be conducted with the help of other provisions on ascertainment of contents of foreign law discussed below.

III. Preliminary (Incidental) Question

The issue of preliminary (incidental) questions in private international law (PIL) arises when the following conditions are met cumulatively:[41]

(a) In order to decide on a main question, it is required first to take a decision on some preliminary question. For example, in order to determine whether a claimant is entitled to inherit assets or to receive maintenance (main issue), it may be necessary to evaluate the validity of a marriage or establish whether an adoption of a child took place (preliminary question);
(b) The main question is governed by a foreign *lex causae*;
(c) Application of conflict rules of the *lex fori* and *lex causae* leads to diverging results in terms of the law applicable to the preliminary question and the substantive result of the preliminary question.

[38] For a detailed discussion of the concept of functional characterisation see, eg, L Mistelis, *Charakterisierungen und Qualifikation im internationalen Privatrecht: zur Lehre einer parteispezifischen Qualifikation im Kollisionsrecht der privaten Wirtschaft* (Tübingen, Mohr Siebeck, 1999).

[39] Articles 1205 and 1205.1(1) of the Civil Code.

[40] Paragraph 7 of the Resolution of the Plenum of the Supreme Court dated 9 July 2019 No 24.

[41] C Bernitt, *Die Anknuepfung von Vorfragen im europaischen Kollisionsrecht* (Tübingen, Mohr Siebeck, 2010); A Bonomi, 'Incidental (Preliminary) Question' in J Basedow, G Ruehl, F Ferrari and PM Asensio (eds), *Encyclopedia of Private International Law* Vol 2 (Cheltenham, Edward Elgar Publishing, 2017) 912–13.

In theory, there are two competing solutions to the preliminary question. The first one is called the '*lex fori* approach' (or independent connection). According to the first solution, the preliminary question is dealt with in the same manner as if it were the main issue. This means that the court applies its own conflict rules to the preliminary question. It helps to apply the *lex fori* conflict rules in a consistent manner, which does not depend on the context in which the relevant question arises (as a main or preliminary issue).

The second solution is called the '*lex causae* approach' (or dependent approach). Under this solution, the preliminary question is treated as if it were a matter of interpretation of the law applicable to the main issue. This means that the preliminary issue shall be resolved in the manner which the court of the *lex causae* would apply – most frequently using the conflict rules of *lex causae*. This solution helps to promote international harmony of judgments – the approach of the court of the *lex fori* will coincide with the approach of the court of the *lex causae*.

Neither Russian legislation nor Russian case law gives a clear answer to the issue of the preliminary question. As for the doctrine, traditionally it favours the *lex fori* approach (independent connection).[42] Russian commentators stress that the conflict solution should not differ depending on whether one and the same issue arises as a main or preliminary question.

IV. *Renvoi*

In theory, when a conflict rule provides for the application of foreign law, this reference can be interpreted in two different ways.[43] The first interpretation implies that the reference is made to foreign substantive law only – excluding any foreign conflict rules. This interpretation denies any form of *renvoi*.

According to the second possible interpretation, the reference to foreign law is made to the foreign legal system as a whole, including its conflict rules. Under this interpretation, there might be several scenarios. If a foreign conflict rule accepts the reference and does not indicate any other legal system, then no issue of *renvoi* arises. Other option is that a foreign conflict rule may refer back to the *lex fori* (this option is called 'remission' or '*renvoi* of the first degree'). Finally, a foreign conflict rule may refer to a legal system of some third state (this option is called 'transmission' or '*renvoi* of the second degree').

[42] L Lunts, *Kurs mezhdunarodnogo chastnogo prava (Course of Private International Law)* in 3 vols. (Moscow, Spark, 2002) 241.

[43] M Sonnentag, 'Renvoi' in J Basedow, G. Ruehl, F Ferrari and PM Asensio (eds), *Encyclopedia of Private International Law* Vol 2 (Cheltenham, Edward Elgar Publishing, 2017) 1537–39; M Sonnentag, *Der Renvoi im Internationalen Privatrecht* (Tübingen, Mohr Siebeck, 2001) 15f; J Sauveplanne, 'Renvoi' in K Lipstein (ed), *International Encyclopedia of Comparative Law, Vol III: Private International Law* (Tübingen, JCB Mohr 1990) chapter 6.

There is no uniform solution to the *renvoi* problem across the world. Russian PIL takes a middle approach. It does not accept transmission (*renvoi* of the second degree).[44] As a general rule, it also does not accept remission (*renvoi* of the first degree), but makes an important exception allowing remission on matters related to the individual's personal status.[45] This is a compromise solution, which is used in some other jurisdictions as well.[46] The Russian legislator expressly confirms that its preference for remission (in comparison with transmission) is based on the homeward trend and convenience of returning to the application of Russian law in the Russian courts.[47]

Under the 2013 legislative reform, references to particular articles of the Civil Code were removed from the exception rule. This is explained by the desire to apply remission not only in the context of conflict rules on the individual's personal status from the Civil Code, but also to conflict rules dealing with the individual's capacity from the separate Family Code.[48] For example, Article 156 of the Family Code addresses, inter alia, the issue of marriage capacity, and the concept of remission may be invoked here.[49]

V. Non-Unified Legal Systems (Reference to the Law of a Composite State)

A conflict rule may refer to the law of a state in which different private-law regimes apply in different territorial units (a state with non-unified legal systems or 'composite state'). Multi-unit states can either be federal states (eg the USA), or unitary states with composite private-law systems (eg the UK). The multiplicity of legal systems may also be associated with different groups of individuals – depending on their ethnicity, religion, etc.

In Russia, civil legislation falls within the exclusive competence of the federal Russian state, which prevents interregional conflicts if Russian substantive law is applicable. However, family, labour, land and housing legislation falls within the joint competence of the federal state and its territorial units (so-called

[44] Article 1190(1) of the Civil Code.

[45] Article 1190(2) of the Civil Code.

[46] See, eg, Article 14 of the Swiss Federal Act on Private International Law.

[47] 'Obobscheniya diskussiy rabochei gruppy po podgotovke dopolneniy i izmeneniy v razdel VI "Mezhdunarodnoe chastnoe pravo" GK RF' ('Summary of the Discussions of the Working Group for Preparing Amendments to Section VI "Private International Law" of the Russian Civil Code') (2019) 2 *Civil Law Review* 133, 136.

[48] Ibid.

[49] The example of Article 156 of the Family Code is given in para 9 of the Resolution of the Plenum of the Supreme Court dated 9 July 2019 No 24. See also NI Marysheva, 'Obratnaja otsylka v mezhdunarodnom chastnom prave: rossijskoe zakonodatel'stvo' ('Remission in Private International Law: Russian Legislation') (2018) 11 *Journal of Russian Law* 55–62.

'subjects of the Russian Federation'). In these spheres of private law, legal regimes may differ among various Russian territorial units. Such interregional conflicts are resolved based on specific provisions from the respective branches of law (eg Family Code, Land Code, etc). PIL rules from the Civil Code are not applicable to interregional conflicts, as they are supposed to apply to international conflicts only.

Russian PIL provisions may refer to the law of a composite state. In theory, two different models can be used for such situations.[50] The indirect-reference model provides that the reference is made to the law of a composite state as a whole, while national rules of such a composite state shall determine which of the legal systems within the state governs the dispute. However, there may be no federal rules on interregional conflicts in the state referred to. Then, there is a need for a subsidiary rule, which most commonly provides for the application of the law of a territorial unit that has the closest connection with the dispute.

In contrast, the direct-reference model provides that the conflict rule refers both to the law of a composite state, and to a particular territorial unit within such a state. However, this model also demands an additional solution for connecting factors that are unsuitable for delineating a particular territorial unit (eg nationality).

At first sight, Russian PIL sticks to the indirect-reference model. The express statutory provision sets forth that the referenced law of a composite state shall choose the applicable legal system. If this is impossible, the court applies the legal system which has the closest connection.[51]

However, the Supreme Court's guidance changes the approach. It clarifies that the direct-reference model shall be used in the first place if the connecting factor from the conflict rule points to a specific territorial unit within the composite state (eg the connecting factor of an individual's domicile). The indirect-reference model is used only as a subsidiary solution for situations in which the connecting factors are unsuitable for delineating a particular territorial unit (eg nationality).[52]

There are no express clarifications for interpersonal conflicts when different private-law provisions apply to different groups of individuals in the same territory. Most obviously, here the indirect-reference model would be most appropriate, as connecting factors usually have territorial (geographical) orientation and are unable to select between various groups of persons residing in the same territory.

[50] CG Beilfuss, 'Interregional / Interstate Law' in J Basedow, G Ruehl, F Ferrari and PM Asensio (eds), *Encyclopedia of Private International Law* Vol 2 (Cheltenham, Edward Elgar Publishing, 2017) 1015–19; E Vitta, 'Interlocal Conflict of Laws' in K Lipstein (ed) *International Encyclopedia of Comparative Law, Vol III: Private International Law* (Tübingen, JCB Mohr 1986) chapter 9.

[51] Article 1188 of the Civil Code.

[52] Paragraph 8 of the Resolution of the Plenum of the Supreme Court dated 9 July 2019 No 24.

VI. Public Policy (*Ordre Public*)

PIL rules of any state include the public policy clause (clause on *ordre public*) in order to block the application of foreign substantive provisions if their application would manifestly contradict the basic legal or moral principles of the *lex fori*.

According to the language of statutory provisions of Russian legislation,[53] the public policy clause may be triggered only in 'exceptional cases', where the consequences of application of foreign law 'manifestly' contradict the foundations of the Russian legal order. This double emphasis means that the application of the public policy clause can take place only in rare cases of obvious and insurmountable contradiction. Examples of application of the public policy clause in determining the applicable substantive law can scarcely be found in Russian case law.[54]

However, the same concept of public policy is frequently referred to in cases related to the recognition and enforcement of foreign court judgments and arbitral awards. Unfortunately, in this category of cases, the case law is not uniform, and there are examples of the unfounded broad interpretation of the public policy clause.[55]

When applying the public policy clause, the basics of the Russian legal order must be compared not with a foreign legal rule in the abstract, but with the particular consequences of application of the foreign legal rule. Again, this should limit the scope of the concept of public policy. For example, Russian family law does not recognise polygamous marriages. However, if the polygamous marriage was celebrated in a foreign Islamic country, and one of the wives brings a claim to the Russian court for her maintenance or as an heir to the estate of the deceased husband, then there would be no sufficient grounds to say that such particular consequences of the polygamous marriage are manifestly contrary to the fundamental notions of the Russian family law.

In the theory of PIL, there is a distinction between negative and positive functions of public policy.[56] The negative function consists in refusing to give legal effect to the application of particular provisions of foreign law, to which a conflict rule or parties' choice-of-law agreement refers and which was previously

[53] Article 1193 of the Civil Code and Article 167 of the Family Code.

[54] In the case of *Federal Customs Service v Bank of New-York*, the Russian court came across the issue of granting triple punitive damages under the US law. However, no decision was issued on the merits, as the parties reached a settlement. See S Budilin, 'Process o dvadcati dvuh milliardah, ili Neverojatnye prikljuchenija RIKO v Rossii' ('Case on Twenty Two Billions, or Incredible Adventures of RICO in Russia') (2008) 10 *Corporate Lawyer*.

[55] See Chapters 11 and 12 of this volume for more details.

[56] I Thoma, 'Public Policy (Ordre Public)' in J Basedow, G. Ruehl, F Ferrari and PM Asensio (eds), *Encyclopedia of Private International Law* Vol 2 (Cheltenham, Edward Elgar Publishing, 2017) 1453–60; P Lagarde, 'Public Policy' in K Lipstein (ed), *International Encyclopedia of Comparative Law, Vol III: Private International Law* (Tübingen, Mohr Siebeck, 1994) chapter 11; SV Krochalyov, *Kategorija publichnogo porjadka v mezhdunarodnom grazhdanskom processe (Category of Public Policy in the International Civil Procedure)* (St Petersburg, Publishing House of the Saint-Petersburg State University, 2006).

ascertained by the court. The positive function presupposes that certain substantive rules of the *lex fori* apply directly notwithstanding the reference of conflict rules or the parties' agreement to foreign law and independent of the contents of such foreign law. It is well established that the Russian concept of public policy realises the negative function only,[57] while a mechanism similar to the positive function is used for another concept of overriding mandatory provisions (rules of immediate application).[58]

Under the 2013 legislative reform, the statutory provisions of the Civil Code were amended, and it was added that the concept of public policy shall be applied 'taking into account the nature of relations complicated with a foreign element'.[59] The rationale behind this amendment was to influence the unjustified broadening of the public policy clause that was sometimes demonstrated by Russian courts when dealing with the recognition and enforcement of foreign court judgments and arbitral awards.[60] This amendment implements the classification of public policy into domestic (internal) and international policy, which is known to many other jurisdictions (eg France).[61] According to this classification, for domestic purposes (for cases not involving any foreign element), the courts may use a rather broad understanding of public policy, while for international cases, this concept must be narrowed significantly.

The statutory provisions do not provide for any detailed definition of public policy save for the indication that the definition of Russian public policy is interchangeable with the definition of the basics of the Russian legal system.[62] They also contain a helpful clarification, according to which the refusal to apply rules of foreign law cannot be based solely on the differences between legal, political or economic systems in Russia and those of a foreign state.[63] The Supreme Court develops this guiding principle and indicates that the absence of certain legal norms or legal concepts in Russian law similar to those from the applicable foreign law cannot be *per se* a ground for triggering the public policy clause.[64]

[57] IS Zykin, AV Asoskov and AN Zhiltsov (eds), *'Kommentarij k razdelu VI "Mezhdunarodnoe chastnoe pravo" chasti tret'ej Grazhdanskogo kodeksa Rossijskoj Federacii (postatejnyj)' ('Commentary to Division VI "Private International Law" of Part Three of the Civil Code of the Russian Federation (Article-by-Article)')* (Moscow, Statut, 2021) 107–8.

[58] See section VII below about the concept of overriding mandatory provisions.

[59] Amendments to Article 1193 of the Civil Code in force as of 1 November 2013.

[60] 'Obobscheniya diskussiy rabochei gruppy po podgotovke dopolneniy i izmeneniy v razdel VI "Mezhdunarodnoe chastnoe pravo" GK RF' ('Summary of the Discussions of the Working Group for Preparing Amendments to Section VI "Private International Law" of the Russian Civil Code') (2019) 2 *Civil Law Review* 133, 139.

[61] P de Vareilles-Sommieres and IV Getman-Pavlova, 'Mezhdunarodnyj i vnutrennij publichnyj porjadok pri priznanii i ispolnenii inostrannyh arbitrazhnyh reshenij (pravoprimenitel'nyj opyt Francii i Rossii)' ('International and Domestic Public Policy in the Context of Recognition and Enforcement of Foreign Arbitral Awards (Law-Enforcement Experience of France and Russia)') (2014) 1 *Law: Journal of the Higher School of Economics*, 141–45.

[62] Article 1193(1) of the Civil Code.

[63] Article 1193(2) of the Civil Code.

[64] Paragraph 12 of the Resolution of the Plenum of the Supreme Court dated 9 July 2019 No 24. The same guidance is given by the Supreme Court in the context of application of the public policy

An attempt to give a more detailed explanation of the substance of the concept was made by the Supreme Court in the context of the recognition and enforcement of foreign court judgments and arbitral awards. The Supreme Court explains that 'the public policy is understood as fundamental legal notions (principles) that have the highest imperative, universality, special social and public significance, form the basis for building the economic, political, and legal system of the Russian Federation'.[65] This definition repeats the guidance previously given by the Highest *Arbitrazh* Court in its 2013 Review.[66] Although the above-mentioned definition is difficult to criticise, it is doubtful that it contains clarifications that may really help to increase predictability and legal certainty. In particular, it is not clear whether the 'fundamental legal notion (principle)' in question must be relevant to most fields of Russian law or can be limited to a specific legal sphere or even an isolated legal concept. As a result, notwithstanding this Supreme Court's guidance, the approach of inferior Russian courts remains far from uniform.[67]

If the public policy clause is triggered, the lacuna in regulation is filled with the relevant rule of Russian law 'if necessary'. The latter caveat leaves room for the court's discretion. There might be instances where it is possible to apply other more appropriate rules (that do not contradict to the basics of the Russian legal order) than the applicable foreign law. Only if such a substitution within the framework of the same legal system is impossible in the circumstances, will the Russian court have to fill in the gap using a rule from Russian law.[68]

VII. Overriding Mandatory Provisions (Rules of Immediate Application)

Contemporary PIL in many countries uses a special concept of 'overriding mandatory provisions' (rules of immediate application, internationally mandatory rules) in order to single out those mandatory rules that are applicable irrespective of the *lex causae* indicated in the parties' choice-of-law agreement or by ordinary

clause in the procedure of recognition and enforcement of foreign judgments and arbitral awards – para 51 of the Resolution of the Plenum of the Supreme Court dated 10 December 2019 No 53.

[65] Paragraph 51 of the Resolution of the Plenum of the Supreme Court dated 10 December 2019 No 53.

[66] Paragraph 1 of the Review of the Practice of Arbitrazh Courts in Cases on the Application of the Public Policy Exception as a Basis for Refusal in Recognition and Enforcement of Foreign Court Judgments and Arbitral Awards 26 February 2013 dated 2013 No 156. This Review was commented on in the following article: A Asoskov and A Kucher, 'Are Russian Courts Able to Keep Control over the Unruly Horse? The Long-Awaited Guidance of the Russia's Highest Commercial Court on the Concept of Public Policy' (2013) 30(5) *Journal of International Arbitration* 581–89.

[67] See Chapter 12 of this volume for more details.

[68] IS Zykin, AV Asoskov, AN Zhiltsov (eds), *'Kommentarij k razdelu VI "Mezhdunarodnoe chastnoe pravo" chasti tret'ej Grazhdanskogo kodeksa Rossijskoj Federacii (postatejnyj)' ('Commentary to Division VI "Private International Law" of Part Three of the Civil Code of the Russian Federation (Article-by-Article)')* (Moscow, Statut, 2021) 108.

conflict rules. In this way, overriding mandatory provisions are distinguished from non-derogable rules (domestically mandatory rules), from which the parties may not depart in a purely domestic context, but which may be disapplied by a choice of foreign law in an international contract.

Russian statutory provisions on overriding mandatory provisions were modelled on Article 7 of the Rome Convention.[69] Before the 2013 legislative reform, they had the same ambiguity in terminology, as the general term 'mandatory rules' was used in the heading and the text. This created confusion between overriding mandatory rules (internationally mandatory rules) and non-derogable rules (domestically mandatory rules). The 2013 amendments eliminated this confusion and included the special definition of 'rules of immediate application', which equates to internationally mandatory rules (or 'super-mandatory rules' used in the Russian doctrine).[70]

However, the 2013 amendments did not introduce any substantive changes. The statutory provisions continue to be rather vague on the characterisation of mandatory rules as overriding mandatory provisions. They mention two criteria for the separation of such provisions from non-derogable rules.

First, the rules themselves may contain an indication of their applicability irrespective of other PIL provisions. An example of such a rule is Article 414(2) of the Maritime Code, according to which a choice-of-law agreement cannot entail the elimination or reduction of civil liability of maritime carriers specified in the mandatory rules of the Maritime Code. However, most Russian mandatory rules do not contain such an express indication of the sphere of their application.

Second, mandatory rules may be recognised as overriding mandatory provisions 'due to their special importance, including for ensuring civil rights and legally protected interests'.[71] The Supreme Court gives an important interpretation of this second criterion, which helps to create more certainty. It uses the definition of overriding mandatory provisions from the Rome I Regulation and explains that a mandatory rule has 'special importance', if it has as its main purpose the protection of a public interest connected with the basics of the economic, political, or legal system of the state.[72] This Supreme Court guidance follows the restrictive approach to the concept of overriding mandatory provisions, which has its origins in German case law and academic writings.[73] According to this approach, the concept of overriding mandatory provisions does not cover those mandatory

[69] See Article 1192 of the Civil Code.

[70] 'Obobscheniya diskussiy rabochei gruppy po podgotovke dopolneniy i izmeneniy v razdel VI "Mezhdunarodnoe chastnoe pravo" GK RF' ('Summary of the Discussions of the Working Group for Preparing Amendments to Section VI "Private International Law" of the Russian Civil Code') (2019) 2 *Civil Law Review* 133, 137–38.

[71] Article 1192(1) of the Civil Code.

[72] Paragraph 10 of the Resolution of the Plenum of the Supreme Court dated 9 July 2019 No 24.

[73] Eg M Wilderspin, 'Overriding Mandatory Provisions' in J Basedow, G Ruehl, F Ferrari, PM Asensio (eds), *Encyclopedia of Private International Law* Vol 2 (Cheltenham, Edward Elgar Publishing, 2017) 1330–36.

rules that are designated primarily for the balancing of private interests (eg rules of consumer legislation, of labour legislation, or on the protection of minority shareholders, etc). Typical examples of overriding mandatory provisions include rules on economic sanctions, antitrust and currency control, trade restrictions, protection of the environment, financial markets and other fields with a predominantly public interest. The Supreme Court expressly characterises as overriding mandatory provisions rules of Russian legislation that impose additional restrictions on the acquisition of certain assets by foreign persons (eg land plots, shares and participation interests in Russian companies from strategic sectors).[74] The Supreme Court emphasises that not every mandatory rule of Russian law can be characterised as an overriding mandatory provision.[75]

There is an important distinction in the way Russian courts apply overriding mandatory provisions of the *lex fori*, on the one hand, and overriding mandatory provisions of third countries, on the other hand. The application of overriding mandatory provisions of the *lex fori* is binding for the Russian court if the territorial and personal scope of the relevant Russian internationally mandatory rule covers the dispute.[76]

In contrast, giving effect to a foreign overriding mandatory provision is a matter of discretion for the Russian court.[77] The court shall exercise its discretion taking into account the following criteria: (i) a close connection between the dispute and the state that enacted the relevant mandatory rule; (ii) the purpose and nature of the mandatory rule; and (iii) the consequences of its application or non-application. The Supreme Court adds that the Russian court is obliged to ignore a foreign overriding mandatory provision if its purpose and nature are inconsistent with the basics of the Russian legal order (Russian public policy), or it negatively affects the sovereignty or security of the Russian Federation, or it violates the constitutional rights and freedoms of Russian individuals and legal entities.[78] For example, Russian courts tend not to give effect to foreign sanctions oriented against Russian persons or sectors of the Russian economy.[79]

If the Russian court does not give effect to a foreign mandatory provision as a legal rule of immediate application, it is still unsettled whether the existence of such a provision and its influence on the parties can be taken into account as a factual circumstance under the *lex causae* (eg as a *force majeure*, ground for the termination of an obligation due to impossibility of performance, ground

[74] Paragraph 10 of the Resolution of the Plenum of the Supreme Court dated 9 July 2019 No 24.

[75] Ibid.

[76] Article 1192(1) of the Civil Code, para 11 of the Resolution of the Plenum of the Supreme Court dated 9 July 2019 No 24.

[77] Article 1192(2) of the Civil Code.

[78] Paragraph 11 of the Resolution of the Plenum of the Supreme Court dated 9 July 2019 No 24.

[79] Postanovlenie Arbitrazhnogo suda Moskovskogo okruga ot 21 ijunja 2018 (Resolution of the Arbitrazh Court of the Moscow District) dated 21 June 2018 No Ф05-6057/2018 in case No A40-126531/2017.

for the amendment or termination of a contract due to a substantial change of circumstances, etc). The Russian doctrine speaks in favour of using this concept.[80]

If the court applies an overriding mandatory provision, this does not mean that the choice-of-law agreement or ordinary conflict rules lose their effect completely. An overriding mandatory provision ousts the application of rules of *lex causae* only on the issue regulated by such provision. All other aspects of the dispute shall still be governed by the *lex causae* determined via the choice-of-law agreement or ordinary conflict rules.[81]

VIII. Ascertainment of Foreign Law

Various states use different theoretical approaches to pleading and proof of foreign law.[82] One group of countries (mostly common law states) use factual characterisation and generally equate foreign-law issues with factual circumstances of the case. As a result, the application of foreign law must be pleaded by the parties, who bear the burden of proving the contents of foreign law. Superior courts cannot reconsider the findings of trial courts on the contents of foreign law.

Another group of countries (mostly Continental states) use legal characterisation and generally do not differentiate between the application of foreign and domestic law. As a result, they stick to the principle '*jura novit curia*' ('the court knows the law'), which means an active role of the court in the ascertainment of foreign law, application of conflict rules *ex officio* (even if not pleaded by any party), and judicial control of superior courts over the application of foreign law in trial courts.

However, in practice, many countries use compromise solutions which include certain elements from both approaches. Russia is among such countries. The starting point is the legal characterisation, which is rather natural for Russian law as a Continental legal system. Russian courts must apply conflict rules *ex officio* and play an active role in the ascertainment of foreign law. As a general rule, it is the right of the parties (but not an obligation) to help the court to ascertain the applicable foreign law.[83]

However, the statutory provisions make an important step towards another approach. If the dispute relates to commercial activities of both parties, then the court may oblige the parties to submit information about applicable foreign law.[84]

[80] AV Asoskov, *Osnovy kollizionnogo prava (Basics of Conflict of Laws)* (Moscow, Infotropic Media, 2012) 177–90.

[81] Paragraph 10 of the Resolution of the Plenum of the Supreme Court dated 9 July 2019 No 24.

[82] C Esplugues and G Palao, 'Foreign Law, Application and Ascertainment' in J Basedow, G Ruehl, F Ferrari and PM Asensio (eds), *Encyclopedia of Private International Law* Vol 1 (Cheltenham, Edward Elgar Publishing, 2017) 769–78; M Jantera-Jareborg, 'Foreign Law in National Courts: a Comparative Perspective' (2003) 204 *Recueil des Cours* 199 ff.

[83] Article 1191(2)(2) of the Civil Code.

[84] Article 1191(2)(3) of the Civil Code.

The Supreme Court clarifies that such instruction by the court to the parties must be fixed in a court's ruling. Issuing this ruling does not free the court from its duty to take steps for the ascertainment of foreign law, but the party that does not follow the court's instruction cannot refer to misapplication of foreign law on appeal.[85]

The Supreme Court adds that parties may submit expert reports about foreign law on their own initiative, which is a method of ascertainment of foreign law typical for the common law jurisdictions. If an expert report of one party contains sufficient information on foreign law and is not rebutted by their opponent with a reference to other admissible evidence, the court may consider the content of foreign law ascertained.[86] It is important to note that the expert report on foreign law must contain a description of applicable foreign rules and the practice of their application, but it cannot evaluate the evidence from the case file or make conclusions on relations of the parties, which is the sole prerogative of the court.[87]

The PIL provisions contain a list of mechanisms which are available for the court to collect information on foreign law. The court can make a request to the Russian Ministry of Justice or other competent bodies in Russia or abroad, as well as engage a court-appointed expert.[88] By the 'competent bodies', this provision means, inter alia, foreign authorities which are involved in the exchange of information on applicable law according to multilateral and bilateral international treaties. Among the multilateral treaties, the most important are: the 1968 European Convention on Information on Foreign Law[89] and the 1993 Minsk Convention on Legal Assistance and Legal Relations in Civil, Family and Criminal Law Matters. Many bilateral treaties on legal assistance in civil and family matters in force between Russia and other states also contain provisions on the exchange of information about applicable law. However, in practice, these mechanisms are not efficient, as they are very time-consuming, and the quality of responses is far from ideal.[90] In view of that, Russian courts prefer to rely upon expert reports submitted by the parties on their own initiative, or presented by a court-appointed expert, if this method of ascertainment of foreign law is available.

If the applicable foreign law cannot be ascertained by the Russian court within a reasonable period of time, the Russian court should apply Russian law.[91] Russian PIL provisions do not allow for any alternative options for resolving such a deadlock (eg application of a legal system from the same legal family and having the same historical roots).

[85] Paragraph 44 of the Resolution of the Plenum of the Supreme Court dated 27 June 2017 No 23.
[86] Ibid. Last sentence in para 44.
[87] Paragraph 46 of the Resolution of the Plenum of the Supreme Court dated 27 June 2017 No 23.
[88] Article 1191(2)(1) of the Civil Code.
[89] 720 UNTS 147.
[90] IS Zykin, AV Asoskov and AN Zhiltsov (eds), '*Kommentarij k razdelu VI "Mezhdunarodnoe chastnoe pravo" chasti tret'ej Grazhdanskogo kodeksa Rossijskoj Federacii (postatejnyj)*' ('*Commentary to Division VI "Private International Law" of Part Three of the Civil Code of the Russian Federation (Article-by-Article*')) (Moscow, Statut, 2021) 76–77.
[91] Article 1191(3) of the Civil Code.

4

Persons

IVAN CHUPRUNOV

This chapter deals with the key Russian PIL rules applicable to individual and legal entities. It describes how Russian PIL uses different connecting factors and other legislative techniques to determine the legal status of individuals (excluding family law matters). In addition, this chapter deals with the PIL rules applicable to legal entities, including issues relating to shareholders' agreements and similar arrangements.

I. Individuals

PIL rules on the legal status of individuals (legal capacity, various restrictions applicable to foreign persons, etc) are set out in a few Russian statutes as well as international treaties to which Russia is a party. However, the general principles as well as key operative rules in this sphere are all set out in Chapter 67 of the Civil Code, which is the primary focus of this chapter.

A. General Remarks

Similarly to some other countries' national PIL rules, the Civil Code operates the general notion of personal law (sometimes also called 'personal statute') (*личный закон*) of an individual (*lex personalis*).[1] This personal law is determined on the basis of a set of connecting factors and governs a few aspects of an individual's legal status. Nonetheless, as will be discussed below, some areas are carved out from the scope of the individual's personal law, and law applicable thereto may be determined under separate conflict-of-laws rules.

[1] Cf Art 23(1) of the Minsk Convention which does not provide for a general concept of a personal law of an individual.

Interestingly enough, although Russian PIL rules applicable to individuals may appear somewhat out-of-date,[2] they were practically unaffected by the 2013 Reform.

B. Determination of the Personal Law. Connecting Factors

Compared to a few other national European PIL rules, the Civil Code rules on determination of the personal law of an individual are fairly complex and a bit confusing as they focus primarily on the nationality of an individual. However, contrary to an opinion sometimes expressed,[3] the Civil Code is not using it as the predominant connecting factor, but rather in combination with other connecting factors.

The Civil Code provides for separate connecting factors to determine the personal law for the following categories of individuals: (i) individuals who are nationals of a state; (ii) stateless persons (*apatrides*); and (iii) refugees.

Where an individual is a national of a country, the main connecting factor used by the Civil Code for determination of their personal law is the law of such country (*lex nationalis* or *lex patriae*) (Article 1195(1)). On this basis, it is often argued that the Russian PIL follows the continental European tradition of using *lex nationalis* as the main connecting factor (as opposed to *lex domicile*, used primarily in common law jurisdictions).[4] If an individual is a national of more than one country, including the Russian Federation, their personal law would be Russian law (Article 1195(2)). These rules indeed embody the *lex nationalis* principle historically preferred by the Soviet and then Russian legislators. This hard and fast connecting factor is (i) relatively easy to use in practice since the courts would normally have no problems identifying the nationality of an individual, and (ii) less susceptible to any changes and, therefore, promotes legal certainty. Furthermore, it is sometimes argued that the Russian legislators favoured the *lex nationalis* to ensure protection of many Russian nationals residing abroad following the collapse of the Soviet Union[5] (although there may be doubts whether this is indeed an appropriate and effective instrument for these purposes).

In spite of the *lex nationalis* being the key connecting factor, the other provisions of the Civil Code significantly erode it and make the place where

[2] See subsection I.B of this chapter.

[3] See eg O Vorobieva, *Private International Law in Russia* (Alphen aan den Rijn, Kluwer Law International BV, 2012) para 150.

[4] See eg TE Abova, MM Boguslavskiy and AG Svetlanov (eds), *Kommentariy k Grazhdanskomu Kodeksu Rossiyskoy Federatsii, chasti tret'ei (postateynyi)* (*Commentary to the Civil Code of the Russian Federation, Part Three (Article-by-Article)* (Moscow, Urait, 2004) Commentary to Article 1195 para 3.

[5] See eg IS Zykin, AV Asoskov and AN Zhiltsov (eds), *Kommentariy k Razdelu VI 'Mezhdunarodnoe Chastnoe Pravo' Grazhdanskogo Kodeksa Rossiyskoy Federatsii (postateynyi)* (*Commentary to Section VI 'Private International Law' of the Civil Code of the Russian Federation (Article-by-Article)* (Moscow, Statut, 2021) 125.

an individual resides also an important connecting factor in certain cases. First, the personal law of a foreigner residing in Russia would be Russian law (Article 1195(3)). Furthermore, for both a foreign person with more than one nationality (Article 1195(4)) and an *apatride* (Article 1195(5)), their personal law is the law of the country of their residence. Finally, the Civil Code declares that the *lex personalis* of a refugee is the law of the country that granted their asylum (Article 1195(6)) (which, from a purely practical perspective, is likely to be the country of their new residence).[6]

As a practical result of application of the nationality principle and the principle of residence, in most disputes involving individuals that fall within jurisdiction of the Russian courts, such individuals' personal law would be Russian law. This may even be seen as an instrument of unilateral PIL logic employed by the Russian legislator – though a Russian judge would almost always be using the multilateral rules of Article 1195 described above, in practice, it would still result in application of the *lex fori* in most of the cases. The dominance of the unilateral approach here is further evidenced by the fact that (i) the legal status of individuals is the *only* sphere where *renvoi* is permitted under the Civil Code and only to the extent that this leads to application of Russian law (Article 1190(2)), and (ii) the continuation of the use of *renvoi* in this sphere found further support from the 2013 Reform.[7]

As a consequence, under the Russian PIL rules, the personal law of an individual would almost always be the law of the country where they reside. The only two significant exceptions to this are the cases of (i) foreign persons who only have one nationality and do not reside in Russia, and (ii) Russian nationals residing abroad. With respect to the first category, application of Article 1195(1) of the Russian Civil Code may have somewhat idiosyncratic results as this would be the only case where a foreigner's personal law would be determined exclusively based on their nationality without regard to the place of their residence. As to the second category, application of Russian law as the personal law of a Russian national living abroad may also seem a rather counter-intuitive result of Article 1195(1). For example, if the relevant dispute relates to whether this individual had capacity to enter into a transaction abroad,[8] application of the *lex nationalis* alone ignores a clear turn by many countries towards a more significant use of the habitual residence as the main connecting factor for the legal status of individuals.[9]

[6] Article 1195(6) should be treated as the *lex specialis* in respect of Art 1195(1) and, therefore, should prevail in cases where the refugee retains the nationality of their country of origin.

[7] 'Obobscheniya diskussiy rabochei gruppy po podgotovke dopolneniy i izmeneniy v razdel VI "Mezhdunarodnoe chastnoe pravo" GK RF' ('Summary of the Discussions of the Working Group for Preparing Amendments to Section VI "Private International Law" of the Russian Civil Code') (2019) 2 *Civil Law Review* 136.

[8] Cf the approach set out in Art 1197(2) of the Civil Code – see section I.C.(ii) of this chapter.

[9] See K Siehr, https://max-eup2012.mpipriv.de/index.php/Personal_Law (accessed 13 January 2024) (the author expects that, within the European Union, the principle of nationality will soon be very much reduced on account of various factors) and D Baetge, https://max-eup2012.mpipriv.de/index.php/Habitual_Residence (accessed 13 January 2024).

Therefore, in the modern world, it is becoming much harder to justify nationality as the most significant tie or the closest connection between an individual and a legal order.[10] This is especially true in the post-pandemic world of remote working and mass migration.

In any case, one should be mindful of the fact that neither of these two categories of cases frequently arises in Russian courts, which, pragmatically speaking, makes the described idiosyncrasies much less significant as a matter of practice.

Although the Civil Code uses the residence of an individual as a connecting factor that is alternative to *lex nationalis*, there is no wide consensus on what 'residence' means in this context,[11] including whether this should have exactly the same meaning as the 'habitual residence', a connecting factor widely used in national legislation and international instruments. This raises a difficult PIL question of 'characterisation' (qualification).[12]

According to the general rules of characterisation (Article 1187(1)), the meaning of 'residence' is to be determined under Russian law. Pursuant to Article 20 of the Civil Code, the place of residence of an individual (for those purposes that are not PIL-specific) is a place where they 'permanently or predominantly live'. This definition is not equivalent to the common law term of art 'domicile', as the former would be primarily concerned with the *factual matters*, ie with where the person in fact permanently or predominantly lives, and would arguably apply irrespective of their intentions, legal capacity etc.[13] Russian courts tend to use the same definition of 'residence' both for individuals living in Russia and abroad.[14] However, many aspects of how residence should be determined as a matter of Russian law still remain unclear – in particular, what 'permanently' or 'predominantly' means in this context, at which point in time an individual changes the country of their residence (and whether their relevant intention is to be taken into consideration at all), whether a newborn automatically acquires the residence of their parents, whether there may be an individual without a residence, etc.

Furthermore, characterisation of who qualifies as an 'individual' will also likely be governed by the same general rules of the Civil Code (Article 1187). Therefore, for instance, the moments of birth and death of an individual (which may be

[10] For this reason habitual residence is used as the key connecting factor eg in Rome I Regulation (see eg Art 4).

Furthermore, it is almost impossible to apply the *lex nationalis* (without the use of some form of other connecting factor) where an individual concerned is a national of a jurisdiction with multiple legal systems or has several nationalities.

[11] See eg IS Zykin, AV Asoskov and AN Zhiltsov (eds), *Commentary to Section VI*, n 5 above, 126–30; O Vorobieva, *Private International Law in Russia*, n 3 above, para 150.

[12] See section III.B of Chapter 3 of this volume.

[13] Cf L Collins, J Harris et al (eds), *Dicey, Morris and Collins on the Conflict of Laws*, 16th edn (London, Sweet & Maxwell, 2022) chapter 6.

[14] Paragraph 8 of Postanovlenie Plenuma Verkhovnogo Suda RF (Resolution of the Plenum of the Supreme Court) dated 9 July 2019 No 24 'O primenenii norm mezhdunarodnogo chastnogo prava sudami Rossiyskoy Federatsii' ('On the Use of Private International Law Norms by the Courts of the Russian Federation') ('Plenum Resolution No 24').

relevant eg in inheritance matters) are arguably to be determined in accordance with the general rules of Russian substantive law and not in accordance with the *lex causae*.

C. Scope of Application of the Personal Law

According to the Civil Code, the personal law of an individual covers primarily the following aspects of their legal status: (i) legal capacity, (ii) capacity to act, (iii) guardianship (*опека*) and curatorship (*попечительство*) matters, and (iv) the right to one's name.

(i) Legal Capacity

Under Article 1196 of the Civil Code, legal capacity (*правоспособность*), ie capacity to be a subject of civil rights and duties (*Rechtsfähigkeit*, *capacité de jouissance*, *capacità giuridica*), of an individual is subject to their *lex personalis*. However, the second sentence of the same Article 1196 additionally states that foreign nationals and stateless persons enjoy the same legal capacity as Russian nationals, unless the law provides otherwise (the so-called 'national treatment regime').

No universal consensus exists among Russian scholars on the juxtaposition between *lex personalis* and the national treatment regime. In particular, it is not clear whether an individual whose capacity is limited under their *lex personalis* (eg they may not own certain types of property) may benefit from less restrictive provisions of Russian law due to the national treatment regime.[15] Perhaps the better view is that the national treatment regime set out in Article 1196 of the Civil Code is merely a unilateral mechanism preventing discrimination against individuals who do not have Russian nationality and that, beyond this context, legal capacity of such individuals shall still be determined under the *lex personalis*.[16] However, given that in the modern world there are hardly any significant differences between national laws regulating the legal capacity of an individual, this remains primarily an academic issue.

The national treatment regime remains subject to a significant number of deviations and limitations set out in various laws and regulations. For example, a non-Russian national may not (i) own agricultural land plots[17] or land plots near the border of Russia,[18] (ii) be a parent in case of surrogacy by a Russian mother in Russia (unless the other parent is Russian too),[19] or (iii) own (together

[15] See eg O Vorobieva, *Private International Law in Russia* (n 3 above) para 141.
[16] Ibid, para 140.
[17] Article 3 of the Federal Law dated 24 July 2002 No 101-ФЗ 'On Transfers of Agricultural Lands'.
[18] Article 15(3) of the Land Code.
[19] Article 51(4) of the Family Code.

with other non-Russian nationals) over 20 per cent of interest in a mass media company (whether directly or indirectly).[20] These limitations sometimes apply notwithstanding the Russian nationality and, as one could expect, have become substantially more numerous during wartime.

As indicated above, there is also a potentially difficult question of characterisation relating to an individual's legal capacity – is there indeed an individual? For example, although Russian civil law provides for certain rules that expressly apply to an unborn child (*nasciturus*), they are generally not recognised as a civil law subject *sensu proprio*.[21] Therefore, irrespective of the provisions of the *lex nationalis*, an unborn child will not have legal capacity under Article 1196 of the Civil Code. However, they may still have some civil rights under the *lex causae* determined under other PIL provisions, such as the right to inherit or the right to claim damages in tort.[22] Nevertheless, none of these matters appear to have been resolved in Russian legal scholarship or court practice.

A similar analysis should arguably apply to the determination of when an individual passes away, ie this may be seen as a question of characterisation that is subject to Russian substantive law.

Unlike certain other national PIL rules,[23] in case of declaration of presumed death of a missing person in the Russian Federation, Russian law deviates from application of the *lex personalis* and subjects this matter to the rules of *lex fori* (Article 1200 of the Civil Code). This deviation from *les personalis* appears to lack substantial justification, but does not seem to result in significant practical issues.

(ii) Capacity to Act

From the Russian conflict of law perspective, an individual's capacity to act (*дееспособность*), ie capacity to take legal actions, including to enter into legal transactions (*Geschäftsfähigkeit, capacité d'exercice, capacità da agire*), is governed by the *lex personalis* (Article 1197(1) of the Civil Code). Therefore, *lex personalis* will apply to questions of validity of transactions in case of a breach of limitations relating to the individual's capacity to act.[24]

However, this is a very complex PIL area, as questions arising in practice will almost always be somewhere on the borderline between the capacity rules and the sphere of application of the *lex causae*. Perhaps it is not surprising that the Civil Code provides for a few rules deviating from application of the *lex personalis* principle in favour of the *lex causae*. For instance, in respect of the

[20] Article 19.1 of the Law of the Russian Federation dated 27 December 1991 No 2124-1 'On Mass Media'.

[21] See eg DV Lorents and EK Shott, 'Pravosposobnost' nastsiturusa: nasledstvenno-pravovoi aspect' ('Legal Capacity of the Nasciturus: Succession Law Aspect') (2015) 3 *Law of Succession* 24, 24–28.

[22] Cf Art 34 of the Swiss PIL Act, which provides that passive capacity is governed by Swiss law, but the beginning and the end of legal personality are governed by *lex causae* that presupposes legal capacity.

[23] Cf Art 9 of the German Introductory Act.

[24] Paragraph 42 of Plenum Resolution No 24 (n 14 above).

capacity to commit a tort (Article 1220(1)) and capacity to make or cancel a will (Article 1224(2)), *lex causae* prevails over *lex personalis* (and these rules derogate from Article 1197(1) as *lex specialis*).

Furthermore, Article 1197(2) of the Civil Code provides for a further carve-out from the application of the *lex personalis* regarding capacity to act. An individual who is not capable to act under the *lex personalis* may not invoke such incapacity if they have capacity under the laws of the place where the transaction is concluded, unless they can prove that the counterparty knew or should *manifestly* (*заведомо*) have known of such incapacity. While similar PIL rules embodying the *favor negotii* principle are well-known to the national legislation of a few states as well as Rome I Regulation (Article 13), there are a few nuanced differences between most of them and Article 1197(2).

First, this carve-out from the *lex personalis* normally applies only if both parties to a transaction are located in the same state.[25] Furthermore, in the case of many other PIL rules, there is no requirement to prove that the counterparty should *manifestly* have known of the relevant incapacity (and thus the knowledge may be imputed on the basis of pure negligence). This makes the Civil Code even more protective of the interests of counterparties, as it makes it almost impossible to invalidate a transaction under the *lex personalis*. In fact, there appear to be no examples of such invalidation in the Russian court practice.[26]

Although Article 1197(2) of the Russian Civil Code may be interpreted to only apply to parties' capacity to enter into contracts (ie, transactions that have a counterparty), the Russian legal scholarship tends to interpret it broadly and, in particular, apply it to certain unilateral transactions.[27]

Unlike certain other national PIL rules, the Civil Code does not include an express provision permitting an individual to retain their capacity obtained under *lex personalis*, regardless of any future change of such *lex personalis*.[28]

Article 1197(3) of the Civil Code provides that Russian courts shall apply the *lex fori* when declaring an individual's incapacity (or limited capacity) to act. This deviation by the Russian legislation from application of the *lex personalis* does not seem to be properly justified.

(iii) Guardianship and Curatorship Matters

The Civil Code provides for nuanced PIL rules in relation to various aspects of guardianship and curatorship over an individual. Establishment of the

[25] Article 13 of Rome I Regulation; Art 12 of the German Introductory Act; Art 23(2) of the Italian PIL Act.

[26] At the same time, Art 1197(2) does not provide for certain express carve-outs from this rule that are known to other PIL sets of rules – eg for transactions pertaining to family or inheritance law matters.

[27] Cf Art 23(3) of the Italian PIL Act (which provides for a perhaps more elegant solution in this respect).

[28] Cf Art 35 of the Swiss PIL Act; Art 7(2) of the German Introductory Act.

guardianship / curatorship is governed by the *lex personalis* of an individual (Article 1199(1)), while the duty to accept the guardianship / curatorship is subject to the *lex personalis* of the potential guardian / curator (Article 1199(2)). In practice, Russian courts are likely to apply *lex fori* in most of cases, since in most of the case it would be the *lex personalis* of both the individual concerned and their potential guardian / curator.

However, the legal relationships between an individual and their guardian / curator are not subject to *lex personalis*. They would be governed by the laws of the country where guardianship / curatorship was established, or, if this individual resides in the Russian Federation, under Russian law, provided it is more beneficial for such individual (Article 1199(3) of the Civil Code).

(iv) Name

Another aspect of the status of an individual that national PIL rules often make subject to the *lex personalis* is their right to their name. The Civil Code is not different in this regard – Article 1198 provides that the *lex personalis* applies to the individual's right to their name as well as to its use and protection. Although protection of the individual's name is governed by the *lex personalis*, in reality, given that a breach of the right to their name usually constitutes a tort, some believe that the relevant matters shall be subject to the PIL tort rules.[29]

D. Matters Outside of the Scope of the Personal Law

An unusual feature of the Russian Civil Code is that it provides for specific PIL rules on determination of the law applicable to an individual's capacity to get involved in entrepreneurial activities. According to Article 1201, the laws of the country where an individual entrepreneur is registered govern their capacity to carry out entrepreneurial activity. Alternatively, if there are no applicable state registration requirements, such matters are subject to the laws of the country where such individual has their main place of business.

E. Nationality / Citizenship

Given that *stricto sensu* nationality is not viewed in Russia as a matter of PIL, it is worth mentioning that obtaining Russian citizenship is subject to the provisions of the Russian Constitution (Article 6) as well as a few more technical requirements set out in the Federal Law 'On Citizenship of the Russian Federation'[30] and is based

[29] IS Zykin, AV Asoskov and AN Zhiltsov (eds), *Commentary to Section VI* (n 5 above) 148.
[30] Federal Law dated 31 May 2002 No 62-ФЗ 'On Citizenship of the Russian Federation'.

primarily on the *jus sanguinis* principle (though the *jus soli* principle also has its more limited sphere of application).

II. Legal Entities

This section focuses on the personal law of legal entities and the sphere of its application, including its interaction with the law applicable to shareholder agreements and similar arrangements.

A. Personal Law of a Legal Entity. Connecting Factors

According to Article 1202(1) of the Civil Code, the personal law of a legal entity (*lex societatis*) is the law of the country of its incorporation (registration). This means that Russian law follows the so-called incorporation theory (*lex incorporationis*). This approach is sometimes criticised, as state registration of a legal entity does not appear to always be a strong connecting factor in the modern world. Nevertheless, it promotes greater legal certainty and stability than the use of the real seat (*Realsitz*) as a connecting factor and is currently a predominant connecting factor used in various jurisdictions.

Similarly to most national PIL rules, the Russian conflict-of-laws rules on the legal status of a legal entity are much less complex than those relating to individuals – almost all of the issues are governed by the *lex societatis*. Perhaps the main reason for this is that a legal entity is often viewed as a fictitious person, a creation of a certain national legal order, and, therefore, the key aspects relating to its subjecthood are derived from a recognition by such legal order.

The main exception to application of the *lex incorporationis* is set out in Article 1202(4) of the Civil Code, which provides for a unilateral conflict-of-laws rule applicable to any foreign incorporated legal entity that carries out its activities primarily in the Russian Federation. According to this rule, the liability of (i) participants or founders of a legal entity, and (ii) persons able to give binding instructions to such entity (or otherwise determine its actions), to the extent such liability is towards a third party in relation to such legal entity's obligations, shall be governed by Russian law or – at the discretion of such third party – the *lex societatis*. This provision was introduced as part of the 2013 Reform and seems to have been inspired by similar PIL rules from other European PIL legislations, most importantly Article 159 of the Swiss Private International Law Act[31] (although it has a much broader scope, as it also apply to foreign entities 'managed from' Switzerland, thus capturing 'Swiss-controlled' legal entities registered outside of Switzerland).

[31] 'Summary of the Discussions of the Working Group' (n 7 above) 140–42.

It is often argued that if a legal entity qualifies as a legal entity under the *lex incorporationis*, it would also be automatically recognised as such in the Russian Federation.[32] However, according to Article 1202(2)(1) of the Civil Code, the *lex societatis* governs, inter alia, the status of an 'organisation' as a legal entity. This reference to an 'organisation' here may raise doubts as to whether a legal subject that is not an organisation may be characterised as a legal entity from the perspective of Russian PIL.[33] In such a case, Article 1203 of the Russian Civil Code may still apply (see Section III of this chapter).

Subject to certain conditions, Russian law allows for re-domiciliation of foreign legal entities via their re-incorporation in Russia in the form of an 'international company' or an 'international fund'.[34] Further, it permits limited application of the original *lex societatis* to certain aspects of the corporate relations following re-domiciliation.

B. Scope of the Personal Law

Similarly to many other national PIL rules, the scope of *lex societatis* in Russia is determined by way of listing in Article 1202(2) of the Civil Code the following specific areas that it governs: However,

- status of the organisation as a legal entity;
- the legal form;
- requirements towards the name of the legal entity;
- issues relating to incorporation, reorganisation, transformation, and liquidation, including legal succession;
- contents of the legal capacity;
- the procedure for acquisition of civil rights and duties;
- internal affairs, including relations between the legal entity and its participants;
- ability of the legal entity to be liable for its obligations; and
- liability of the founders (participants) of a legal entity in respect of such legal entity's obligations.

This list is not exhaustive, which means that there may be quite a few borderline questions with the relevant *lex causae*. Russian courts have not yet developed any

[32] IS Zykin, AV Asoskov and AN Zhiltsov (eds), *Commentary to Section VI* (n 5 above) 163.

[33] On differences between the concept of a legal entity in different jurisdictions, see eg P Behrens, 'Connecting Factors for the Determination of the Proper Law of Companies' in P Mankowski and W Wurmnest (eds), *Festschrift für Ulrich Magnus zum 70. Geburtstag* (Otto Schmidt/De Gruyter, 2014) 353–54. Cf F Wedemann, 'Der Begriff der Gesellschaft im Internationalen Privatrecht. Neue Herausforderungen durch den entrepreneur individual à responsabilité limitée' (2011) 75 *RabelsZ* 541, 541–80.

[34] Federal Law dated 3 August 2018 No 290-ФЗ 'On International Companies and International Funds'.

clear approach on how to deal with many of those, which means that they are to be resolved on an ad hoc basis.

Most of the items listed in Article 1202(2) perhaps do not require any detailed commentary – so we will focus only on the ones that are less clear.

As a general rule, the *lex societatis* governs all issues relating to the legal capacity (Article 1202(2)(5)), capacity to act (Article 1202(2)(6))[35] – including liability for its obligations (Article 1202(2)(8))[36] –, requirements regarding its legal name (Article 1202(2)(3)), and re-organisations, transformations and liquidation of the legal entity (Article 1202(2)(4)). However, there are a few caveats.

First, as in the case of individuals and notwithstanding the national treatment regime applicable to foreign legal entities,[37] there are a few restrictions regarding the rights that such entities (as well as entities under foreign control) may hold and/or the types of activities that they may be involved in. These restrictions are usually characterised as overriding mandatory provisions[38] and, as such, apply regardless of the provisions of *lex societatis*.

Article 1202(3) of the Civil Code provides for the following important carve-out from application of the *lex societatis* to the questions of capacity to act:[39] a legal entity may not invoke *lex societatis* limitations on the authority of its corporate body or representative where such limitations are unknown to the law of the country where such corporate body or representative entered into a transaction, unless such legal entity is able to prove that the counterparty knew or should manifestly (*заведомо*) have known of these limitations. Although according to the prevailing doctrine, the claimant needs to prove knowledge that the counterparty knew (or should manifestly have known) that such limitations are known *lex societatis*,[40] Russian courts seem to interpret Article 1202(3) differently and believe that the claimant needs to prove the counterparty's knowledge as to the fact that these limitations apply in relation to the specific transaction.[41]

Russian court practice extends application of Article 1202(3) of the Civil Code to any ultra vires acts (not just transactions),[42] and the prevailing doctrine further supports the application of Article 1202(3) to unilateral transactions (at least where they require perception by another party).[43] It is important to note that one of the pre-requisites for application of Article 1202(3) is that the relevant *lex societatis* limitations are not known to the law of the jurisdiction where a legal entity's

[35] Paragraph 14 of Plenum Resolution No 24 (n 14 above).

[36] Paragraph 14 of Plenum Resolution No 24 (n 14 above).

[37] Article 4(1) of the Federal Law dated 9 July 1999 No 160-ФЗ 'On Foreign Investments in the Russian Federation'.

[38] Zykin, Asoskov and Zhiltsov (eds), *Commentary to Section VI* (n 5 above) 166.

[39] See analysis of Art 1197(2) in section I.C.(i) of this chapter, which provides for a similar rule, but in respect of individuals.

[40] Zykin, Asoskov and Zhiltsov (eds), *Commentary to Section VI* (n 5 above) 176–77.

[41] Opredelenie Sudebnoi Kollegii po Ekonomicheskim Sporam Verkhovnogo Suda RF (Resolution of the Commercial Chamber of the Supreme Court) of 15 December 2014 Case No 309-ЭС14-923.

[42] Also see para 16 of Plenum Resolution No 24 (n 14 above).

[43] Zykin, Asoskov and Zhiltsov (eds), *Commentary to Section VI* (n 5 above) 174–75. An example of a unilateral transaction that can be set-off.

body or representative enters into a transaction, which can differ from the *lex loci actus* of the transaction (Article 1197(2) of the Civil Code) and does not require that the other counterparty is present in this jurisdiction.[44] These peculiarities of Article 1202(3) inevitably raise a question of whether its scope of application should in fact be teleologically reduced to exclude cases where a transaction is entered into remotely, as in those cases there are arguably no grounds for the counterparty to reasonably rely on the absence of the limitations in question.[45]

As regards a legal entity's liability for its obligations, although under Article 1202(2)(8) of the Civil Code it is subject to the *lex societatis*, capacity relating to tortious liability would still be governed by *lex specialis* rules of Article 1220(1) of the Civil Code (see Chapter seven of this volume).

Furthermore, although Article 1202(2)(4) expressly indicates that the *lex societatis* governs legal succession in rights and/or obligations as a result of re-organisation, transformation or liquidation, this is not always the case. In particular, legal succession in rights *in rem* in respect of real estate shall be governed by the *lex rei sitae* (see Article 1224(1) for such carve-out in the context of hereditary succession[46]). Also, though Russian law is unclear on this point, similar carve-outs from application of the *lex societatis* would be appropriate for succession in other rights that are subject to registration (eg shares in another legal entity).

Finally, while the *lex societatis* governs a solvent liquidation of a legal entity (Article 1202(2)(4) of the Civil Code), an insolvent liquidation is a much more complex situation, which calls for application of a special set of PIL insolvency rules and principles. No such set of rules currently exists in Russian law, which makes the relevant matters very controversial both in scholarly writings and in court practice.

Perhaps the most complex item expressly covered by the scope of the *lex societatis* is the 'internal affairs' ('*внутренние отношения*') of a legal entity, which includes relations between the legal entity and its participants (Article 1202(2)(7)). According to paragraph 15 of Plenum Resolution No 24, this covers (i) corporate governance, including the formation of corporate bodies and the liability of the relevant members, and (ii) certain types of relationships among participants – eg issues relating to disposal of an interest in a legal entity by a participant (including rights of first refusal, restrictions regarding sale or other disposal, consequence of a breach of such restrictions etc).[47] In this author's opinion, the better view is that 'corporate governance' here should be interpreted

[44] Cf Art 13 of Rome I Regulation.

[45] Cf AV Asoskov, 'Kollizionnoe regulirovanie voprosov pravosposobnosti yuridicheskogo litsa i polnomochiy ego organov: kak naiti balans mezhdu interesami uchastnikov yuridicheskogo litsa i potrebnostyami grazhdanskogo oborota?' ('Conflict of Law Regulation of the Capacity Matters of a Legal Entity and of the Authorities of Its Organs: How to Find Balance between the Interests of the Participants of the Legal Entity and the Needs of the Civil Commerce') (2014) 4 *Civil Law Review* 7, 38–45.

[46] See section I.A of Chapter 9 of this volume.

[47] See para 15 of Plenum Resolution No 24 (n 14 above).

even more broadly to cover (i) voting and passing corporate resolutions, (ii) rights and duties of a participant of a legal entity vis-à-vis both such entity and other participants, (iii) dividends and other distributions (including limitations thereto), and (iv) ability of a participant to bring a derivative claim in the name of the legal entity, etc. However, as a matter of Russian law, there are still a few grey areas on the borderline of the *lex societatis* and *lex causae* (such as piercing the corporate veil or directors' liability for torts).

Under Article 1202(2)(9) of the Civil Code, the liability of participants of a legal entity for its obligations is subject to the *lex societatis* – however, as indicated above, this rule remains subject to additional rules set out in Article 1202(4) and anyway, covers only statutory liability, as opposed to additional undertakings that may be given by a participant for the benefit of a third party (eg liability under a guarantee).

Although Article 1202(2) of the Civil Code does not expressly state this, there are a few other items that, in this author's opinion, would by their nature have to be governed by the *lex societatis*. Those include (i) all issues regarding maintenance of corporate registers, including transfer of shares, their acquisition in good faith or by prescription, opposability and correction of entries in corporate registers etc; (ii) triggers for a mandatory tender offer in case of acquisition of a significant stakeholding of shares in a public corporation; (iii) capital requirements and maintenance; and (iv) disclosure matters. Perhaps the better view is that *lex societatis* should also govern liability of the founders of a company for the pre-incorporation (or pre-reorganisation) matters.

C. Law Applicable to Shareholder Agreements and Similar Agreements

Unlike most national PIL legislation, the Civil Code includes special rules applicable to agreements on incorporation of a legal entity and agreements on exercise of corporate rights / shareholder agreements[48] (SHAs). Under Article 1214(1) parties to an SHA are free to choose governing law, but their choice shall be without prejudice to mandatory rules (as opposed to overriding mandatory provisions[49]) of the *lex societatis* in respect of the matters set out in Article 1202(2) (see section II.B of this chapter). Furthermore, pursuant to Article 1214(2)) in the absence of such choice, the *lex societatis* shall apply anyway.

[48] The latter term is sometimes understood broadly to include sale and purchase agreements (see eg Zykin, Asoskov and Zhiltsov (eds), *Commentary to Section VI* (n 5 above) 370–74). This approach is not entirely convincing as it is based on an overbroad (and unconventional) interpretation of what an 'agreement on exercise of corporate rights' (cf K Csach, 'Cross-border Shareholders' Agreements and Private International Law' in S Mock, K Csach and B Havel (eds), *International Handbook on Shareholders' Agreements* (Berlin, De Gruyter, 2018).

[49] 'Summary of the Discussions of the Working Group' (n 7 above) 158–59.

The current wording of Article 1214(1) is the result of the 2013 Reform and is not entirely free of contradictions that do, at times, lead to confusion in the PIL scholarship. For example, it is sometimes argued that the choice of foreign governing law in respect of an SHA is 'seriously restricted', as 'most corporate law issues are governed by mandatory rules of Russian law which cannot be derogated [from] by a choice of a foreign law'.[50] It is hard to agree with this view, since the prevailing position in the contemporary Russian corporate law scholarship is that an SHA has mainly a contractual effect *inter partes* and, subject to few exceptions, is not enforceable by or against third parties. An SHA cannot replace or amend a legal entity's articles of association, which are the main source of rules in respect of the matters falling within the scope of the *lex societatis*. From this perspective, it is not entirely clear how an SHA could prejudice the *lex societatis* rules at all which, as demonstrated above, do not go as far as to cover any contractual matters between participants that somehow relate to a legal entity. Perhaps a better reading of Article 1214(1) should be that the parties' choice of the law applicable to an SHA should be subject to any mandatory *lex societatis* rules applicable to SHAs. Examples of relevant rules in Russian law are the prohibition on setting out the structure of corporate bodies in an SHA, the participant's right to challenge corporate decisions taken in breach of an SHA signed by all participants of a legal entity; other forms of enforceability of an SHA by/against the company or third parties, etc.[51]

The formal validity of an SHA is always subject to the 'special requirements' of the *lex societatis* under Article 1209(2). For example, under Russian substantive law, an SHA needs to be signed as a single document to be valid.

III. Unincorporated Bodies

The Russian PIL recognises situations where an organisation may have certain elements of legal capacity, while not being a legal entity. Examples of such organisations given by the Supreme Court in its abstract recommendations for lower courts are the German OHG (*Offene Handelsgesellschaft*) and KG (*Kommanditgesellschaft*).[52] Another example could be 'pre-incorporation' organisations that in certain jurisdictions (eg Austria or Germany) possess certain elements of legal personhood before incorporation is complete. Pursuant to the first paragraph of Article 1203 of the Russian Civil Code, any such organisation's

[50] AA Kostin and DL Davydenko, 'Russia' in K Hobér and Y Kryvoi (eds), *Law and Practice of International Arbitration in the CIS Region* (Alphen aan den Rijn, Kluwer Law International, 2017) para 1.49.

[51] Cf Zykin, Asoskov and Zhiltsov (eds), *Commentary to Section VI* (n 5 above) 367–69; Csach, 'Cross-border Shareholders' Agreements' (n 48 above) 94–97.

[52] Paragraph 17 of Plenum Resolution No 24 (n 14 above).

personal law would be the law of the country where it was 'founded'. According to the Russian doctrine, such place is the country where the founders enter into a foundation agreement.[53]

The second paragraph of Article 1203 of the Russian Civil Code further provides that unincorporated organisations shall be treated as legal entities for the purposes of application of Russian substantive law (unless the law expressly provides otherwise).[54]

[53] Zykin, Asoskov and Zhiltsov (eds), *Commentary to Section VI* (n 5 above) 186.
[54] Also see ibid, 186–87.

5

Contractual Obligations: Party Autonomy

DARIA LEVINA

This chapter deals with one of the most important domains of private international law (PIL), ie, contractual obligations. It looks into the concept of party autonomy in Russian PIL and the rules and the limitations surrounding the choice of law by the parties to a contract. The chapter starts by introducing the principle of party autonomy and its distinction from related concepts. After that, it discusses the Russian PIL approach to determining the admissibility of choice of law, its existence, validity, and interpretation, as well as express and implied choice of law agreements. Lastly, the chapter examines the restrictions on party autonomy in Russian PIL.

I. Party Autonomy in Russian PIL

A. Introduction

The principle of party autonomy is of paramount importance to Russian PIL.[1] Safeguarded in Article 1210(1) of the Civil Code, this principle provides that parties to a contract may choose the law applicable to their rights and duties under the contract by agreement among themselves. Party autonomy may be exercised by agreement or unilaterally, for instance in cases concerning product liability where the victim may choose the law governing the liability of a person responsible for the harm caused.[2]

[1] S Lebedev, 'New Russian Legislation on Private International Law' (2002) 4 *Yearbook of Private International Law* 130; A Asoskov, 'National Report on Russian Federation' in J Basedow, G Rühl, F Ferrari and P De Miguel Asensio (eds), *Encyclopedia of Private International Law* (Cheltenham, Edward Elgar Publishing, 2017) 2459; O Vorobieva, *Private International Law in Russia* (Alphen aan den Rijn, Kluwer Law International BV, 2012) (National Report) 79.

[2] See Article 1221(1) of the Civil Code.

Party autonomy should be distinguished from related but distinct concepts, such as incorporation of rules into a contract by reference, also known as substantive law reference.[3] Incorporation means integration of foreign law rules into the text of a contract and allows the parties to complement and substantiate contractual terms. This can be done by integrating foreign norms verbatim into the contract or by referencing them. The parties can, eg, agree to incorporate the French *code civil* or an international convention.[4] Incorporated rules apply as ordinary contractual terms and do not replace mandatory rules of objectively applicable law, ie, the law that would apply in the absence of the parties' agreement on the basis of conflict-of-laws rules.[5]

Party autonomy in the PIL sense of the word, also known as reference to foreign law, operates differently.[6] First, it entirely replaces objectively applicable law. Foreign law rules, being incorporated into a contract, cease to be rules of law and become contractual terms; they govern the contract only as long as they do not contradict mandatory rules of objectively applicable law. In contrast, when party autonomy is exercised, it replaces all objectively applicable law, including its mandatory rules. Second, after being incorporated into the contract, foreign rules remain unaffected by legislative amendments of relevant laws, unless the parties revise contractual terms accordingly. The exercise of party autonomy means that chosen law applies to the contract as a living system, with all the changes that occur and accumulate over time.[7] Throughout this chapter, references to 'party autonomy' and 'choice of law' mean reference to foreign law in the abovementioned sense, rather than incorporation by reference.

The above distinctions find expression in the Russian scholarship and court practice.[8] For instance, in a case heard by the Highest *Arbitrazh* Court, the parties agreed on the application of the 1988 Regulation on the Supply of Industrial and Technical Goods, adopted by the Council of Ministers of the USSR ('*Polozhenie o postavkakh produktisii proisvodstvenno-tekhnicheskogo znacheniya*').[9] Based on

[3] A Asoskov, *Kollizionnoe regulirovanie dogovornykh obyazatel'stv* (*Conflict of Laws of Contract*) (Moscow, Infotropik Media, 2012) 9–10; see, similarly, German author Wilhelm Haudek, *Die Bedeutung des Parteiwillens im internationalen Privatrecht* (Berlin, Julius Springer, 1931) 2 (calling party autonomy in the broader sense of the word 'false reference' – 'unechte Verweisung'). See also: A Mills, *Party Autonomy in Private International Law* (Cambridge, Cambridge University Press, 2018) 13–14 ('such rules are not … true examples of party autonomy, which involves the parties contractually choosing … the law to govern their legal relations').

[4] See, eg, Mills (n 3 above) 23, referring to incorporation as 'a shorthand way of drafting the contract, equivalent in legal effect to cutting and pasting the text of those rules into the pages of the contract'.

[5] Asoskov (n 3 above) 11.

[6] Asoskov (n 3 above) 12.

[7] The exception is when the parties decide to 'cement' applicable law at a particular point in time, the admissibility of which will be discussed later.

[8] Asoskov (n 3 above) 13; N Trigubovich, *Avtonomia voli v mexhfunarodnom chastnom prave* (*Party Autonomy in Private International Law*) (Dissertation for the obtainment of a degree of candidate of legal sciences, Saratov, 1999) 25.

[9] Adopted and approved by the Postanovlenie Sovmina SSSR ot 25.07.1988 No 888 'Ob Utverzhdenii Polozhenia o postavkah produktsii proizvodstvenno-tekhnicheskogo znacheniya' (Decree of the Council of Ministers of the USSR dated 25 July 1988).

contractual wording, the court concluded that the parties had incorporated the Regulation's provisions into their contract, which applied as regular contractual terms. At the same time, the parties had not chosen Russian law as applicable law, which is why the court proceeded to determine the latter on the basis of conflict-of-laws rules of the forum.[10]

The underlying idea of party autonomy is that for the most part, cross-border contracts only concern the individual interests of their parties. It is therefore natural for legislatures to give them the capacity to choose the best for themselves, providing for restrictions on party autonomy if third-party interests are involved.[11] The source and legal nature of the principle of party autonomy have been debated in Russian PIL over the years. Soviet law took a strictly positivist approach, meaning that party autonomy was understood solely as a legislative norm enacted by the authority of the state.[12] Some contemporary authors still support this view by arguing that party autonomy is just another connecting factor, determining that the applicable law is the law chosen by the parties (*lex voluntatis*).[13] This line of reasoning, however, is problematic because the legal provision authorising the parties' choice of law is actually anything *but* a traditional conflict-of-laws norm: for instance, it does not determine the governing law of the contract as such but rather refers to the source – ie, the parties' agreement – as the basis of the choice of applicable law.[14]

The debate over the legal nature of party autonomy is not merely academic but also has important practical implications. The understanding of party autonomy as a conflict-of-laws norm would entail, inter alia, parties' inability to choose applicable law for different parts of the contract separately: since regular conflict-of-laws rules usually refer to a single applicable law, the parties should be required to do the same.[15] It would further mean the inadmissibility of choice of non-state law, such as the Principles of European Contract Law (PECL) or the UNIDROIT Principles of International Commercial Contracts, because regular Russian PIL rules do not permit it.

In this light, the majority of scholars agree that party autonomy is not merely a legal norm enacted by the state but rather a *sui generis* concept of PIL, ie, a concept 'of its own kind'. Its only similarity to a traditional conflict-of-laws rule is that, like

[10] See para 11 of Informatsionnoe Pismo Presidiuma Vysshego Arbitrazhnogo Suda ot 16.02.1998 No 29 'Obzor sydebno-arbitrazhnoy praktiki razresheniya sporov po delam s uchastiem inostrannykh lits' (Information letter of the Presidium of the Highest *Arbitrazh* Court dated 16 February 1998 No 29 'Overview of the Court Practice Regarding Disputes Concerning Foreign Persons').

[11] Asoskov (n 3 above) 25. This principle is not absolute. The limitations to party autonomy are discussed further below.

[12] L Lunts, *Kurs mezhdunarodnogo chastnogo prava* (*Course of Private International Law*) (Moscow, Spark, 2002) 212–13.

[13] V Tolstykh, *Mezhdunarodnoe chastnoe parvo: kollizionnoe regulirovanie* (*Private International Law: Conflict of Laws Regulation*) (Izd-vo R. Aslanova 'I͡Uridicheskiĭ t͡sentr' Press, 2004) 119.

[14] Asoskov (n 3 above) 40.

[15] Asoskov (n 3 above) 43–44.

regular conflict-of-laws rules, party autonomy aims to resolve a conflict-of-laws issue, ie, to determine the governing law of a contract.[16] Such an understanding of party autonomy makes it possible to avoid unnecessary restriction of the parties' choices regarding the design of their contractual relations.

B. The Law Applicable to a Choice of Law Agreement

Structurally, the concept of party autonomy consists of two elements, namely the substantive rules of forum law that sanction the choice of law and define its limits, and the choice of law agreement itself.[17] Russian PIL regards the choice of law agreement as autonomous and separate from the underlying contract.[18] Consequently, the questions of admissibility of a choice of law agreement, its existence, interpretation, and validity are determined separately from those of the underlying contract, and themselves require the ascertainment of applicable law.

For a state court, the possibility of applying foreign law is opened up by the national PIL (ie, forum law). Forum law is therefore regarded as a natural starting point for determining the admissibility of the choice of law (see Article 1186(1) of the Civil Code).[19] Forum law, inter alia, governs the existence and interpretation of the choice of law agreement,[20] as well as its formal validity. There is a debate, however, regarding the exact provisions governing the formal validity of choice

[16] Asoskov (n 3 above) 42, 45; S Tretyakov, *Yuridicheskaya Priroda Avtonomii Voli v Mezhdunarodnom Chastnom Prave* (*Legal Nature of Party Autonomy in International Private Law*) (Dissertation for the obtainment of a degree of Candidate of Legal Sciences, Moscow, 2003) 106–7; Vorobieva (n 1 above) 81–82.

[17] Asoskov (n 3 above) 41; Tretyakov (n 16 above) 106–7; see similarly G Ivanov and A Makovskiy, *Mezhdunarodnoe chastnoe morskoe parvo* (*International Private Maritime Law*) (Leningrad, Sudostroenie, 1984) 26.

[18] The autonomy of a choice of law agreement is widely supported in the Russian PIL doctrine. See, for instance, A Rubanov, '"Avtonomia Voli" v Mezhdunarodnom Chastnom Prave Kak Teoretichestkaya Problema' ('Party Autonomy in International Private Law as a Theoretical Problem') (1986) *Sovetskiy Ezhegodnik Mezhdunarodnogo Prava (Soviet Yearbook of International Law)* 214, 216; Vorobieva (n 1 above) 82; IS Zykin, 'Commentary to Article 1210 of the Civil Code' in A Makovskiy and E Sukhanov (eds), *Kommentariy k Chasti Tretiey Grazhdanskogo Kodeksa Rossiyskoy Federatsii* (*Commentary to Part III of the Civil Code of the Russian Federation*) (Moscow, Yurist, 2002) 429–30; A Komarov, 'Commentary to Article 1210 of the Civil Code' in N Marysheva and K Yaroshenko (eds), *Kommentariy k Grazhdanskomy Kodeksy Rossiyskoy Federatsii, Chasti Tretiey* (*Postateyniy*) (*Article-by-Article Commentary to the Civil Code of the Russian Federation, Part III*) (Moscow, Kontrakt, 2009) 479–80. Arbitral tribunals constituted under the MKAS auspices and adjudicating disputes under Russian law support the autonomy of a choice of law agreement as well. See M Rozenberg (ed), *Praktika Mezhdunarodnogo Kommercheskogo Arbitrazhnogo Suda pri TPP RF za 2001–2002 gg* (*Practice of the International Commercial Arbitration Court of the Russian Chamber of Industry and Commerce for 2001–2002*) (Moscow, Statut, 2004) 148–53 (in particular the award dated 5 November 2001 in case No 66/2001). See, however, the alternative view in: A Pokrovskaya, *Soglashenie o prave, primenimom k chastnopravovym otnosheniyam, oslozhnennym inostrannym elementom* (*Agreement on Law Applicable to Private Relations with Foreign Element*) (Dissertation for the obtainment of a degree of candidate of legal sciences, Moscow 2006) 21.

[19] Asoskov (n 3 above) 47, 55.

[20] Asoskov (n 3 above) 60, 88.

of law. First, Article 1210(2) of the Civil Code defines general requirements as to the choice of law. Mirroring Article 3(1) of the Rome I Regulation, it provides that a choice of law agreement 'must be directly expressed or must definitely follow from the terms of the contract or the totality of the circumstances of the case'.[21] Simultaneously, there is Article 1209 of the Civil Code regarding the formal validity of a contract. It has been suggested that since a choice of law agreement is a distinct contract in and of itself, it should therefore be subject to the requirements of Article 1209 as well.[22] This approach, however, would result in cumulative application of Articles 1209 and 1210(2) of the Civil Code and, as a consequence, heighten requirements of choice of law agreements. This would inevitably lead to more frequent invalidations of choice of law agreements on formal grounds – a scenario undesirable from a policy perspective. The prevailing opinion is therefore that formal validity of choice of law is exclusively subject to Article 1210(2) of the Civil Code.[23]

C. Express and Implied Choice of Law

Russian PIL recognises express and implied choice of law. An example of an express choice of law is the parties' explicit agreement on the application of a particular law to a contract. Express choice of law can also take form of a reference to another contract between the same parties that contains an explicit choice of law clause, or to a legal act containing a provision on applicable law, provided that the parties' intention regarding the choice of law follows from such reference.[24]

The admissibility of implied choice of law is envisaged by Article 1210(2) of the Civil Code and has been part of the national PIL for quite some time.[25] Soviet PIL, for instance, took into account the parties' intentions regarding the choice of law that were expressed through their actions rather than expressly stipulated in a contract.[26] A peculiar instance of an implied choice of law concerned the parties'

[21] Article 1210(2) of the Civil Code.

[22] Asoskov (n 3 above) 82; Komarov in Marysheva and Yaroshenko (n 18 above) 479 believes that in the absence of a special rule in Russian law regarding the form of a choice of law agreement, general rules on the form of a contract should apply as long as they do not conflict with the character and purpose of choice of law agreement.

[23] Asoskov (n 3 above) 86.

[24] Vorobieva (n 1 above) 79; See, eg, on practice of arbitral tribunals constituted under the auspices of the International Commercial Arbitration Court at the Chamber of Commerce and Industry of the Russian Federation: M Rozenberg (ed), *Praktika Mezhdunarodnogo Kommercheskogo Arbitrazhnogo Suda pri TPP RF za 1996–1997 gg* (*Practice of the International Commercial Arbitration Court of the Russian Chamber of Industry and Commerce for 1996–1997*) (Moscow, International Center of Financial-Economic Development, 1998) 172–74.

[25] See views to the contrary: Komarov in Marysheva and Yaroshenko (n 18 above) 478; also E Kabatova, 'Commentary to Article 1210 of the Civil Code' in T Abova, M Boguslavskiy and A Svetlanova (eds), *Kommentariy k Grazhdanskomy Kodeksy Rossiyskoy Federatsii, Chasti Tretiey, Tom 3* (*Commentary to the Civil Code of the Russian Federation, Part III*) (Moscow, Urait-Izdatelstvo, 2004) 400.

[26] Lunts (n 12 above) 499.

agreements on the place of contracting. Such agreements were routinely regarded as evidence of the parties' intentions to apply the law of the place of contracting.[27] The reason may be that the Soviet PIL norms at the time used the place of contracting as the main connecting factor for determining the law applicable to contractual obligations in the absence of the parties' agreement. An arbitral award of the Arbitration Commission for Foreign Trade (*Vneshnetorgovaya arbitrazhnaya komissiya*) in case No 6/1970 dated 14 May 1970 is illustrative of this approach: the case concerned a dispute between an English firm (claimant) and a Soviet state enterprise (respondent). The contract was signed in London but contained a term according to which Moscow was to be considered the place of contracting for legal purposes. On this basis, the arbitral tribunal concluded that the parties had made an implied choice of Russian law as the governing law of the contract.[28]

Even though the admissibility of an implied choice of law is not in question, the range of circumstances that may be interpreted as such is debatable. Some scholars suggest that circumstances indicating an implied choice of law must depend on the parties' will in order to be interpreted as a manifestation of their intention to choose a particular law.[29] This means, inter alia, that they do not extend to factors such as the law determining the legal status of the parties to a contract, even if both parties share this law, or their habitual residence, or the location of a contractual object.[30]

Choice of court is one of the circumstances that can be interpreted as indicating implied choice of law. Although the Russian courts traditionally do not regard a choice of court agreement as a standalone indicator of an implied choice of law[31] (meaning that a choice of Russian court will not automatically mean submission to Russian law),[32] they do consider choice of court to be one of the factors that, in conjunction with other circumstances of the case, can cumulatively indicate the parties' intention to submit to a certain law.[33]

[27] Asoskov (n 3 above) 103.

[28] This approach continued to be used for contracts negotiated before 1992, ie until the relevant PIL was repealed. M Rozenberg (ed), *Praktika Mezhdunarodnogo Kommercheskogo Arbitrazhnogo Suda pri TPP RF za 1999–2000 gg* (*Practice of the International Commercial Arbitration Court of the Russian Chamber of Industry and Commerce for 1999–2000*) (Moscow, Statut, 2002) 207–12.

[29] Asoskov (n 3 above) 109.

[30] This approach is suggested, eg, by VA Kanashevskiy, *Vneshneekonomicheskie sdelki: material'no-pravovoe i kollizionnoe regulirovanie (Foreign Economic Transactions: Substrative and Conflict of Law Regulation)* (Alphen aan den Rijn, Wolters Kluwer, 2008) 106–8.

[31] For historical background see: Lunts (n 12 above) 217; for current practice see: para 12 of the Review by the Presidium of the Highest *Arbitrazh* of Court Practice on Certain Matters Related to the Proceedings Involving Foreign Persons dated 9 July 2013 No 158 (Informatsionnoe pismo Presidiuma VAS RF ot 9.07.2013 No 158).

[32] See para 5 of Informatsionnoe Pismo Presidiuma Vysshego Arbitrazhnogo Suda ot 16.02.1998 No 29 'Obzor sydebno-arbitrazhnoy praktiki razresheniya sporov po delam s uchastiem inostrannykh lits' (Information letter of the Presidium of the Highest *Arbitrazh* Court dated 16 February 1998 No 29 'Overview of the Court Practice Regarding Disputes Concerning Foreign Persons'); Postanovlenie Presidiuma Vysshego Arbitrazhnogo Suda Rossiiskoy Federatsii ot 16.06.2009 No 2088/09 (Resolution of the Presidium of the Highest *Arbitrazh* Court dated 16 June 2009 No 2088/09).

[33] See, eg, Zykin in Makovskiy and Sukhanov (n 18 above) 423–24; M Boguslavskiy, *Mezhdunarodnoe Chastnoe Pravo: Uchebnik* (*International Private Law: Textbook*), 6th edn (Moscow, Norma, 2009) 310;

The previous course of dealings of the parties concerning other contracts between them that include an express choice of law can be regarded either as a standalone or a cumulative indicator of an implied choice of law.[34] Simultaneously, the use in a contract of expressions and terms common to a certain system of law can be regarded as a standalone indicator of an implied choice of law.[35] For instance, conscious use of a standard form of a contract known to be governed by a particular law is usually believed to sufficiently prove the intentions of the parties and therefore indicate the choice of law. The agreement on the place of performance, in contrast, is only regarded as one of the cumulative indicators of an implied choice of law.[36] Reference to a particular system of law in the course of court proceedings can be regarded as an implied choice of law and has been interpreted as such by the Russian courts:[37] parties' statements in court have been interpreted this way even in the presence of an explicit choice of law clause in the contract.[38]

II. Restrictions on Party Autonomy

Russian PIL, while recognising the fundamental ability of the parties to choose the applicable law, nonetheless provides for certain restrictions on party autonomy. Restrictions are usually dictated by the need to account for conflict-of-laws interests other than those of the parties to a contract.[39] This section addresses the three most important categories of restrictions: those aiming to protect an economically weaker party, those aiming to protect third parties who are not parties to a contract, and those aiming to protect the regulatory interests of the state.

A. Restrictions Aiming to Protect Economically Weaker Parties

Restrictions aiming to protect an economically weaker party pertain primarily to choice of law in consumer contracts. The approach of Russian PIL to consumer

N Marysheva (ed), *Mezhdunarodnoe Chastnoe Pravo: Uchebnik* (*International Private Law: Textbook*), 3rd edn (Moscow, Statut, 2011) 358.

[34] Asoskov (n 3 above) 126.

[35] Komarov in Marysheva and Yaroshenko (n 18 above) 478.

[36] Asoskov (n 3 above) 125.

[37] Asoskov (n 3 above) 151; Asoskov (n 1 above) 2459; see also: Postanovlenie Federalnogo Arbitrazhnogo Suda Moskovskogo Okruga ot 5.12.2003 po dely No A40-47669/02-69-492 (Judgment of the Federal *Arbitrazh* Court of Moscow Region dated 5 December 2003 in case No A40-47669/02-69-492); Postanovlenie Devyatogo Arbitrazhnogo Apellaytsionnogo Suda ot 18.01.2010 po dely No A40-57346/09-70-210 (Judgment of the 9th *Arbitrazh* Court of Appeals dated 18 January 2010 in case No A40-57346/09-70-210.

[38] See examples of this line of reasoning here: Postanovlenie Federalnogo Arbitrazhnogo Suda Moskovskogo Okruga ot 10.08.1999 No KG-A40/2425-99 (Judgment of the Federal *Arbitrazh* Court of Moscow Region dated 10 August 1999 No KG-A40/2425-99).

[39] Asoskov (n 3 above) 157.

contracts is similar to that of the European PIL, providing that consumers cannot be deprived of their rights or otherwise be constrained by a contract with a professional, or business party. Russian law defines a consumer as a natural person who uses, obtains, or orders movable property, works or services for personal, family, household, and other needs without a business purpose.[40] In contrast, the professional, or business party is usually an entrepreneur or a merchant providing services, goods, or works to the consumer.

Rules defining the professional party were substantially amended during the 2013 Reform. Purely territorial criteria that had been used previously, such as the physical presence of the professional party on the territory of the consumer's country, were deemed no longer suitable for determination of applicable law.[41] The reformed provisions account for developments in the European PIL, in particular Article 6(1) of the Rome I Regulation,[42] which implements the criterion of directed activity for the classification of a party as a professional party in a consumer contract. Accordingly, the current Article 1212(1) of the Civil Code defines the professional party as a counterparty of the consumer, who conducts activity in the consumer's country of residence or in any manner directs its activity toward the territory of this country or territories of several countries, including the country of the consumer's place of residence, provided that the contract is connected to such activity of the professional party.

The crucial requirement is the targeting of the professional party's activity toward the territory of the consumer's place of residence. The physical presence of the professional party on the territory of the consumer's country of residence is therefore irrelevant. If the professional party organises her business in a way that attracts the interest of consumers from a certain country, and the contract is associated with business activities of this party, such directed activity will be sufficient for determining applicable law. The criterion also encompasses activities of the professional party in electronic commerce, such as selling goods or providing services through a website.[43] The presumption is that if the professional party maintains a website targeting consumers from a particular country, she directs her activities to the territory of the country of the consumer's place of residence. As per the Supreme Court's clarification,[44] the website is considered

[40] Preamble of Zakon Rossiyskoy Federatsii ot 7.02.1992 No 2300-1 'O Zaschite Prav Potrebiteley' (Law of the Russian Federation 'On protection of Consumers' Rights' dated 7 February 1992 No 2300-1).

[41] 'Obobscheniya diskussiy rabochei gruppy po podgotovke dopolneniy i izmeneniy v razdel VI "Mezhdunarodnoe chastnoe pravo" GK RF' ('Summary of the Discussions of the Working Group for Preparing Amendments to Section VI "Private International Law" of the Russian Civil Code') (2019) 2 *Civil Law Review* 133 (Summary of Discussions) 155.

[42] Regulation (EC) No 593/2008 of the European Parliament and of the Council of 17 June 2008 on the law applicable to contractual obligations (Rome I Regulation). See on their influence on the reform: Summary of Discussions (n 41 above) 155.

[43] Summary of Discussions (n 41 above) 155.

[44] Postanovlenie Prenuma Verkhovnogo Suda Rossiyskoy Federatsii ot 9.07.2019 No 24 'O Primenenii Norm Mezhdunarodnogo Chastnogo Prava Sudami Rossiyskoy Federatsii' (Resolution of the Plenum

to be directed at Russian consumers if it has official translation to the Russian language, its prices are displayed in the Russian currency, or the contact numbers have Russian codes. This list is not exhaustive, and other indicators may be invoked to prove the directed nature of a business activity. For instance, if the website owner ordered services aimed at increasing the visits to her site by Russian Internet users, she will be considered to be targeting consumers on Russian territory.

In line with the principle of party autonomy, parties to a consumer contract may choose the applicable law. However, the choice of law in consumer contracts is subject to certain restrictions. In particular, under Article 1212(1) of the Civil Code, the express choice of law in a consumer contract cannot deprive the consumer of her rights granted by the mandatory rules of the law of the country of her place of residence. In this context, the term 'mandatory rules of the law' means all mandatory rules of the Russian law that cannot be derogated from by the parties (Article 422(1) of the Civil Code) rather than the overriding mandatory provisions that have extraterritorial application in the sense of Article 1192 of the Civil Code. Mandatory rules of Russian consumer law are found primarily in the Federal Law 'On Protection of Consumers' Rights', the Civil Code, and some other applicable laws. If the parties to a consumer contract do not choose the applicable law, the law of the country of the consumer's residence applies.[45]

The above choice of law rules regarding consumer contracts do not extend to contracts of carriage and contracts for the performance of works or the provision of services if the work has to be performed or the services rendered exclusively in a country other than the country of the place of consumer's residence.[46]

B. Restrictions Aiming to Protect Third Parties

Restrictions on party autonomy that aim to protect parties who are not parties to a contract (third parties) include primarily those pertaining to the admissibility of subsequent choice of law, ie, choice of law made after the conclusion of the contract, and the retroactive force of such choice of law. These restrictions on party autonomy are essentially a conflict-of-laws continuation of a principle of substantive law that accounts for the interests of third parties. In Russian law this principle is reflected, inter alia, in Article 308(1) of the Civil Code, under which an obligation, contractual or non-contractual, cannot create duties for persons who are not parties to such obligation.[47]

of the Supreme Court 'On the Application of Private International Law Rules by the Courts of the Russian Federation' dated 9 July 2019 No 24).

[45] Article 1212(2) of the Civil Code.

[46] Article 1212(3) of the Civil Code. See commentary in: Summary of Discussions (n 41 above) 156–57.

[47] Asoskov (n 3 above) 223.

The analysis of individual conflict-of-laws interests of the parties lends itself to a conclusion that favours permitting the choice of law not only at the moment of conclusion of a contract but also afterwards (subsequent choice of law).[48] The parties may need it, for instance, to adapt the contract to the circumstances that have changed, eg, because the parties entered into another contract that is closely connected with the previously concluded contract and they want to subject both contracts to a different law, or the parties may want to optimise procedural costs and therefore choose a different law during the court proceedings. Further, given that parties can terminate the existing contract at any time and enter into a new one, effectively choosing new law for the new contract, it would be hard to justify a prohibition, only to reach the same result in a much simpler way, ie, by choosing a new law for the existing contract without entering into a new one.[49]

In view of the above, subsequent choice of law is permitted under Russian PIL and is subject to the same rules as the choice of law made at the moment of conclusion of the contract.[50] Under Article 1210(3) of the Civil Code, subsequent choice of law has retroactive effect. The latter, however, has been criticised by scholars. Indeed, the retroactive force of the newly chosen law may not always be what the parties wanted. To ensure the flexibility of the conflict-of-laws regulation and take account of the parties' intentions, scholars suggest presuming that the newly chosen law has retroactive force unless the parties' intentions, the essence of the contract, and the totality of the circumstances show that the subsequent choice of law was meant to have prospective force only.[51] To support such an approach in light of the statutory provisions of Article 1210(3) of the Civil Code, which provide for no exceptions, scholars rely on the analogous provision of Article 116(3) of the Swiss Private International Law Act, which is interpreted by commentators to mean that the parties can still agree in an express or implied manner that the subsequent choice of law will have prospective force only.[52] A different conclusion would contradict the principle of party autonomy, and unnecessarily limit its

[48] Asoskov, National Report (n 1 above) 2459.

[49] See, eg, Mills (n 3 above) 370 ('there does not seem to be any essential reason not to permit a subsequent choice of law, at least to the extent that the choice would have been permissible at the time of entering into the agreement').

[50] Asoskov (n 3 above) 216.

[51] Asoskov (n 3 above) 221; *Münchener Kommentar zum Bürgerlichen Gesetzbuch. Bd 10. Internationales Privatrecht. Rom-I Verordnung. Rom-II Verordnung. Einführungsgesetz zum Bürgerlichen Gesetzbuche (Artt 1–24)* 490; C Reithmann and D Martiny (eds), *Internationales Vertragsrecht. Das internationale Privatrecht der Schuldverträge* (OttoSchmidt, 2010) 129; MB Jaspers, *Nachträgliche Rechtswahl im internationalen Schuldvertragsrecht: unter besonderer Berücksichtigung der Rechtspraxis in England, Frankreich, Dänemark und Deutschland – Saarbrücker Studien zum Privat- und Wirtschaftsrecht. Bd 30* (Frankfurt, Peter Lang, 2002) 151; see also P Nygh, *Autonomy in International Contracts* (Oxford, Oxford University Press, 1999) 102 (suggesting to abandon presumptions and instead determine whether the parties had intended the subsequent choice of law to have retroactive force on the basis of the circumstances of a particular case).

[52] H Honsell, NP Vogt, A Schnyder and S Berti, *Basler Kommentar Internationales Privatrecht*, 2nd edn (Basel, Helbing & Lichtenhahn, 2007) 840; F Vischer, L Huber and D Oser, *Internationales Vertragsrecht*, 2nd edn (Bern, Vischer, 2000) 105; Asoskov (n 1 above) 2459.

exercise by the parties. Furthermore, retroactive force of the change in applicable law may in some instances affect the already existing rights and duties of the third parties who did not express their consent to such a change. The above proposition intends not only to protect parties to the contract but also prevent an adverse effect on third parties as well.[53]

C. Restrictions Aiming to Protect the Regulatory Interests of the State

Restrictions of this type aim to protect conflict-of-laws interests such as the uniformity of judgments, the predictability of outcome, and legal certainty. In this section, I discuss restrictions such as the limitations of choice of law for purely domestic contracts, the requirement of an objective connection of a contract with the chosen law, the admissibility of choosing different laws for different parts of the contract (*dépeçage*), and the admissibility of choosing non-state law.

(i) Choice of Law for Purely Domestic Contracts

A number of countries impose restrictions on choice for law for purely domestic contracts, ie, contracts with no foreign connection. Since choice of law by the parties effectively replaces objectively applicable law, including its mandatory rules, restrictions of this kind aim to protect the regulatory interest of the state to have its mandatory rules complied with. Permitting the choice of law for purely domestic contracts would lead to a scenario where the existence of mandatory rules in a legal system would entirely lose its meaning, because the parties would be easily able to avoid them by simply agreeing on the application of foreign law. This, in turn, would encourage countries to promote all of their regular mandatory rules to the status of overriding mandatory provisions that parties cannot derogate from. To avoid scenarios like this, the interest of the state in making sure its mandatory rules are complied with in a purely domestic contract leads to differentiation between purely domestic contracts on the one hand and contracts with a foreign connection on the other hand, with limited party autonomy for the former.[54]

[53] Asoskov (n 3 above) 223. See similarly: Art 3(2) of the Rome Convention and Rome I Regulation Art 1210(3) of the Civil Code, Art 116(3) of the the Swiss Private International Law Act.

[54] Asoskov (n 3 above) 234; D Solomon, 'The Private International Law of Contracts in Europe: Advances and Retreats' (2008) 82 *Tulane Law review* 1709, 1727; S Egeler, *Konsensprobleme im internationalen Schuldvertragsrecht* (St Gallen, Dike, 1994) 53; see similarly: Mills (n 3 above) 475 ('The autonomy of the parties is contrained because it is considered that, in a purely domestic case, the state objectively connected has an overriding interest in the mandatory provisions of its contract law governing the relationship between the parties, although otherwise the parties remain free to make a choice of foreign law').

Russian PIL employs an approach similar to the European PIL;[55] namely, Article 1186(1) of the Civil Code indicates that the issue of applicable law can only arise regarding legal relations with a foreign connection (a 'foreign element' in Russian terminology). Further, Article 1210(5) of the Civil Code specifies, regarding purely domestic contracts, that:

> If at the time of choice by the parties to a contract of the applicable law all circumstances concerning the essence of the relations of the parties are connected only with one country, the choice by the parties of the law of another country may not alter the effect of the mandatory rules of law of the country with which all the circumstances concerning the essence of the relations of the parties are connected.

Thus, although the Russian PIL allows for a choice of law for purely domestic contracts, this choice can only amount to incorporation of foreign law norms into the contract and does not displace the mandatory rules of the objectively applicable law.

(ii) Requirement of an Objective Connection of a Contract with the Chosen Law

In today's world, 'the law is applied simply because it is the law under which the parties have expressly or impliedly agreed to contract'.[56] This is the approach generally followed by Russian law: neither Soviet nor Russian PIL required a contract to have an objective connection with the chosen law as a condition of the parties' exercise of their autonomy.[57] Presumably, the rationale behind this policy is that previously, in the Soviet era, it was important for the government to be able to choose a neutral law to govern its trade with capitalist countries. Accordingly, the PIL norms had to ensure the possibility to do so, without requiring the contract to have a link to the country whose law was chosen.

[55] Under Article 3(3) of the Rome I Regulation, the parties to a purely domestic contract, as a rule, may choose applicable law but their choice will be regarded as incorporation of the chosen law into the text of the contract rather than actual reference to foreign law, and the governing law of the contract will still be objectively applicable law. See more: O Lando, 'Party Autonomy in the EC Convention on the Law Applicable to Contractual Obligations' in F Rigaux and P Bourrel (eds), *The Influence of the European Communities upon Private International Law of the Member States* (Bruxelles, Larcier, 1981) 194; K Lipstein, 'Introduction: the Preliminary Draft Convention on the Law Applicable to Contractual and Non-Contractual Obligations' in K Lipstein (ed), *Harmonization of Private International Law by the E.E.C* (London, Institute of Advanced Legal Studies, 1978) 4; A Overbeck, 'Contracts: the Swiss Draft Statute Compared with the E.E.C. Convention' in P North (ed), *Contract Conflicts: The E.E.C. Convention on the Law Applicable to Contractual Obligations: a Comparative Study* (Amsterdam, North-Holland Publishing Co, 1982) 271.

[56] Mills (n 3 above) 367.

[57] Asoskov (n 3 above) 268; Lunts (n 12 above) 217, 501–2; Zykin in Makovskiy and Sukhanov (n 18 above) 427. See, though, an argument to the opposite: Tolstykh (n 13 above) 120.

*(iii) Choice of Different Laws for Different Parts of the Contract (*Dépeçage*)*

Russian PIL, as a rule, allows for a split of the applicable law (*dépeçage*).[58] In this vein, the Civil Code, in its Article 1210(4), explicitly provides that 'the parties may choose the applicable law both for the contract as a whole as well as for individual parts thereof'. There are no additional requirements as to the parties' agreement on the split of applicable law: it can be either explicit or implicit, entered into simultaneously with the formation of the contract or afterwards.[59]

The limits of such split, however, still require discussion. The split of applicable law can be vertical or horizontal. A vertical split occurs when a contractual obligation has several objects; for instance, when various types of goods are supplied or leased, or the objects of the contract are located in different countries, or the works and services are to be performed in different countries. In other words, a vertical split of applicable law is a split performed with respect to 'vertically' separable parts of the contract, where in principle, the parties could enter into a distinct contract regarding each of these parts. Vertical split of applicable law can be employed in mixed contracts that contain elements of various contractual types. A mixed contract is governed by the law of the country with which the contract, taken in its entirety, is most closely connected. If, however, it follows from the law, the contract, or the totality of the circumstances that different parts of a mixed contract are more closely connected with different laws, then the court at its discretion can apply different laws to different parts of such a contract.[60]

In contrast, a horizontal split occurs when different aspects of a single contract, such as its conclusion and validity, are subject to different laws. Such a split of the applicable law can produce a clash between conflict-of-laws interests of the parties and those of the state, such as the uniformity of judgments and legal certainty. This can be illustrated by adhesion contracts. In some jurisdictions, the protection of a weaker party to an adhesion contract takes the form of entitling her to demand invalidation of unfair contractual terms or the entire contract. In contrast, under Article 428 of the Russian Civil Code, the weaker party can only demand an amendment or termination of such contract, but not its invalidation. In a scenario where different aspects of an adhesion contract are governed by different laws, and the invalidity of a contract is governed by Russian law and its amendment and termination by another law, the weaker party might be left with no means of recourse against the economically stronger party.[61] Therefore, to protect a weaker

[58] Asoskov (n 3 above) 273.

[59] Asoskov (n 3 above) 273.

[60] Article 1211(10) of the Civil Code. See a similar approach in: Report on the Convention on the Law Applicable to Contractual Obligations by Mario Giuliano and Paul Lagarde para 8 of the commentary to Article 4 of the Rome Convention.

[61] Asoskov (n 3 above) 282.

party, in case of a horizontal split of applicable law, it is presumed that the parties intended to only choose one law as the applicable law. If they chose separate laws for different aspects of the contract, it is presumed that the choice of the second law operates as incorporation rather than choice of foreign law. This logic works well in the context of the Civil Code, as the wording of Article 1210(4) does not just allow the choice of applicable law for any part of the contract but rather for an individual part of the contract only.[62] This is interpreted to mean a separable *part* of a contract, such as in the case of a vertical split of applicable law, rather than a certain *aspect* of a contract, such as in the case of a horizontal split of applicable law.

(iv) Choice of Non-state Law

Although arbitral tribunals constituted under the auspices of the International Commercial Arbitration Court (*Mezhdunarodniy kommercheskiy arbitrazhniy sud*) apply non-state law on a regular basis,[63] scholars have traditionally been sceptical of the choice of non-state law in state court proceedings, the latter including but not limited to international treaties that have not yet entered into force, model laws, collections of customary practices, religious sources not sanctioned by the state, and the like.[64] For instance, a prominent Soviet scholar, August Rubanov, argued that 'the nature of international cooperation does not allow the law to sanction agreements where the parties determined that their [legal] relation should be governed by [quasi-legal] norms …'.[65] Russian scholar Natalia Trigubovich continues this line of thought by positing that the choice of non-state law cannot amount to the exercise of party autonomy, but instead operates as incorporation by reference.[66] Ivan Zykin and Aleksandr Komarov in their respective commentaries on the Civil Code reason that Article 1210 of the Civil Code

[62] Asoskov, National Report (n 1 above) 2459.

[63] See generally A Muranov (ed), *Mezhdunarodnuy Kommercheskiy Arbitrazh: Oput Otechestvennogo Regulirovaniya/Samoregulirovaniya* (*International Commercial Arbitration: Experience of Domestic Regulation/Self-Regulation*) Vol I (Moscow, Infotropic, 2012); A Zhiltsov, 'Primenenie Razdela VI Chasti Tretiey GK RF v Praktike MKAS pri TPP RF' ('Application of Section VI of Part III of the Civil Code of the Russian Federation in Practice of the ICAC at the Chamber of Commerce and Industry of the Russian Federation') (2014) 2 *Vestnik Mezhdunarodnogo Kommercheskogo Arbitrazha* 13. See similarly: Mills (n 3 above) 492.

[64] See generally: IS Zykin, *Vneshneekonomicheskie Operatsii: Pravo i Praktika* (*Foreign Economic Operations: Law and Practice*) (Moscow, International Relations Publishers, 1994); M Mazhorina, 'Primenime Pravo v Mezhdunarodnykh Kommercheskikh Kontraktakh: Sovremennoe Tolkovanie i Prognoziruemaya Praktika Mezhdunarovnykh Kommercheskikh Arbitrazhei i Natsionalnukh Sudov' ('Applicable Law in International Commercial Contracts: Contemporary Interpretation and Prognosed Practice of International Commercial Arbitral Tribunals') (2015) 6 *Zakonodatel'svo* 79; O Fonotova, 'Printsypy UNIDROIT Kak "Primenimoe Pravo" (Prakticheskiy Aspekt)' ('UNIDROIT Principles as "Applicable Law" (Practical Aspect)') (2017) 10 *Pravo i Ekonomika* 56.

[65] Rubanov (n 18 above) 218.

[66] Trigubovich (n 8 above) 72.

talks about the choice of law *by the parties*, whereas the law means an objectively existing system of norms that qualifies as such due to it being sanctioned *by state authority*.[67] Zykin advances a further argument against the choice of non-state law in state court proceedings, stating that such norms cannot ensure effective and fair regulation of the parties' relations, given that the sources of non-state law often do not contain mandatory rules to protect public interests or the interests of weaker parties, and therefore are not balanced enough. The unlimited freedom to choose them as rules governing the parties' relations might potentially lead to abuse of power by the parties with stronger bargaining positions.[68]

Other scholars do not find the above arguments convincing, and argue for a more liberal approach, especially regarding contracts entered into by business parties within the framework of their commercial activities. For instance, Anton Asoskov observes that legal science no longer limits the law exclusively to the norms sanctioned by a legislative authority of a state but rather interprets the law more broadly.[69] The argument about potential abuse of power reflects important regulatory interests of the state, in particular the interest in the internal uniformity of judgments, and as such is worthy of consideration. The regulatory interests of the state, however, are still not sufficient to entirely prohibit the choice of non-state law, primarily because they can be effectively protected by the application of overriding mandatory provisions, permitting the choice of non-state law for

[67] Zykin in Makovskiy and Sukhanov (n 18 above) 426–27; Komarov in Marysheva and Yaroshenko (n 18 above) 480–81; see also authors arguing the inadmissibility of choice of non-state law for disputes arising out of commercial contracts and heard in state courts: N Vilkova, 'Rol' MKAS pri TPP RF v Stanovlenii I razvitii sovremennogo kollizionnogo regulirovaniya dogovornykh otnosheniy s inostrannym elementom' ('The Role of MKAS of the Russian Chamber of Commerce and Industry in the Creation and Development of Modern Conflict of Law Regulation of Contractual Relations with Foreign Element') in A Komarov (ed), *Mezhdunarodniy Kommercheskiy Arbitrazh: Sovremennie Problemy i Resheniya: Sbornik Statey k 75-letiyu Mezhdunarodnogo Kommercheskogo Arbitrazhnogo Suda pri Torgovo-Promyshlennoy Palate Rossiyskoy Federatsii Federatsii* (*International Commercial Arbitration: Contemporary Problems and Solutions: Collection of Articles for the 75th Anniversary of MKAS of the Russian Chamber of Commerce and Industry of the Russian Federation*) (Moscow, Statut, 2007) 121–22. See also: A Komarov, *Printsypy Mezhdunarodnykh Kommercheskikh Dogovorov UNIDROIT 2010* (*UNIDROIT Principles 2010 in International Commercial Contracts*) (Moscow, Statut, 2013) VIII; A Komarov, 'Reference to the UNIDROIT Principles in International Commercial Arbitration practice in the Russian Federation' (2011) 16(3) *Uniform Law Review* 657. See discussion of a similar argument in: Mills (n 3 above) 496, in particular with the reference to the traditionally cited theoretical underpinning of this position found in the judgment of the Permanent Court of International Justice in the Serbian Loans Case: 'any contract which is not a contract between States in their capacity as subjects of international law is based on the municipal law of some country', *Serbian Loans Cases, France v Yugoslavia* (1929) PCIJ Series A, No 20, 41.

[68] IS Zykin, 'Commentary to Article 1210 of the Civil Code' in AV Asoskov and AN Zhiltsov (eds), *Kommentariy k Razdelu VI 'Mezhdunarodnoe Chastnoe Pravo' Grazhdanskogo Kodeksa Rossiyskoy Federatsii (postateynyi) (Commentary to Section VI 'Private International Law' of the Civil Code of the Russian Federation (Article-by-Article)* (Moscow, Statut, 2021) 292; see similarly: S Symeonides, 'Party Autonomy and Private-Law Making in Private International Law: The Lex Mercatoria that Isn't' in *Festschrift für Konstantinos D. Kerameus 1397–1423* (Athens/Brussels, Ant. N. Sakkoulas and Bruylant Publishers, 2009).

[69] See, eg, Mills (n 3 above) 495 ('modern theorists … frequently take the view that the legal status of a norm is conferred through a collective understanding of a community that the norm is binding').

cross-border commercial contracts only, and other conflict-of-laws mechanisms. Protection of private interests, on the other hand, can be ensured by establishing additional requirements to sources of non-state law that the parties can choose, an example being a requirement that the content of a relevant source of non-state law is 'balanced and protected against evasion and abuses by certain mandatory rules'.[70] Further, the argument concerning the incomplete nature of non-state sources of law as compared to state law does not hold true with respect to at least some of them, eg, such codifications as the Principles of European Contract Law or the UNIDROIT Principles of International Commercial Contracts. Moreover, the latter have an important advantage over state law, as they are specifically designed for cross-border commercial contracts, unlike the national law that is largely devised for domestic needs and not well-suited to international business demands. Even so, non-state law does not have to provide comprehensive coverage: this can always be resolved by subsidiary application of national law.[71] In Asoskov's opinion, there are therefore no sufficient grounds to justify prohibition of a choice of non-state law for cross-border commercial contracts, at least when it comes to state court proceedings.[72] That being said, although some academics advocate for a liberal approach to the choice of non-state sources of law, it has to be acknowledged that they are not in the majority. A state court in Russia, faced with such a choice by the parties, will most probably treat it as incorporation by reference and apply it to the extent that does not contradict objectively applicable law.

[70] See a comprehensive list of suggested requirements in: Max Planck Institute for Comparative and International Private Law: 'Comments on the European Commission's Green Paper on the Conversion of the Rome Convention of 1980 on the Law Applicable to Contractual Obligations into a Community Instrument and its Modernization' (2004) 68(1) *The Rabel Journal of Comparative and International Private Law* 33.

[71] Asoskov (n 3 above) 337.

[72] Asoskov (n 3 above) 340.

6

Contractual Obligations: Applicable Law in the Absence of the Parties' Agreement

DARIA LEVINA

This chapter deals with the rules governing the determination of law applicable to contractual obligations in the absence of the parties' choice under Russian PIL. It starts by analysing the general principle of the characteristic performance applicable under Article 1211 of the Russian Civil Code and the ways in which this principle expresses itself as regards different types of contracts. The chapter proceeds to look at exceptions from the general principle such as construction contracts and contracts relating to intellectual property rights. It closes with a discussion of the subsidiary principle of the closest connection and determining the law applicable to mixed contracts.

I. The General Principle: Application of the Law of Characteristic Performance

The general rule is that the law shall apply of the country of residence or principal place of business of the party rendering performance that has decisive significance for the content of the contract.[1] The place of residence and the principal place of business are determined as of the time of contracting.[2] Functionally, the term 'the performance that has decisive significance for the content of the contract' (*испо лнение, имеющее решающее значение для содержания договора*) is equivalent to the concept of 'characteristic performance' in the European PIL.[3] The unusual

[1] Article 1211(1) of the Civil Code.

[2] The reference to timing was introduced during the 2013 reform of the Civil Code.

[3] A Asoskov, *Kollizionnoe regulirovanie dogovornykh obyazatel'stv* (*Conflict of Laws of Contract*) (Moscow, Infotropic Media, 2012) 419; A Asoskov, 'National Report on Russian Federation' in J Basedow, G Rühl, F Ferrari and P De Miguel Asensio (eds), *Encyclopedia of Private International Law* (Cheltenham, Edward Elgar Publishing, 2017) 2459; O Vorobieva, *Private International Law in Russia*

translation of the term has historical origins: it appeared in the 1970 draft bill on the Soviet PIL, developed by a prominent conflict-of-laws scholar, Lazar Lunts.[4] The draft bill did not, however, become law, and until 1991 the dominant connecting factor employed to determine applicable law in the absence of parties' agreement was a rather archaic place of contracting.[5] There were, though, some exceptions: for instance, the 1968/1988 General Terms of Supply of the Council for Mutual Economic Assistance (Общие условия поставок стран Совета экономической взаимопомощи 1968/1988) mandatorily provided for the application of the law of the seller.[6] The concept of characteristic performance as a default rule for most contract types appeared for the first time in legislation in the 1991 Fundamentals of Civil Legislation.[7]

Currently, the rules for determining the law applicable in the absence of parties' choice are contained in Article 1211 of the Civil Code, to a large extent inspired by relevant provisions of the Rome I Regulation.[8] Structurally, Article 1211 is quite straightforward:

- paragraph 1 stipulates the general principle of characteristic performance;
- paragraph 2 concretises application of the principle in respect of a specific contract;
- paragraphs 3 to 8 contain exceptions from the general principle applicable to construction contracts, contracts relating to intellectual property rights, etc;
- paragraph 9 supplements the general principle of characteristic performance with the principle of the closest connection, providing the court with discretion to deviate from the default rules;

(Alphen aan den Rijn, Kluwer Law International BV, 2012) 83–84. To compare with the European PIL, see, eg, paras 19 and 21 of the preamble and Article 4(2) of the Rome I Regulation.

[4] Asoskov, *Conflict of Laws of Contract* (n 3 above) 419.

[5] The connecting factor of the place of contracting was employed, inter alia, by the Fundamentals of Civil Legislation of the USSR (Article 129) and the 1964 Civil Code of the Russian Soviet Federative Socialist Republic (the legal name of Russia during its membership in the USSR) (Article 566). See more in: SN Lebedev and EV Kabatova (eds), *Mezhdunarodnoe Chastnoe Pravo: Uchebnik* (*Private International Law: Textbook*) (Moscow, Statut, 2015) vol 2, 208.

[6] Lebedev and Kabatova (n 5 above) 211; Asoskov, *Conflict of Laws of Contract* (n 3 above) 419.

[7] Article 166 of the Foundations; both the Foundations and the Civil Code retained the wording of the 'performance having decisive significance for the contract'; Asoskov, *Conflict of Laws of Contract* (n 3 above) 419; GK Dmitrieva, *Mezhdunarodnoe Chastnoe Pravo: Uchebnik (Private International Law: Textbook)*, 4th edn (Moscow, Prospekt, 2016) 312.

[8] 'Obobscheniya diskussiy rabochei gruppy po podgotovke dopolneniy i izmeneniy v razdel VI "Mezhdunarodnoe chastnoe pravo" GK RF' ('Summary of the Discussions of the Working Group for Preparing Amendments to Section VI "Private International Law" of the Russian Civil Code') (2019) 2 *Civil Law Review* 133, 151. Cf Article 4 of the Rome I Regulation: 'the contract shall be governed by the law of the country where the party required to effect the characteristic performance of the contract has his habitual residence'. The previous, pre-reform edition of Article 1211 of the Civil Code was respectively modelled on Article 4 of the Rome Convention. See, eg, M Badykov, 'The Russian Civil Code and the Rome Convention: Applicable Law in the Absence of Choice by the Parties' (2005) 1(2) *Journal of Private International Law* 270; Vorobieva (n 3 above) 84; N Vilkova, *Dogovornoe pravo v mezhdunarodnom oborote (Contract Law in International Context)* (Moscow, Statut, 2004).

- paragraph 10 contains a special conflict-of-laws rule for mixed contracts;
- finally, paragraph 11 clarifies that reference to trade customs in the contract is to be interpreted as the parties' agreement to apply such trade customs, unless the contract provides otherwise.

To identify the law applicable to contractual obligations under Article 1211(1) of the Civil Code, an obligation needs to be determined that has decisive significance for the content of the contract, ie, a characteristic obligation; in other words, an obligation that 'characterises' the contract.[9] Identification of such an obligation depends on the contract type. For unilateral contracts, ie, contracts giving rise to only one main obligation, the performance of such an obligation will be deemed characteristic. An example can be a contract of donation or gift. For reciprocal contracts, ie, contracts under which both parties undertake mutual obligations, and where the main obligation of one party is of a monetary nature and the obligation of another party is of a non-monetary nature, the performance of the latter will generally be regarded as characteristic. Usually, this is the performance for which the payment is due. The reasoning behind this is that a monetary obligation is typical of most contractual types; it therefore does not 'characterise' the contract, at least not as much as the non-monetary obligation does.

A question might arise if both parties to a reciprocal contract undertake obligations in monetary form – which one of them is deemed to be characteristic? In this case, the performance needs to be identified that functions as remuneration for performance of another obligation from the economic perspective; the latter will be regarded as characteristic.[10] For instance, in a loan contract the payment of interest by the borrower functions as remuneration for the lender's services – hence, the characteristic performance is rendered by the lender. In an insurance contract, the premium paid by the client is the remuneration for insurer's services – therefore, the insurer renders the characteristic performance; and so on.[11]

Notably, the principle of characteristic performance points not to the place of the characteristic performance itself but rather to the residence or the principal place of business of a *party* rendering such performance.[12] In the context of

[9] See A Asoskov, 'Commentary to Article 1211' in IS Zykin, AV Asoskov and AN Zhiltsov (eds), *Kommentariy k Razdelu VI 'Mezhdunarodnoe Chastnoe Pravo' Grazhdanskogo Kodeksa Rossiyskoy Federatsii (postateynyi)* (*Commentary to Section VI 'Private International Law' of the Civil Code of the Russian Federation (Article-by-Article)*) (Moscow, Statut, 2021) 314. See also (pre-reform): Badykov (n 8 above) 270–71.

[10] Asoskov, 'Commentary to Article 1211' (n 9 above) 314.

[11] Asoskov, 'Commentary to Article 1211' (n 9 above) 315.

[12] Postanovlenie Plenuma Verkhovnogo Suda RF (Resolution of the Plenum of the Supreme Court) of 9 July 2019 No 24 'O primenenii norm mezhdunarodnogo chastnogo prava sudami Rossiyskoy Federatsii' ('On the Use of Private International Law Norms by the Courts of the Russian Federation') para 33. See more on the evolution of the connecting factor of the place of performance and transition to the principle of characteristic performance: D Levina *Lex propria in foro proprio*: *Parallelizatsiya kriteriev opredeleniya primenomogo prava i mezhdunarodnoi podsudnosti dlya dogovornykh obyazatelstv* (*Lex propria in foro proprio: Parallel Criteria for Determining the Applicable Law and International Jurisdiction in Contractual Obligations*) (Moscow, Infotropic, 2021) 39–80; D Levina, 'Jurisdiction

Article 1211, the concept of residence only applies to natural (physical) persons. Residence of a natural person is defined as a place where such person permanently or predominantly lives.[13] If the natural person is registered as an individual entrepreneur and their principal place of business is different from their place of residence, the place of business takes precedence.

For legal entities, their principal place of business takes precedence. Historically, the 1991 Fundamentals of Civil Legislation allowed for two possibilities: the application to the contract of the law of the country of the party's principal place of business or that of the place of its formal incorporation.[14] The Civil Code, however, retained only reference to the party's principal place of business. The connecting factor of Article 1211(1), therefore, is not identical to the place of formal incorporation of the company, although the latter is still used for determining the personal law of a legal entity under Article 1202 of the Civil Code.[15]

Unlike residence for natural persons, place of business for legal entities is not legislatively specified.[16] The authors of the current version of the Civil Code interpret this term to be a projection of similar concepts employed by the UNCITRAL documents – such as the 1980 Vienna Convention on contracts for the international sale of goods or the 2015 United Nations Convention on use of electronic communications in international contracts – and suggest using them as a point of reference.[17] For instance, Article 4(h) of the United Nations Convention on the use of electronic communications in international contracts defines 'place of business' as encompassing 'any place where a party maintains a non-transitory establishment to pursue an economic activity other than the temporary provision of goods or services out of a specific location'. The above emphasis on the actual place of business activities is especially important in the Russian context: for a long time, courts tended to confuse the two and relied on the formal place of incorporation to determine the governing law of the contract. Presumably, this was an echo of the absence of separation of the actual place of activity of a legal entity and its place of incorporation in the Soviet legal tradition.[18] This approach has been widely criticised in the literature, especially

at the Place of Performance Revisited: A Case for the Theory of Characteristic Performance in the European Civil Procedure' (2022) 18(2) *Journal of Private International Law* 266–95.

[13] See Article 20(1) of the Civil Code.

[14] Article 166 of the Fundamentals of Civil Legislation.

[15] Under Article 1202(1) of the Civil Code the personal law of a legal entity is the law of the place of its incorporation; it determines questions such as the status of the organisation as a legal person, the organisational-legal form of the legal person, the legal person's rights to its name, the questions of creation, reorganisation, and liquidation of the legal person, including issues of legal succession, etc.

[16] The Civil Code does define in Article 54 the registered place of a legal entity which is its formal place of incorporation but it does not amount to a place of business for conflict of law purposes.

[17] Asoskov, 'Commentary to Article 1211' (n 9 above) 316–17; Asoskov, *Conflict of Laws of Contract* (n 3 above) 429–30. Russia is a party to the 1980 Vienna Convention on contracts for the international sale of goods but not to the 2015 United Nations Convention on use of electronic communications in international contracts.

[18] See Vorobieva (n 3 above) 85.

regarding the cases where a legal entity – a party to a contract – was incorporated in an offshore jurisdiction such as the British Virgin Islands or Cyprus and for purposes of benefiting from the simplified tax regime of such jurisdiction did not engage in any economic activity on its territory.[19] The Supreme Court addressed this criticism by the Resolution of the Plenum of the Supreme Court 'On the Application of Private International Law Rules by the Courts of the Russian Federation' dated 9 July 2019 No 24 that explicitly clarifies the separate content of the place of business and formal place of incorporation and the use of the former for determining the governing law of the contract.[20]

Both residence of a natural person and the principal place of business of a legal entity are determined as of the time of contracting,[21] meaning that if a party's residence or its place of business changes after conclusion of the contract, such change will not affect the applicable law. The previous, pre-2013 edition of Article 1211 did not contain the timing component, therefore producing conflicts in the contractual rights and duties of the parties due to uncertainty in and /or change of applicable law (a problem known in PIL as the 'mobile conflict' – *conflit mobile, Statutenwechsel*). The current wording, modelled on the Rome I Regulation,[22] aims to uphold reasonable expectations that the parties may have when entering into a contract as regards the applicable law.[23]

For specific/ certain contract types, the general rule of the application of the law of the party rendering characteristic performance is further concretised in Article 1211(2) of the Civil Code. For instance, for a contract of sale, the party rendering characteristic performance is the seller – hence, the law of the seller's residence or place of business applies; in a contract of lease – the lessor; in a contract for the performance of works (*договор подряда*) – the party doing the works;[24] and so on. Under the principle of *lex specialis*, the provisions of Article 1211(2) supersede those of Article 1211(1) for the enumerated contractual types.

[19] Asoskov, *Conflict of Laws of Contract* (n 3 above) 431; VA Kanashevskiy, *Vneshneekonomicheskie sdelki: material'no-pravovoe i kollizionnoe regulirovanie* (*Foreign Economic Transactions: Substrative and Conflict of Law Regulation*) (Moscow, Wolters Kluwer, 2008) 22.

[20] Postanovlenie Plenuma Verkhovnogo Suda RF (Resolution of the Plenum of the Supreme Court) of 9 July 2019 No 24 'O primenenii norm mezhdunarodnogo chastnogo prava sudami Rossiyskoy Federatsii' ('On the Use of Private International Law Norms by the Courts of the Russian Federation') para 33.

[21] This, as mentioned above, applies as of 2013. The pre-reform version of Article 1211 did not include a timing component, which led to uncertainty for the parties regarding applicable law.

[22] Asoskov, *Conflict of Laws of Contract* (n 3 above) 318; Summary of the Discussions (n 8 above) history of negotiations. Rome I, Article 19(3).

[23] Summary of the Discussions (n 8 above) 151.

[24] In the classification of contractual types under Russian law, a contract for the performance of works (*договор подряда*), as defined in Article 702 of the Civil Code, is distinguished from a service contract (Article 779 of the Civil Code). The key differentiating criterion is that in a contract for the performance of works, a contractor undertakes to achieve a certain result. An example is a construction contract. In a service contract, by contrast, the contractor undertakes to provide the agreed upon service to the best of her abilities. This difference accordingly determines the extent of liability in case of non-performance or poor performance.

If there is an international treaty that has conflict-of-laws norms differing from those stipulated by Article 1211 of the Civil Code, the former take precedence.[25] Among such treaties are the Kiev Convention on Settling Disputes Related to Commercial Activities, of 20 March 1992, and the Minsk Convention on Legal Assistance and Legal Relations in Civil, Family and Criminal Law Matters, of 22 January 1993. The above treaties, however, provide for the application of the law of the place of contracting rather than the law of characteristic performance (Article 11(e) of the 1992 Kiev Convention or Article 41 of the 1993 Minsk Convention) and do not allow for the court's discretion to apply the law mostly closely connected with the contract. Their application, though, is limited to situations where both parties to a treaty are located on the territories of the respective contracting parties. The above conventions also do not apply to consumer contracts, contracts relating to immovable property, agreements on the creation of a legal entity, assignment of rights, or subrogation; to these types of contracts, the Civil Code applies.[26]

If a particular type of contract is not covered by Article 1211 of the Civil Code and the general rule of Article 1211(1) is not applicable due to the impossibility of identifying a party rendering characteristic performance, then the law most closely connected to the contract applies (Article 1186(2) of the Civil Code). An example is the contract of exchange or any other contract of a barter nature that assumes a mutual exchange by parties of non-monetary performances (eg, one party assigns a property right and another reciprocally renders services). To determine the legal system with which the contract is most closely connected, the court should consider the entirety of the circumstances of the case.[27]

II. Exceptions to the Principle of Characteristic Performance

The general principle of characteristic performance under the Civil Code has a number of exceptions, relating eg to construction contracts, simple partnerships, contracts concluded at a stock exchange, and contracts regarding intellectual property rights.[28] In this subsection, I discuss them in turn.

For construction contracts, there is a separate conflict-of-laws rule, providing that such contracts shall be governed by the law of the country where the results envisaged by the contract are predominantly created. This conflict-of-laws rule

[25] Article 1186 of the Civil Code; Lebedev and Kabatova (n 5 above) 207.

[26] Postanovlenie Plenuma Verkhovnogo Suda RF (Resolution of the Plenum of the Supreme Court) of 9 July 2019 No 24 'O primenenii norm mezhdunarodnogo chastnogo prava sudami Rossiyskoy Federatsii' ('On the Use of Private International Law Norms by the Courts of the Russian Federation') para 4.

[27] Asoskov, 'Commentary to Article 1211' (n 9 above) 333.

[28] Article 1211(3)–(8) of the Civil Code.

is devised to take account of the specifics of this contract type, because normally construction contracts have to comply with a variety of technical rules and regulations that are in force at the location where they are to be carried out; further, contractors often hire local experts and workers to ensure the completion of the contract. This enhances the close connection of the contract with the place where the results of such works are created. Concurrence of the governing law of the contract and the applicable technical rules therefore reduces the complexities that might have arisen otherwise, if these sets of rules were to differ.[29] If construction works are carried out simultaneously on the territories of several countries, priority is given to the law of the country where the major part of the works is performed.[30]

Another exception to the principle of characteristic performance concerns simple partnership (*простое товарищество*). Here, the applicable law is that of the country where the activities of the partnership mainly take place.[31] Further, for contracts entered into at an auction or a stock exchange, the law of the auction or stock exchange applies.[32] The consideration behind this conflict-of-laws choice is that at the time of contracting, participants in the bidding may not even be aware of who the seller is and thus not be able to identify the characteristic performance in a given contract; the effective functioning of a stock exchange therefore can only be ensured if all transactions are subject to a single system of law.[33]

Contracts in relation to intellectual property (IP contracts) represent another important exception. The conflict-of-laws rules governing such contracts went through a significant transformation during the 2013 Reform. Previously, they were fully subject to the principle of characteristic performance; the party rendering characteristic performance was deemed to be the rights-holder. Accordingly, a licence contract was governed by the law of the country of residence of the licensor (or their place of business), a franchise contract was governed by the law of the residence of IP rights, and so on.[34]

The above rules, however, did not prove to be effective in practice. In many IP contracts, it is not the rights-holder who renders the characteristic performance.[35] In a franchise contract, for instance, the franchisee's duties regarding the production of goods or rendering of services under the acquired IP rights are usually more characterising of a contract than those of the franchisor. The same applies to licence agreements where the licensee takes on the duties to produce goods under the licence and pays the royalties depending on profit. It is for this reason that some systems of PIL, such as the European PIL, designate the law of the country

[29] Asoskov, 'Commentary to Article 1211' (n 9 above) 321.
[30] Asoskov, 'Commentary to Article 1211' (n 9 above) 322.
[31] Article 1211(4) of the Civil Code.
[32] Article 1211(5) of the Civil Code.
[33] Article 1211(5) of the Civil Code.
[34] Asoskov, 'Commentary to Article 1211' (n 9 above) 324.
[35] Summary of the Discussions (n 8 above) 153.

of the franchisee's habitual residence as applying to the contract rather than that of the rights-holder.[36]

During the 2013 Reform, the default rule for IP contracts chosen by the working group was the application of the law of the country on whose territory the IP rights were being used.[37] Such a country is deemed to be more closely connected to the contract, as the IP rights are exercised on its territory. Further, this solution ensures the concurrence of the law governing the contract and the law providing legal protection to the IP rights (*lex loci protectionis*).[38] The latter usually contains a host of mandatory norms that apply to the IP rights but fall outside of the scope of the governing law of the contract, such as rules on the permissible ways of disposing of an IP right (eg, the permissibility of alienation and/or assignment of an IP right, the content of an IP right, the time-frame of its validity, etc).[39] Concurrence of the governing laws ensures predictability and certainty of the conflict-of-laws regulation for the parties. Moreover, in the case of IP contracts, state registration is often required, either of the contract itself or of the IP rights arising out of it. Applying the law of the country where the use of the IP rights is permitted simplifies the task of the registering authorities who are relieved of the necessity to determine the contents of foreign law in order to establish the existence and validity of the contract, and other pertinent questions of law.[40]

Finally, this solution also seems to be appropriate in the Russian context. When developing the reform proposal, the working group discovered that a major portion of the IP rights exercised on Russian territory belonged to foreign owners, a large number of whom represented the offshore vehicles used by Russian companies to minimise taxation. As a consequence, scenarios were common where a licence agreement concerning a Russian trademark that enjoyed protection only on Russian territory was concluded between a foreign (offshore) licensor and a Russian licensee and was governed by the law of an offshore jurisdiction. The reformed provision ensured the application of Russian law to such contracts and simplifies the resolution of IP disputes submitted to the Russian courts.[41]

It is important to note that the application of this connecting factor (ie, the law of the country on whose territory the IP rights are used) is limited to cases where

[36] See, eg, Article 4(1)(e) of the Rome I Regulation. See commentary in: Max Planck Institute for Comparative and International Private Law, 'Comments on the European Commission's Proposal for a Regulation of the European Parliament and the Council on the law applicable to contractual obligations' (2007) 71 *The Rabels Journal of Comparative and International Private Law* 257.

[37] Asoskov, 'Commentary to Article 1211' (n 9 above) 325; Summary of the Discussions (n 8 above).

[38] Article 1231 of the Civil Code.

[39] For the full spectrum of issues subject to the IP statute, see Article 1207.2(2) of the Civil Code; see also: Postanovlenie Plenuma Verkhovnogo Suda RF (Resolution of the Plenum of the Supreme Court) of 9 July 2019 No 24 'O primenenii norm mezhdunarodnogo chastnogo prava sudami Rossiyskoy Federatsii' ('On the Use of Private International Law Norms by the Courts of the Russian Federation') para 35.

[40] Asoskov, 'Commentary to Article 1211' (n 9 above) 326.

[41] Asoskov, 'Commentary to Article 1211' (n 9 above) 327; Summary of the Discussions (n 8 above) 153–54.

the IP right is permitted to be used on the territory of a single country; if such use is permitted on the territories of multiple countries, the law of the country of residence or the principal place of business of the rights-holder continues to apply.[42]

III. Principle of the Closest Connection: An Escape Clause

The court has discretion to depart from the principle of characteristic performance or any of the connecting factors envisaged by Article 1211 if it clearly follows from the law, contractual terms, nature of the contract or the entirety of the circumstances of the case that the contract is more closely connected to the law of another country.[43] Rules of Article 1211 therefore are rebuttable presumptions, designed to preserve flexibility of the conflict-of-laws regulation and to take into account the particular circumstances of each case.[44]

The former version of the provision also contained escape clauses, but had a number of disadvantages that prompted its revision in 2013.[45] First of all, the previous version of Article 1211 did not make it clear that the deviation from default rules had to be a rare exception, based on the fact that the law determined on the basis of the principle of characteristic performance was not closely connected to the contract and that there was another law more closely connected to the contract. Further, the court did not have to give reasons as to why and how exactly the contract was more closely connected with the law of another country; the presumption of characteristic performance therefore was not stable enough.[46] Now, the use of 'clearly' in the current wording suggests that the court has to indicate specific grounds for deviating from the default rules and provide reasoning as to why it believes that the contract is more connected to the law of a country other than the one identified through application of default rules.[47] In addition, escape clauses in the former version of Article 1211 of the Civil Code were distributed throughout its different paragraphs; this not only duplicated the regulation in an unjustified manner but led to a mistaken perception that escape clauses had different meanings depending on their location in Article 1211;[48] this problem has now been solved through the introduction of a single escape clause.

[42] See Article 1211(6)–(8) of the Civil Code.

[43] Article 1211(9) of the Civil Code; Dmitrieva (n 7 above) 313.

[44] Asoskov, 'Commentary to Article 1211' (n 9 above) 328; Lebedev and Kabatova (n 5 above) 217; Vorobieva (n 3 above) 84.

[45] Summary of the Discussions (n 8 above) 152.

[46] Asoskov, *Conflict of Laws of Contract* (n 3 above) 423.

[47] Asoskov, 'Commentary to Article 1211' (n 9 above) 329.

[48] See an example of this in: M Badykov, 'The Characteristic Performance Test in the Russian Civil Code and 1980 European Convention on the Law Applicable to Contractual Obligations' in N Erpyleva, M Gashi-Butler and J Henderson (eds), *Forging a Common Legal Destiny: Liber Amicorum in Honour of William E Butler* (London, Simmonds & Hill, 2008) 729–34; for more in-depth discussion of the

The current provision reflects the following analytical algorithm: first, the court establishes the presumably applicable law using the fixed rules of Article 1211(1)–(8); after doing that, the court exercises its discretion under Article 1211(9) to assess the contractual terms, the nature of the contract, and the totality of the circumstances of the case, and determines whether there is a law more closely connected to the contract than the one identified in stage one.[49] When assessing the circumstances of the case, the court only takes into account circumstances that were present at the time of contracting.[50] The working group, when considering the above revisions, took account of the approach adopted in the European PIL as expressed in Article 4(3) of the Rome I Regulation.[51]

IV. The Law Applicable to Mixed Contracts

For mixed contracts, ie, contracts containing elements of multiple contract types, the Civil Code contains a special provision. Under Article 1211(10), the presumption is that applicable law is the law most closely connected to the contract; when determining the closest connection, the court should first check whether it is possible to identify a party rendering characteristic performance and determine a single applicable law on that basis.[52] This legislative choice is based on the consideration that the split of applicable law – *dépeçage* – is often inconvenient for the parties and can lead to contradictions between applicable laws that will be difficult to resolve for the parties or the court. The court, however, retains the discretion to depart from this presumption if it follows from the law, the contractual terms, or the entirety of the circumstances that the applicable law is to be individually determined for each element of the contract.[53]

An example of the latter situation can be a contract for the creation of a legal entity that envisages the transfer to this newly created entity of immovable property on Russian territory. The transfer of immovable property in this case will be mandatorily governed by Russian law.[54] The rest of the contract, however, is more logically governed by the law of the place of incorporation of the legal entity.[55]

problems with escape clauses see: Asoskov, *Conflict of Laws of Contract* (n 3 above) 423–24; D Sotbarn, *Russisches internationales Privatrecht der vertraglichen Schuldverhältnisse* (Hamburg 2010) 65–67.

[49] Asoskov, 'Commentary to Article 1211' (n 9 above) 329.

[50] See also: Postanovlenie Plenuma Verkhovnogo Suda RF (Resolution of the Plenum of the Supreme Court) of 9 July 2019 No 24 'O primenenii norm mezhdunarodnogo chastnogo prava sudami Rossiyskoy Federatsii' ('On the Use of Private International Law Norms by the Courts of the Russian Federation') para 36.

[51] Asoskov, 'Commentary to Article 1211' (n 9 above) 330.

[52] Asoskov, 'Commentary to Article 1211' (n 9 above) 332.

[53] Asoskov, 'Commentary to Article 1211' (n 9 above) 331.

[54] Article 1213(2) of the Civil Code.

[55] Article 1214(2) of the Civil Code.

7

Non-Contractual Obligations

GLEB SUDAREV

The chapter examines PIL regulation of non-contractual obligations, which was significantly reshaped by the 2013 reform, largely inspired (though not uncritically) by the Rome II Regulation. The chapter begins with an examination of connecting factors used for determining the law applicable to obligations arising out of torts and unjust enrichment, including when they are closely connected to a contract. Particular attention is paid to party autonomy in non-contractual contexts, which was significantly extended and encouraged in the course of the said reform. The chapter concludes with a discussion of PIL rules applicable to particular types of non-contractual obligations – such as unfair competition and restriction of competition, product liability, *culpa in contrahendo*, and *negotiorum gestio* – as well as the issue of direct action against the insurer of the person liable.

I. General Rules on Torts

Article 1219(1) of the Civil Code takes as its starting point the rather traditional connecting factor of the place where an action or some other circumstance took place that served as the basis for the claim for damages (*lex loci delicti commissi*). Albeit a classic, this connecting factor is not unproblematic in that it may be impossible to localise a tort (when, for instance, it was committed in a place which cannot be assigned to any particular country), or such localisation may at least be troublesome (when the commission of a tort is 'split' between different countries or when a tort consists of an omission).[1]

Lex loci delicti commissi, however, is further supplemented by the provision that if the harm occurred in another country and it was or should have been foreseen by the tortfeasor, the law of such country may be applied. While *lex loci damni* has been generally described as a more flexible rule, which allows for a broader

[1] See, eg: L Lunts, *Kurs mezhdunarodnogo chastnogo prava* (*Course of Private International Law*) (Moscow, Spark, 2002) 641–44.

consideration of the injured party's interests but at the same time decreases legal certainty,[2] the foreseeability criterion employed by the Civil Code seems to mitigate this issue.[3]

Although it is not specified who is entitled to choose between the two laws, the Supreme Court, when discussing this provision, slightly changed its wording to '*the court* may apply the law …' (emphasis added).[4] But since this provision aims at additional protection of the injured party, it would seem that the choice should be theirs. Closely connected therewith is the (also uncertain) issue of burden of proof. Although the case law is not quite established yet, there has been a case where a libellous article was published by an international news agency on its website, and the court held that 'the defendant, by posting a publication about the claimant on the Internet, foresaw or should have foreseen the occurrence of damage to the business reputation of the claimant precisely on the territory of the Russian Federation.'[5] However, it is unclear whether the court intended to make a more general statement or simply referred to the peculiarities of the case (namely, that it was a 'cyber' tort).

Article 1219(2) of the Civil Code introduces a special conflict-of-laws rule. If the parties to the obligation in tort have their places of residence or principal places of business in the same country, that country's law should apply irrespective of where the action or the circumstance giving rise to liability in tort occurred.[6] Similarly, even if the parties have their places of residence or principal places of business in different countries, but are citizens of or incorporated in the same country, its law should apply. Previously, the Soviet legislation contained a unilateral choice of law rule according to which Soviet law applied where *Soviet citizens or Soviet organisations* were parties to an obligation in tort which arose out of circumstances occurring *abroad*. The modern rule is bilateral in that its application does not require that the common citizenship of the parties is Russian, it could very well be foreign (as well as the place of residence or principal place of business,

[2] E Kabatova, 'Delikty v mezhdunarodnom chastnom prave' ('Torts in Private International Law') (1992) 9 *Gosudarstvo i pravo* (*State and Law*) 105.

[3] In this regard Russian PIL is quite unlike Article 4 of the Rome II Regulation, which chooses 'the law of the country in which the damage occurs irrespective of the country in which the event giving rise to the damage occurred and irrespective of the country or countries in which the indirect consequences of that event occur.' Here the *lex loci delicti commissi* is excluded in favour of the *lex loci damni* (although only regarding direct consequences), and the latter is to be applied irrespective of its foreseeability.

On use of comparative law during the reform of the Civil Code in general, with some methodological comments, see: A Shirvindt, 'Reforming the Russian Civil Code – A Search for a Better Law-Making' in J Basedow, H Fleischer and R Zimmermann (eds), *Legislators, Judges, and Professors* (Tübingen, Mohr Siebeck, 2016) 57–62.

[4] Paragraph 56 of the Resolution of the Plenum of the Supreme Court 'On the Application of Private International Law Rules by the Courts of the Russian Federation' dated 9 July 2019 No 24.

[5] Postanovlenie Arbitrazhnogo Suda Moskovskogo Okruga ot 25 yanvarya 2022 g. (Resolution of the *Arbitrazh* Court of the Moscow Area) of 25 January 2022 no F05-31292/21 case No A40-42722/2021.

[6] Paragraph 53 of the Resolution of the Plenum of the Supreme Court 'On the Application of Private International Law Rules by the Courts of the Russian Federation' dated 9 July 2019 No 24.

which is another direction in which the original rule was widened).[7] Since 2013, the requirement that the tort was committed abroad has also been dropped, which approximates the provision to foreign models.[8]

The idea of a legal space common to the parties allows for a more flexible solution to conflict-of-laws issues.[9] For instance, in one of the cases the defendant wrongly accused the claimant of a criminal offence in front of a Cypriot court, and the claimant, after he was acquitted, claimed his legal costs as damages. Since both parties to the case were Russian citizens, the court applied Russian law.[10]

Article 1219(3) of the Civil Code suggests that if an obligation in tort has close connections with the contract between the victim and the tortfeasor, and that contract was concluded in the course of their entrepreneurial activities, the law applicable to the contract will also apply to the obligation in tort. From both the wording of the rule and the privity of contract doctrine, it follows that the scope of this paragraph does not extend to the claims of third parties.[11]

The scope of the tort conflict-of-laws rule is described in Article 1220 of the Civil Code. In particular, it governs a person's capacity to be liable for the harm caused, the liability of a person for the harm they did not cause, causes of action, grounds of limiting and excluding liability, modes of compensation for harm, and the scope of damages. The list is not exhaustive though.[12] Remarkably, following Article 15 of the Rome II Regulation, the Civil Code chooses to place the capacity to bear tort liability within the scope of the law applicable to torts and not within the scope of the personal law.[13]

II. Unjust Enrichment

As established in Article 1223(1) of the Civil Code, the main connecting factor for obligations arising out of unjust enrichment is the country where the enrichment took place (*lex loci condictionis*). For instance, if the defendant is enriched by

[7] S Lebedev, A Muranov, R Khodykin and E Kabatova, 'New Russian Legislation on Private International Law' (2002) 4 *Yearbook of Private International Law* 117, 142.

[8] E Kabatova, 'The Latest Amendments in the Russian International Private Law' (2014) 4(86) *Zhurnal mezhdunarodnogo chastnogo prava* (*Journal of International Private Law*) 13–14.

[9] A Komarov, 'Commentary to Article 1219 of the Civil Code' in I Zykin, A Asoskov and A Zhiltsov (eds), *Kommentarij k razdelu VI 'Mezhdunarodnoe chastnoe pravo' chasti tret'ej Grazhdanskogo kodeksa Rossijskoj Federacii (postatejnyj)* (*Commentary on Section VI 'Private International Law' of Part Three of the Civil Code of the Russian Federation (article-by-article)*) (Moscow, Statut, 2021) 456.

[10] Opredelenie Tret'ego Kassacionnogo Suda Obshchej Yurisdikcii ot 21 sentyabrya 2020 g. (Decision of the Third Cassation Court of General Jurisdiction) of 21 September 2020 case No 8G-15763/2020[88-14912/2020].

[11] Paragraph 54 of the Resolution of the Plenum of the Supreme Court 'On the Application of Private International Law Rules by the Courts of the Russian Federation' dated 9 July 2019 No 24.

[12] Lebedev, Muranov, Khodykin and Kabatova (n 7 above) 143.

[13] V Zvekov, *Obyazatel'stva vsledstvie prichineniya vreda v kollizionnom prave* (*Conflict of Laws of Torts*) (Moscow, Wolters Kluwer Russia, 2007) 63–64.

receiving funds into their bank account, the country where the enrichment took place would be the place of location of the bank (or its branch or subdivision) serving the creditor, to whose account the funds were credited.[14]

This approach is quite traditional and coincides with the subsidiary rule in Article 10(3) of the Rome II Regulation. However, it has been approached critically in the Soviet doctrine: prominent PIL scientist Professor Lasar Lunts suggested that the enrichment itself cannot be localised, unlike an action or an event that led to it, and thus the latter should serve as a connecting factor. However, with regard to erroneous payments, Lunts argued that they actually take place when (and where) the funds are credited to the receiver's account.[15] In the case law, it is also not uncommon that the two places (of enrichment and of the circumstance leading thereto) coincide, for instance, when the defendant uses the claimant's berth at a port in Norway without concluding a contract and thus becomes enriched by means of economising on rent.[16] Hence, one has reasons to believe that the difference between the two approaches is not as drastic as it may seem.

Article 1223(2) of the Civil Code, resembling Article 10(1) of the Rome II Regulation, states that if the unjust enrichment arose in connection with an actual or putative legal relationship, under which property was acquired or expenses were saved, the law that did or could have applied to that relationship should also govern the obligation arising out of unjust enrichment (law of the underlying relationship, *lex causae condictionis*).

Perhaps the most prominent example here is cases of rescinding failed contracts (that is, not concluded, invalid, or terminated).[17] Thus, although Russian substantive private law does not generally make a distinction between types of enrichment (as German law, with its *Leistungs*- and *Nichtleistungskondiktionen*, does),[18] Russian PIL deems it necessary. This approach should be welcomed

[14] Paragraph 57 of the Resolution of the Plenum of the Supreme Court 'On the Application of Private International Law Rules by the Courts of the Russian Federation' dated 9 July 2019 No 24.

[15] Lunts (n 1 above) 661.

[16] Postanovlenie Arbitrazhnogo Suda Dal'nevostochnogo Okruga ot 7 iyulya 2022 g. (Resolution of the *Arbitrazh* Court of the Far East Area) of 7 July 2022 no F03-2928/22 case No A59-1461/2021 (although in this particular case the court applied Russian law since the content of Norwegian law had not been ascertained in the proceedings).

[17] Paragraph 56 of the Resolution of the Plenum of the Supreme Court 'On the Application of Private International Law Rules by the Courts of the Russian Federation' dated 9 July 2019 No 24. For instance, see: Postanovlenie Arbitrazhnogo Suda Central'nogo Okruga ot 5 iyulya 2018 g. (Resolution of the *Arbitrazh* Court of the Central Area) of 5 July 2018 no F10-1178/18 case No A14-14009/2016 (after the contract was rescinded, the sum of the advance payment was claimed back; the court applied the law applicable to the avoided contract).

[18] Two reservations, however, must be made in this regard: first, and strictly speaking, unwinding of invalid contracts does not fall within the scope of the law of unjust enrichment but rather constitutes a separate remedy of 'restitution' (developed in the Soviet period and different from its foreign namesakes); secondly, it has been argued that all the instances of unwinding of failed contracts should be modelled as a single *contractual* remedy (K Usacheva, *Vozvrashchenie poluchennogo kak posledstvie rastorzheniya narushennogo dogovora: normoobrazuyushchie faktory i ih sootnoshenie pri reshenii konkretnyh voprosov* (*Unwinding as a Consequence of the Termination of the Violated Contract: Norm-Forming Factors and Their Correlation in Solving Specific Issues*) (Moscow, Infotropic, 2020) I-XLV).

as promoting legal certainty and facilitating a more nuanced approach to the conflict-of-laws issues.

Moreover, since Article 1223(2) is formulated much more widely than Article 1219(3) of the Civil Code, it is not limited to contractual relationships. For instance, in one case the defendant, following his brother's death, obtained probate under Sharia law in the UAE and acquired properties as his inheritance share. Soon afterwards, a Russian court invalidated the certificate of probate and distributed the testator's estate under Russian law. The claimant, who was the wife of the deceased, demanded that the defendant (not an 'heir of the first kin' under Russian law) return the properties he had collected. The court applied Russian law under Article 1223(2) of the Civil Code: the argument was that the defendant's unjust enrichment arose in connection with the inheritance relationship governed by Russian law (although the enrichment allegedly occurred in the UAE).[19]

III. Party Autonomy in Non-Contractual Obligations

Until 2013, the scope of party autonomy in non-contractual obligations was limited in that it was only allowed to choose the *lex fori* after the action or the circumstance giving rise to the obligation occurred. However, under the reform, Article 1223.1 ('Choice of law by the parties to an obligation arising as a result of causing harm or unjust enrichment') was introduced into the Civil Code, which significantly broadened it, much in line with the Rome II Regulation.

Under the new regime, it is now possible to choose any law applicable to non-contractual obligations (not only the *lex fori*) after they arose; that is after the action or the circumstance giving rise to the obligation took place. Such choice may be disallowed by the law, as for instance was done in Article 1222(3) of the Civil Code regarding obligations arising out of unfair competition and restriction of competition. The choice of law must also not prejudice third parties.

Under Article 1210(6) of the Civil Code, the provisions applicable to choice of law in contract, including the general restrictions, respectively apply to choice of law for non-contractual obligations.[20] Thus the same problems discussed in Chapter five above may be of relevance here, in particular the issues of implied choice of law, splitting of the applicable law, and choice of non-state law (eg Principles of European Tort Law).

Article 1223.1(2) of the Civil Code imposes an additional restriction on party autonomy. If, at the time when the act was committed or another circumstance occurred that caused harm or unjust enrichment, all circumstances relating to

[19] Opredelenie SK po Grazhdanskim Delam Vtorogo Kassacionnogo Suda Obshchej Yurisdikcii ot 27 oktyabrya 2020 g. (Decision of the Judicial Division for Civil Cases of the Second Cassation Court of General Jurisdiction) of 27 October 2020 case No 8G-20774/2020[88-20073/2020].

[20] Paragraph 58 of the Resolution of the Plenum of the Supreme Court 'On the Application of Private International Law Rules by the Courts of the Russian Federation' dated 9 July 2019 No 24.

the essence of the parties' relationship were connected with only one country, the choice of law cannot exclude the application of mandatory provisions of that law.

Although the provisions of the Civil Code do not allow the law applicable to non-contractual obligations ex ante to be chosen *directly*, it should be emphasised that an '*indirect*' choice is in fact possible under Articles 1219(3) and 1223(2). Unless agreed otherwise, when parties to a contract exercise party autonomy[21] they choose not only the law applicable to the contract but also the law applicable to non-contractual obligations closely connected with the contract. It is mainly because of this possibility that the drafters decided against including in the draft Bill a provision for ex ante choice of law, similar to Article 14(1)(b) of the Rome II Regulation, as this was practically already covered by the named provisions.[22]

The tendency of Russian law to widen the sphere of the *lex voluntatis* should by all means be welcomed. Apart from paying tribute to party autonomy, it also may have a positive side effect of eliminating the tension between conflict rules for torts and unjust enrichment and thus attaining greater legal certainty: as parties to a non-contractual relationship choose the applicable law, the need to characterise the relationship is dramatically decreased. Given the uncertainty of interrelations between actions in tort and unjust enrichment under substantive Russian law, it is not an insignificant advantage.[23]

IV. Other Special Rules on Non-Contractual Obligations

The current section deals with particular types of non-contractual obligations (and related matters) governed by the Civil Code PIL provisions. Although their characterisation as particular instances of tort is rather unproblematic under Russian law (regarding *culpa in contrahendo*, product liability, and private claims arising out of unfair competition or restriction thereof), they, for one or another reason, received special treatment.

Prior to that, however, one should bear in mind that, apart from the Civil Code, there are other PIL sources that may be of relevance for obligations in torts. As a matter of example, Article 420 of the Merchant Shipping Code contains conflict rules for ship collisions, the connecting factors being the *lex loci* (for collisions in the internal waters and in the territorial seas), the *lex fori* (for collisions on the high seas, if Russian court has jurisdiction), or the law of flag – *lex flagi*

[21] Taking into account that Article 1219(3) of the Civil Code only applies when the contract was concluded in the course of the parties' entrepreneurial activities.

[22] I Zykin and others (n 9 above) 607–9.

[23] I Kutashevskaia, 'Princip avtonomii voli kak sposob nivelirovaniya problemy konkurencii vnedogovornyh trebovanij v mezhdunarodnom chastnom prave' ('The Principle of Autonomy of Will as a Way of Leveling the Problem of Concurrence of Non-contractual Claims in Private International Law') (2022) 4 *Vestnik grazhdanskogo prava* (*Civil Law Review*) 101–10.

(for collisions between ships sailing under the flag of the same country).[24] Certain PIL provisions for torts are also contained in the international treaties of the Russian Federation, which, according to Article 7(2) of the Civil Code and Article 15(4) of the Constitution, are to prevail over the national law provisions. Accordingly, Article 11 of the Kiev Agreement on Settling Disputes Related to Commercial Activities, of 20 March 1992, provides that the law applicable to torts should be *lex loci delicti commissi*, unless an action or a circumstance giving rise to the obligation in tort is not unlawful under the *lex fori*. Article 42 of the Minsk Convention on Legal Assistance and Legal Relations in Civil, Family, and Criminal Law Matters of 22 January 1993 employs the *lex loci delicti commissi* and law of common citizenship (but not the law of common place of residence, unlike modern Russian PIL).

A. Direct Action against the Insurer of the Person Liable

In the course of the 2013 reform, there appeared a separate conflict-of-laws rule for admissibility of direct actions against the insurer of the person liable (Article 1220.1 of the Civil Code). It repeats almost verbatim Article 18 of the Rome II Regulation: such an action may be brought if it is allowed either under the law applicable to the obligation in tort or under the law applicable to the insurance contract. This alternative rule provides for a wider protection of the injured party, since it is sufficient that at least one of the available laws allows direct claims,[25] and in cases where the alternative rule of Article 1219(1) of the Civil Code applies, the number of the laws to choose from may even increase. While additionally protecting the victim, it arguably makes the insurers' position much less certain, though.

B. Product Liability[26]

Under Article 1221(1) of the Civil Code, the injured party in the product liability context – including when the harm is caused as the result of untrustworthy or insufficient information on goods, work, or services – is entitled to choose between

[24] S Lebedev and E Kabatova (eds), *Mezhdunarodnoe Chastnoe Pravo: Uchebnik. V 2 t. T. 2. Osobennaya chast* (*International Private Law: Textbook in two volumes. Vol 2. Special Part*) (Moscow, Statut, 2015) 477.

[25] R Hodykin, 'Commentary to Article 1220.1 of the Civil Code' in I Zykin, A Asoskov and A Zhiltsov (eds), *Kommentarij k razdelu VI 'Mezhdunarodnoe chastnoe pravo' chasti tret'ej Grazhdanskogo kodeksa Rossijskoj Federacii (postatejnyj)* (*Commentary on Section VI 'Private International Law' of Part Three of the Civil Code of the Russian Federation (article-by-article)*) (Moscow, Statut, 2021), 468.

[26] It is important to bear in mind that, under Russian law, product liability includes liability not only for goods but also for work and services (unlike eg Council Directive 85/374/EEC of 25 July 1985 on the approximation of the laws, regulations and administrative provisions of the Member States concerning liability for defective products [1985] OJ L210, which limits its scope to movable products in Article 2).

(1) the law of the country where the seller or the manufacturer of the goods, or another person who caused the harm, has their place of residence or principal place of business, (2) the law of the country where the injured party has their place of residence or principal place of business, and (3) the law of the country where the work was performed, or the services were provided, or the goods were acquired.

For instance, in one of the cases decided by the Supreme Court, during a family vacation in Greece, the claimant's child was assaulted and stabbed with a knife at least 20 times by an entertainer employed by the hotel (one of the defendants). The court applied Russian law as the law of the country where the injured party had his place of residence under Article 1221(1) of the Civil Code.[27]

The injured party does not have to justify their choice. However, the right of choice can only be exercised when the case is being considered in the court of first instance, until the court retires to the deliberation room to make a decision.[28] When the claimant does not expressly choose the law but refers to some particular law in their statements, the law referred to in such a manner may be applied.[29]

However, if the person who caused the harm proves that they neither foresaw nor should have foreseen the distribution of goods in the particular country, the respective choices of (2) and (3) are not allowed. The Supreme Court has explained that

> [f]or this purpose, the tortfeasor must prove that the territory of the relevant country apparently does not belong to the territory of distribution of the goods or that the tortfeasor forbade the persons involved in the distribution of the goods (buyers, distributors, etc.) to sell the goods on the territory of the relevant country, and also did not carry out such marketing independently.[30]

If the injured party fails to choose the applicable law, option (1) should apply under Article 1221(3) of the Civil Code as a default rule.

C. Unfair Competition and Restriction of Competition

The law applicable to obligations arising as the result of *unfair competition* should be the law of the country whose market is or may be affected by such competition, unless some other applicable law follows from a statute or the nature of the obligation. As a matter of exception, if only a single individual is affected, will the

[27] Opredelenie SK po Grazhdanskim Delam Verhovnogo Suda RF ot 27 noyabrya 2018 g. (Resolution of the Judicial Division for Civil Cases of the Supreme Court of the RF) of 27 November 2018 no N 5-KGPR18-232.

[28] Paragraph 47 of the Resolution of the Plenum of the Supreme Court 'On the Application of Private International Law Rules by the Courts of the Russian Federation' dated 9 July 2019 No 24.

[29] See, for instance: Opredelenie SK po Grazhdanskim Delam Vtorogo Kassacionnogo Suda Obshchej Yurisdikcii ot 13 dekabrya 2022 g. (Decision of the Judicial Division for Civil Cases of the Second Cassation Court of General Jurisdiction) of 13 December 2022 case No 8G-20218/2022[88-22356/2022].

[30] Paragraph 47 of the Resolution of the Plenum of the Supreme Court 'On the Application of Private International Law Rules by the Courts of the Russian Federation' dated 9 July 2019 No 24.

conflict rules for tort, namely Article 1219 and 1223.1 of the Civil Code, apply (Article 1222(1) of the Civil Code).

In 2013, there appeared a new rule on obligations arising out of *restriction of competition*, establishing as applicable the law of the country whose market is or may be affected by such restriction (Article 1222(2) of the Civil Code).

These rules are relatively new for Russian law and gravitate towards the Rome II Regulation rather than the US approach in that they are bilateral. They allow the court to apply not only Russian, but also foreign law when considering private claims.[31]

Since, under Article 1187 of the Civil Code, legal relationships are characterised under Russian law, the definitions adopted by Russian legislation may be of importance. Unfair competition is defined as

> any actions of economic entities (a group of persons) that are aimed at obtaining advantages in the conduct of entrepreneurial activities, and are contrary to the legislation of the Russian Federation, business practices, the requirements of integrity, reasonableness, and fairness, and have caused or may cause losses to other economic entities – competitors, or have caused or may cause damage to their business reputation [Article 4 of the Federal Law of the Russian Federation 'On Competition' dated 26 July 2006 No. 135-FZ].

However, the application of this definition for PIL purposes has been criticised as being too narrow in only referring to the Russian legislation; it has been suggested instead to use the definition from Article 10-bis of the Paris Convention for the Protection of Industrial Property ('[a]ny act of competition contrary to honest practices in industrial or commercial matters').[32]

D. *Culpa in Contrahendo*

Article 1222.1 of the Civil Code, which contains PIL rules for *culpa in contrahendo* (pre-contractual liability), was first introduced into Russian law with the 2013 reform. The authors of the draft legislation were evidently inspired by Article 12 of the Rome II Regulation, and chose the law that applies to the contract (or the law that would have applied to the contract, had the contract been concluded) as applicable to bad faith negotiations. This also means that if, during the negotiations, the parties managed to effectively choose the law applicable to the future contract, such a law will apply to *culpa in contrahendo*, even if all the other provisions of that contract have not been agreed upon.[33]

[31] N Voznesenskij, 'Commentary to Article 1222 of the Civil Code' in I Zykin, A Asoskov and A Zhiltsov (eds), *Kommentarij k razdelu VI 'Mezhdunarodnoe chastnoe pravo' chasti tret'ej Grazhdanskogo kodeksa Rossijskoj Federacii (postatejnyj)* (*Commentary on Section VI 'Private International Law' of Part Three of the Civil Code of the Russian Federation (article-by-article)*) (Moscow, Statut, 2021) 474–75.

[32] Ibid, 479–81.

[33] Paragraph 55 of the Resolution of the Plenum of the Supreme Court 'On the Application of Private International Law Rules by the Courts of the Russian Federation' dated 9 July 2019 No 24.

Although substantive law rules on *culpa in contrahendo* (Article 434.1 of the Civil Code) only appeared in 2015, the wide scope of legislative provisions for liability in tort would have arguably allowed for such claims even under the pre-reform civil law. Today it is still conceptualised as a liability in tort, which approaches the French law position on the issue. Thus, it is only logical that the subsidiary rule of Article 1222.1(2) of the Civil Code refers to the tort conflict rule of Article 1219 (as well as Article 1223.1). It applies if it is impossible to determine the applicable law under the *lex contractus*.

E. *Negotiorum Gestio*

Current legislation does not contain any PIL provisions on the *negotiorum gestio*, although the relevant substantive law provisions have been part and parcel of the Civil Code since its enactment. The *travaux préparatoires* for the 2013 PIL reform show that such a provision was drafted (quite reminiscent of Article 11 of the Rome II Regulation), but deemed to be unnecessary in view of both the relatively small share of such relationships in modern society and their exceeding intricacy. It was suggested instead that the general rules of Article 1186 of the Civil Code (including the general subsidiary rule of the most closely connected law) or special rules regarding transactions, agency, unjust enrichment, and torts should apply.[34] This corresponds to the view presented in the doctrine.[35]

[34] I Zykin, A Asoskov and A Zhiltsov (eds), *Kommentarij k razdelu VI 'Mezhdunarodnoe chastnoe pravo' chasti tret'ej Grazhdanskogo kodeksa Rossijskoj Federacii (postatejnyj)* (*Commentary on Section VI 'Private International Law' of Part Three of the Civil Code of the Russian Federation (article-by-article)*) (Moscow, Statut, 2021), 609–11.

[35] Lunts (n 1) 662–63.

8

Property

TATIANA LYUBARSKAYA AND GEORGY SHASHERO

I. Introduction

This chapter deals with general conflict-of-laws issues in relation to real property rights in Russia, and reveals peculiarities involving movable and immovable property, mobile equipment, and securities and trusts.

II. Law of Property

The law of property in each state is to a large extent a reflection of the historical development of that society and has its own distinctive features.

According to the Russian principles of conflict of laws, the competent legal system governing a particular type of private legal relationship is called a 'statute'.[1] In other words, a statute is a general rule of law governing a particular type of relationship. The statute is determined on the basis of the conflict rules to which it refers[2] and helps to define the scope of those rules and the list of matters to which they apply, thus contributing to the systematisation of the conflict rules and providing certainty and predictability.[3] The scope of the conflict-of-laws rule determines the range of relationships covered by the rule ('the scope of the rule'). The binding nature of the conflict-of-laws rule determines the applicable law ('the content of the statute').[4]

Russian law distinguishes between the following types of statutes: personal statute, property statute (*in rem* statute), contract statute, tort statute, unjust

[1] L Lunts, *Mezhdunarodnoe Chastnoe Pravo. V 3-h tomah. Tom 1* (*International Private Law. In 3 volumes. Vol 1*) (Moscow, Spark, 2002) 157.

[2] H Koch, U Magnus and P Von Morenfels, *Mezhdunarodnoe chastnoe pravo i sravnitel'noe pravovedenie* (*International Private Law and Comparative Law*) (translated from German into Russian by Y Umasheva, Moscow, Mezhdunarodnyye otnosheniya, 2001) 411.

[3] V Zvekov, *Kollizii zakonov v mezhdunarodnom chastnom prave* (*Conflicts of Laws in Private International Law*) (Moscow, Wolters Kluwer, 2007) 156.

[4] Ibid, 158.

enrichment statute, inheritance statute, etc. Generally speaking, a property statute is the law applicable to the regulation of property and other rights *in rem*.[5]

Under Russian law, *lex rei sitae* applies, ie, ownership and other rights *in rem* are determined by the law of the country where the property is located: 'The right of ownership and other rights in things to immovable and movable property shall be determined by the law of the country where this property is located.' (Article 1205(1) of the Russian Civil Code). Application of the *lex rei sitae* has received various explanations in the Russian legal scholarship. According to one approach, *lex rei sitae* flows from the general understanding of rights *in rem* as rights of dominion over property.[6] Another approach views it flowing from the desire of states to subject to their jurisdiction any property located on their territory.[7]

In Russian law, the scope of the right of ownership includes the following matters (Article 1205(1) of the Russian Civil Code[8]):

A. Types of Objects of Property Rights and their Negotiability

Under Russian law, the *lex rei sitae* determines (1) the types of property rights, (2) the classification of property as movable or immovable, consumable or non-consumable, simple or complex, individually and generally defined, negotiable and limited in circulation.

(i) Classification of Property

Traditionally, only specified things are recognised as property.[9] These are individually defined things that are distinguished from other generic things by their inherent features. For example, an apartment is individualised through its address and the total area. In its turn, every car is individualised through a particular model, year of manufacture, engine number, etc. These unique features allow a thing to be customised. The specified things are also irreplaceable, whereas generic things bear the features inherent in all the things of the same kind and are determined by traits such as a number, weight, measure and are thus easily substitutable

[5] G Dmitrieva (ed), *Mezhdunarodnoe chastnoe parvo: Uchebnik* (*International Private Law: Textbook*) (Moscow, Prospekt, 2016) 257.

[6] Lunts (n 1 above) 231.

[7] S Borodkin, 'Novyj podhod k klassifikacii ob'ektov veshchnyh prav' ('A new approach to the classification of objects of property rights') (2018) 2 *Zhurnal rossijskogo prava* (*Journal of Russian Law*) 53.

[8] The Russian Civil Code (Part Three) of 26.11.2001 N 146-FZ (ed of 01.07.2021). Collection of Legislation of the Russian Federation, 49, Art 4552.

[9] E Sukhanov, *Veshchnoe pravo: Nauchno-poznavatel'nyj ocherk* (*Property Law: A Scientific and Educational Essay*) (Moscow, Statut, 2017) 70.

in commercial transactions. As a general rule, it is not possible to have the right of ownership over a generic thing at all in Russian law. The origin or transfer of the ownership with respect to generic things is possible only if such things are separated from other things of the same kind.

(ii) Qualification of Objects

The division between movable and immovable property is crucial for resolving conflicts of laws. According to Russian law, immovable property includes land plots, subsoil plots, and everything firmly attached to the land, ie, objects that cannot be moved without unreasonable damage to their purpose, including buildings, structures, and unfinished constructions (Article 130(1) of the Russian Civil Code). Immovable property also includes aircraft, sea and inland vessels, as well as enterprises consisting of assets that are subject to the requirement of state registration (Article 132(1) of the Russian Civil Code). Russian law defines movable property according to the residual principle, covering things that are not related to immovable property, including money and securities.

With respect to transfer of property,[10] Article 129 of the Russian Civil Code applies under the Russian law. Generally, property within the Russian Federation may be freely transferred from one person to another. However, laws or regulations may impose various restrictions on assignment (for example, such restrictions are imposed on natural resources in Russia).

B. Types of Rights *In Rem* and their Content

The principle of *lex rei sitae* determines the scope of rights *in rem*. Russian law distinguishes between ownership – the most comprehensive right in terms of its content – and the following limited rights *in rem*: easement, usufruct, right of permanent residence, lifetime lease, right of development, right of economic and operational management, pledge (and its variations), retention, and right of first refusal to purchase of real estate. Most of the limited property rights only apply to real estate and are subject to state registration.[11] The list of rights *in rem* is exhaustive and, according to the principle of *numerus clausus*, it is not possible to classify certain legal rights as rights *in rem* unless expressly provided for by law.[12]

The content of rights *in rem* is defined by the powers (possession, use, disposal), the scope and content of which may vary from one type of right to another.

[10] B Gongalo (ed), *Grazhdanskoe pravo: Uchebnik. V 2-h tomah. Tom 1* (*Civil Law: Textbook. In 2 volumes. Vol 1*), 2nd edn (Moscow, Statut, 2017) 201.

[11] Sukhanov (n 9 above) 210.

[12] Ibid, 211.

C. Creation and Termination of Rights *In Rem*, Including Questions of Transfer of Ownership

Lex rei sitae also determines the basis for creation, termination, and transfer of rights *in rem*.[13]

D. Exercise and Protection of Property Rights

Exercise of property rights means action by the owner of the property in order to exercise property rights granted to him.[14] For example, in accordance with Article 209(2) of the Russian Civil Code, the owner has the right, at his discretion, to perform any acts with respect to his or her property that are not contrary to the law and not breaching the rights of others, including acts to transfer property or the rights to it, to use and dispose of the property, etc.

Remedies for protection of real property rights are also governed by the law of the country in which the property is located. Previously, Russian law allowed the owner to choose among (1) the law of the country where the property was located, or (2) the law of the country where the claim was filed, or (3) the law of the country where the property (eg a motor vehicle) was registered in the State Register.[15] As of today, the law of the country where the property is located applies in all matters of protection. Russian legislation provides for the protection of property rights of both the owner and the person who is not the owner but holds the property on another legal basis, for example, the person who leases certain property or the person who holds the property acquired by inheritance, via economic management, business management, or other grounds established by law or contract (Articles 304 and 305 of the Russian Civil Code).

The list of issues covered by the property statute defined in Article 1205 of the Russian Civil Code is not exhaustive and may be expanded by law enforcement authorities if there are relevant grounds for doing so. At the same time, it should be noted that the scope of application of the law of property in Russian

[13] However, this approach has not always existed in Russia in relation to movable property. For example, during the Soviet period, taking into account the limited economic contacts at the international level and the fact that foreign trade transactions were relevant mainly for specialised organisations, the issues of the creation and termination of the right of ownership of goods arose precisely within the framework of transactions, which is why the creation and termination of the right of ownership of property were determined on the basis of contractual statutes (Article 126(2) and (3) of the Civil Code of the Russian Soviet Federated Socialist Republic of 1961, Article 164(3) of the Civil Code of the Russian Soviet Federated Socialist Republic of 1991). I Zykin, 'K voprosu o sootnoshenii veshchnogo i obyazatel'stvennogo statutov' ('On the Correlation between Property and Obligations Statutes') in M Kozyr and A Makovsky (eds), *Grazhdanskoe pravo sovremennoj Rossii* (*Civil Law of Modern Russia*) (Moscow, Statut, 2008) 46.

[14] N Marysheva (ed), *Mezhdunarodnoe chastnoe pravo: uchebnik* (*International Private Law: Textbook*), 4th edn (Moscow, IZiSP Kontrakt, 2018) 203–24.

[15] Ibid.

conflict of laws does not include the issues of the legal capacity of the owner of the property or of the parties to a transaction having an effect on the law of property.[16] These issues are resolved on the basis of the personal statute (Articles 1195, 1202 of the Russian Civil Code). Inheritance under Russian conflict-of-laws rules is also excluded from the property statute and is included within the scope of the special and separate inheritance statute (Article 1224 of the Russian Civil Code). In addition, the regulation of property relations between a husband and wife is also based on the conflict-of-laws rules of family law (Article 161 of the Russian Family Code), which take precedence over the conflict-of-laws rules applicable to property (Article 1205 of the Russian Civil Code).[17] Thus, the scope of application of property law in the Russian conflict of laws has its own peculiarities, which may create additional difficulties.[18]

In determining the scope of application of property law, the most important issue is the distinction between property law and contract law. If the subject-matter of an agreement is the transfer of ownership interests in property, or if the performance of an agreement gives rise to differing effects with regard to property law, both the law of property (property statute) and the law of contract (contract statute) apply simultaneously.[19] If both laws deal with the question of the transfer of property within the scope of the law of property, there are usually no difficulties. However, if both the property law and the contract law regulate this issue, but at the same time establish different models for the transfer of property, the effects of the transaction in terms of property law may be different. For example, if the applicable law according to the contract statute establishes the 'consensual system' (ownership is transferred from the moment the parties reach an agreement),

[16] The English and US conflict-of-laws traditions define more broadly the range of relations falling within the scope of the property statute, applying it also to the legal capacity of the parties in the event of the transfer and acceptance of a thing and, as a consequence, the transfer of title. See G Zaphiriou, *The Transfer of Chattels in Private International Law: A Comparative Study* (University of London, The Athlone Press, 1956) 66–67. As noted by Cheshire, North and Fawcett, if the person does not, in accordance with the law of location of the thing, possess the capacity necessary to acquire ownership of immovable property, he cannot be a party to the transaction of acquisition of ownership. The same applies to the transfer of immovable property pursuant to contracts of sale, gift or mortgage. See J Fawcett and J Carruthers, *Cheshire, North & Fawcett, Private International Law*, 14th edn (Oxford, Oxford University Press, 2008) 1202. In German law, the property statute also extends to capacity and representation in transactions involving the disposal of property. See Koch, Magnus and Von Morenfels (n 2 above) 196.

[17] V Kanashevskiy, 'Kollizionnye voprosy razdela mezhdu suprugami sovmestno nazhitogo imushchestva, nahodyashchegosya za rubezhom' ('Collision Issues of Division between Spouses of Jointly Acquired Property Located Abroad') (2020) 2 *Zakon* (*The Law*) 181.

[18] A clear separation of the scope of statutes increases certainty and predictability of court decisions and contributes to the development of uniform jurisprudence, its stability and systematisation. See Zvekov (n 3 above) 162.

[19] Koch, Magnus and Von Morenfels (n 2 above) 196; A Skoryukin, 'Yuridicheskie riski zaloga s inostrannym elementom' ('Legal Risks of Pledge with a Foreign Element') (2016) 1 *Yuridicheskaya rabota v kreditnoj kooperacii* (*Legal Work in Credit Institutions*), http://futurebanking.ru/reglament-bank/article/3510; T Lyubarskaya and N Lashkov, 'Problemy kollizionnogo regulirovaniya zaloga v Rossii i za rubezhom' ('Contemporary Issues in the Law Applicable to the Security Interests in Movable Property in Russia and Abroad') (2018) 8 *Zakon* (*The Law*) 156.

then ownership is transferred to the buyer from the moment a contract of sale is concluded; however, if the applicable law according to the property statute establishes the 'transfer system' (ownership is transferred from the moment the thing is transferred), then the buyer becomes the owner from the moment the thing is delivered.[20] In order to avoid legal uncertainty, it is therefore important to analyse the 'compatibility' of the property and contract laws when concluding a transaction.

Another inconsistency between property and contract statutes is the interpretation of such concepts as 'movable property', 'immovable property' and 'legal capacity', etc. If interpretation of these concepts is carried out not according to the law of the forum but according to the rules of contract and property statutes,[21] there is a risk of conceptual incompatibility between the rules of the two legal systems and, as a result, potential inability to achieve the result the parties hoped for.

In sum, determining the scope of the property statute under Russian PIL has certain peculiarities. At the same time, taking into account the unique approaches of different jurisdictions and potential overlap of issues regulated by the property, contract and personal statutes, it is important to clearly distinguish the scope of application of these statutes in each individual case.

III. Special Conflict-of-Laws Rules Concerning Property Rights

A. Conflict of Laws Regarding Immovable Property

As noted above, under Russian law, ownership and other proprietary rights to immovable property are determined by the law of the country in which the property is located (Article 1205 of the Russian Civil Code). In addition, the *lex rei sitae* applies to the issue outside the scope of the property statute – the form of the transaction in relation to immovable property. According to Article 1209(4) of the Russian Civil Code, the form of a transaction concerning immovable property is determined by the law of the country where the property is located. All immovable property gets registered and entered into the State Register in Russia. The conflict-of-laws rule provides that Russian law is the only law applicable to the question of the form of the transaction relating to such property. The Russian

[20] V Plekhanov, *Perekhod prava sobstvennosti po dogovoru mezhdunarodnoj kupli-prodazhi tovarov* (*Transfer of Ownership under a Cross-Border Contract for the Sale of Goods*) (Dissertation for the PhD degree / degree of Candidate of Legal Sciences, Moscow 2008) 121–22.

[21] E Lorenzen gives an overview of the various approaches to the qualification of 'movable property', 'immovable property', 'legal capacity', 'domicile', 'form' and others. See E Lorenzen, 'The Theory of Qualifications and the Conflict of Laws' (1920) 20(3) *Columbia Law Review* 247.

Civil Code also provides that in the absence of an agreement between the parties on the law applicable to a contract concerning immovable property, the law of the country in which the immovable property is located shall apply, unless that law, the terms or the essence of the contract, or the circumstances of the case provide otherwise (Article 1213(1) of the Russian Civil Code). Thus, the Russian law, to ensure legal certainty, seeks to exclude the application of the norms of different legal systems when regulating issues of contract and property law. At the same time, while parties to a real estate transaction are allowed to choose the law applicable to their contract, the Russian Civil Code does not provide for such discretion with respect to the property.

Application of the *lex rei sitae* in relation to immovable property has traditionally been seen as uncontroversial because:

1) The principle of territorial application and certainty of the applicable law in advance corresponds to parties' expectations.[22] This advantage of the *lex rei sitae* is reflected in the principle of territorial sovereignty, which means that property is subject to the exclusive regulation of the state in which it is located.[23] In today's reality, where the number of disputes on states' borders is minimal and the interpretation of the concept of the 'location of a thing' is uncontroversial, application of the *lex rei sitae* in property disputes leads to a high degree of legal certainty.[24]
2) There are no major difficulties in determining the precise location of immovable property and hence of the applicable law. Immovable property, by virtue of its physical characteristics, is generally incapable of changing its location.[25]
3) There is no need to assess the property law effects of cross-border transactions involving immovable property according to a law other than that of the place where the property is situated. The *lex rei sitae* rule requires that the legality of the title to the property be verified only according to the law of one jurisdiction, ie the country in which the property is located. Any other solution to the conflict-of-laws problem would force potential purchasers of real estate to verify title not only under the law of the place where the property is located and the relevant local registry, but also under foreign law and in foreign registries.[26] Representatives of the school of economic analysis of law also point out that the *lex rei sitae*, by virtue of its conciseness and stability, provides 'certainty of title', which makes real estate even more valuable.[27]

[22] J Carruthers, *The Transfer of Property in the Conflict of Laws* (Oxford, Oxford University Press, 2005) 196–97, 199.
[23] Ibid, 196.
[24] Plekhanov (n 20 above) 86.
[25] Carruthers (n 22 above) 197–98.
[26] Plekhanov (n 20 above) 88.
[27] P Hay, R Weintraub and P Borchers, *Conflict of Laws. Cases and Materials*, 14th edn (Galeta, Foundation Press, 2013) 762.

4) The transparency of civil transactions is ensured. This advantage follows organically from the previous ones. In the legal scholarship, there is a strong argument in favour of the *lex rei sitae* because it ensures the transparency of civil transactions.[28] In this context, Martin Wolff has stated that rights *in rem* must be as unambiguous as possible; any third party wishing to acquire rights in an object must be protected against the risk that such property may be subject to regulation by foreign law under which the transaction in question may be declared void.[29]
5) The *lex rei sitae* enjoys immunity from manipulation. Because immovable property cannot be moved and because the territorial principle of the register of rights to immovable property, it is unrealistic to move immovable property to another state in order to change the statute of the property. This cannot be excluded in the case of movable property.

The justifiability of the application of the law of the country of location to immovable property is also noted by Russian scholars.[30] A logical exception to this rule is the conflict-of-laws regulation of property issues in relation to such immovable property as aircraft, sea and inland waterway vessels, and space objects subject to state registration. Pursuant to Article 1207 of the Russian Civil Code, ownership and other property rights to such objects are determined by the law of the country in which such vessels and objects are *registered*. This approach of the Russian legislator is explained largely by the fact that these objects have a significant material value, but due to their mobility they may find themselves at any time on the territory of another state, which may lead to their future fate being determined in a somewhat arbitrary manner. This solution is broadly in line with the international view on the regulation of conflicts of title in respect of mobile equipment as reflected in the 1948 Geneva Convention on the International Recognition of Rights in Aircraft,[31] the 1988 UNIDROIT Convention on International Financial Leasing, adopted in Ottawa in 1988,[32] and the 2001 UNIDROIT Convention on International Interests in Mobile Equipment, adopted in Cape Town in 2001.[33]

[28] Carruthers (n 22 above) 196.

[29] M Wolff, *Private International Law*, 2nd edn (Oxford, Clarendon Press, 1950) 511, citing Carruthers (n 22 above) 196.

[30] Plekhanov (n 20 above) 136.

[31] Convention on the International Recognition of Rights in Aircraft (concluded at Geneva on 19 June 1948). In fact, the Geneva Convention establishes an alternative connecting factor *lex registrationis*, which is not as cumbersome and provides greater legal certainty in comparison to the *lex rei sitae*. M Polak, 'Recognition, Enforcement and Transformation of Foreign Proprietary Rights' in U Drobnig, H Snijders and E Zippro (eds), *Divergences of Property Law, an Obstacle to the Internal Market* (Munich, Sellier European Law Publishers, 2006) 126.

[32] UNIDROIT Convention on International Financial Leasing (concluded in Ottawa on 28 May 1988). The Ottawa Convention does not choose the *lex rei sitae* as the primary connecting factor, but takes a differentiated approach to determining the applicable law depending on the specifics of the object of the financial lease itself.

[33] Convention on International Interests in Mobile Equipment (concluded in Cape Town on 16.11.2001). The Cape Town Convention provides uniform rules ensuring protection of rights in rem

B. Conflict of Laws Regarding Movable Property

In Russian law, *lex rei sitae* is generally a connecting factor applying to issues involving ownership of movable property (Article 1205 of the Russian Civil Code). According to Article 1206(1) of the Russian Civil Code, the origin and termination of property rights and other rights to property are determined by the law of the country where the property was located at the time of the act or other circumstance causing such origin or termination, unless otherwise provided by law. However, despite this rule, which is clearly more relevant for movable property, the application of the conflict rule to movable property may in some cases lead to uncertainty in the conflict rule and to a haphazard result for the parties to the transaction, which rightly calls into question the universality of the *lex rei sitae* as a conflict rule.

Indeed, the ability of movable things to change their location in space may give rise to a number of difficulties in a situation where the legal facts necessary for the transfer of ownership and the creation of other rights *in rem* have been determined under one property statute, but then it changes, because of the new location of the thing,[34] to another statute under *lex rei sitae*. This problem of change of law is referred to in the literature as a 'mobile conflict' (*conflit mobile*)[35] and raises a number of practical issues.

One such issue is the permissibility of recording under a new property statute those legal facts that were previously 'accumulated'. In 2019, the Russian Supreme Court of the Russian Federation clarified[36] that in case of transfer of goods to another country before transfer of ownership, the elements of the set of facts which occurred in the first country (for example, entering into a contract, transfer, etc) should be taken into account when determining whether all the necessary legal conditions for transfer of ownership existed under the *lex rei sitae*.[37] This approach seems reasonable.

Another problem in practice is an assessment of the possibility of producing a relevant legal effect in the jurisdiction to which the thing has been moved, based on previously determined legal elements regarding the thing. Currently, there is no regulation of this question in Russian law or court practice. However, taking into account the explanations in the above-cited Resolution of the Plenum of the

in transactions with mobile equipment (pledge, sale with reservation of title, lease) on the basis of international registration of such rights. See Marysheva (n 14 above) 203–24.

[34] Plekhanov (n 20 above) 97–98.

[35] Zaphiriou (n 16 above) 54.

[36] Postanovlenie Plenuma Verhovnogo Suda Rossijskoj Federacii ot 09.07.2019 No 24 'O primenenii norm mezhdunarodnogo chastnogo prava sudami Rossijskoj Federacii' (Resolution of the Plenum of the Supreme Court of the Russian Federation No 24 of 9 July 2019 'On the Application of Rules of International Private Law by the Courts of the Russian Federation').

[37] A Efimov holds a similar position, but with certain clarifications. See A Efimov, 'Priznanie i adaptaciya veshchnyh obespechenij v mezhdunarodnom chastnom prave' ('Recognition and Adaptation of Property Security in Private International Law') (2018) 17(2) *Vestnik mezhdunarodnogo kommercheskogo arbitrazha* (*Bulletin of International Commercial Arbitration*) 43.

Supreme Court, it can be assumed that the Russian courts will give an affirmative answer in cases where the legal elements are the same, and will focus on the 'new' legal element in cases where they are different.

The situation of the *conflit mobile* is equally acute in the case of security instruments for movable property with a property law effect (eg, a pledge),[38] which become ineffective at the border crossing if they do not meet the requirements set in the foreign country (eg, the publicity rule).[39]

The 2013 reform of the Civil Code attempted to address the problems that may arise from the transferability of movable property. The amended Article 1206 of the Russian Civil Code provides that creation and termination of ownership and other property rights under a transaction with respect to movable property in transit shall be determined by the law of the country from whence the property is sent, unless otherwise provided by law (Article 1206(2) of the Russian Civil Code). At the same time, paragraph 3 of the same article provides for the right of the parties to agree on application to their transaction of the law governing the creation and termination of title and other proprietary rights to movable objects, without prejudice to the rights of third parties. Thus, the law allows party autonomy in determining the law applicable to ownership of movable property.

C. Conflict of Laws Regarding Securities

Russian law is largely silent on the issue of cross-border regulation of civil transactions involving securities. Because, under Article 130(2) of the Russian Civil Code, all securities are classified as things and movables, the only legal norm directly applicable to the regulation of securities is the *lex rei sitae* set out in Article 1205 of the Russian Civil Code. As explained above, with respect to rights *in rem* to both immovable and movable property, the *lex rei sitae* indicates the law of the place where the property is located.

However, determining the place where a security is deemed to be located is not always an easy task. This is because securities nowadays tend to be 'dematerialised', ie they do not have any embodiment in the form of a paper document and are recorded in a complex system, involving a beneficial owner, a nominal holder of the securities, a registrar, a depository, and other securities market participants, each of whom could be located in a different jurisdiction.

In this regard, the Plenum of the Supreme Court of the Russian Federation recently attempted to clarify the *lex rei sitae* in Article 1205:

> Unless otherwise stipulated by an international treaty, the legislation of the Russian Federation or arising from the essence of the relations, the rules of conflict of laws on determining the property statute also apply to certificated and uncertificated securities. For uncertificated securities, the country where the property is located is considered

[38] Lyubarskaya and Lashkov (n 19 above) 154.
[39] Koch, Magnus and Von Morenfels (n 2 above) 198.

> the country where the rights to such securities are recorded. Therefore, when resolving disputes related to uncertificated securities recorded in the share register or depository records maintained in the territory of the Russian Federation, courts should apply Russian law on the issues specified in Article 1205.1 of the Civil Code of the Russian Federation.[40]

As we can see, it recognises application of two different connecting factors within the *lex rei sitae*: (1) for certified securities, the place where the certificates are located (the *lex cartae sitae*), (2) for uncertified securities, the law of the place where the rights to such securities are recorded. Sadly, it is not clear what 'the country where the rights in such securities are registered' means.[41]

Some specific rules on the cross-border regulation of securities can also be found in the Federal Law 'On the Securities Market' No 39-FZ dated 22 April 1996. Its Article 8.4 accepts the application of the personal statute of the foreign legal entity for determining its rights with regard to the registration of ownership rights and transfer of title to securities listed in Russia:

> A foreign organisation that has the right to record and transfer rights to securities shall record and transfer rights to Russian securities in accordance with its personal law. The designation of a person as an owner of securities or other person exercising rights to Russian securities registered on a depo account of a foreign nominee holder shall be made in accordance with the personal law of such persons. A foreign organisation that is not a legal entity under the law of the country where the organisation is incorporated may be the holder of the above securities.

As has been rightly pointed out, the said provision seems to be inherently contradictory and dubious, since, on the one hand, its first sentence refers to the application of the *lex personalis* of the foreign intermediary, whereas the second part refers to the *lex personalis* of the owner of the securities.[42]

There are also a few national laws and international treaties that deal with the regulation of the cheques and bills of exchange dating from the Soviet era, namely, the Convention for the Settlement of Certain Conflicts of Laws in Connection with Bills of Exchange and Promissory Notes (Geneva, 7 June 1930)[43] and the

[40] Postanovlenie Plenuma Verhovnogo Suda Rossijskoj Federacii ot 09.07.2019 No 24 'O primenenii norm mezhdunarodnogo chastnogo prava sudami Rossijskoj Federacii' (Resolution of the Plenum of the Supreme Court of the Russian Federation No 24 of 9 July 2019 'On the Application of Rules of International Private Law by the Courts of the Russian Federation'), para 18.

[41] See more discussion on the vagueness of para 18 of the Resolution of the Plenum of the Supreme Court with regard to the construction of the *lex rei sitae* and its application to securities in: I Podkopalov, 'Nekotoryye aspekty pravovogo regulirovaniya transgranichnogo oborota tsennykh bumag, uchityvayemykh cherez posrednika' ('Some Aspects of the Legal Regulation of Cross-Border Transactions with Securities through an Intermediary') (2021) 12 *Vestnik ekonomicheskogo pravosudiia Rossiiskoi Federatsii* (*Bulletin of Economic Justice of the Russian Federation*) 73, 74.

[42] Y Bezborodova, *Kollizionnoye regulirovaniye transgranichnykh operatsiy s tsennymi bumagami v Rossii i zarubezhnykh stranakh* (*Conflict of laws regulation of cross-border transactions with securities in Russia and foreign countries*) (Dissertation for the PhD degree / degree of Candidate of Legal Sciences, Moscow, 2019) 167.

[43] This Convention is still in force in the Russian Federation.

Regulation on Cheques, approved by a Decree of the Central Executive Committee and Council of People's Commissars of the Union of Soviet Socialist Republics of 6 November 1929. Both of these legal sources are notable for their acceptance of the *renvoi* principle, which is not a common feature of Russian PIL.[44]

Despite the existence of the above-mentioned rules that aim to regulate cross-border securities transactions, the case law of the Russian courts in this area remains scarce and underdeveloped. Therefore, Russian scholars traditionally remain critical of the state Russian law on cross-border securities transactions. This is especially relevant considering that a number of foreign legal systems have developed and introduced into their legal systems various other private law institutions dealing with the increasingly complex world of securities.

D. Conflict of Laws Regarding Trusts and Similar Legal Instruments

The first legislative attempts to incorporate trust as a common law concept into Russian law were made in the early 1990s. At that time, Presidential Decree No 2296 of 24 December 1993 'On Trust Property (Trust)' was enacted.[45] It provided for the adoption of trusts as institutions of property law associated with the transfer of the ownership title from the owner to a trustee. Part II of the Russian Civil Code superseded the Decree in 1996. The new Chapter 53 of the Russian Civil Code regulated fiduciary property management agreements,[46] which would not involve the transfer of property title from the owner. Though short-lived, the very idea of adopting trust as a property law institution has been heavily criticised by Russian scholars.[47]

The Russian legal approach to trusts seems rather formalistic. As Professor Kanashevsky has claimed, 'Russian civil law only recognises a legal title holder, but it does not "see" the beneficial rights that flow from the right of equity'.[48] Since there is no provision in the Russian law directly applicable to trusts in the common law sense, the Russian courts, when faced with declarations of trust or similar legal

[44] See 'Commentary to Article 1190 of the Russian Civil Code' in MM Boguslavsky, BM Gongalo, AV Demkina et al (ed by PV Krasheninnikov), *Grazhdanskiy kodeks Rossiyskoy Federatsii. Mezhdunarodnoye chastnoye pravo. Postateynyy kommentariy k razdelu VI* (*Civil Code of the Russian Federation. Private International Law. Article-by-article commentary to Part VI*) (Moscow, Statut, 2014) 44, 45.

[45] Collected Acts of the President and Government of the Russian Federation, 03.01.1994, No 1, Art 6.

[46] The Russian Civil Code (Part Two) of 29.01.1996 N 14-FZ (ed. of 01.07.2021). Collection of Legislation of the Russian Federation, 5, Art 410.

[47] Eg see S Kolesnikova, 'O doveritel'noy sobstvennosti (traste), ili 15 let spustya' ('On trusts, or 15 years later') (2007) 10 *Zakon* (*The Law*) 188. See also Sukhanov (n 9 above) 130, fn 1.

[48] V Kanashevskiy, *Pravovoy rezhim ofshornykh kompaniy i trastov* (*Legal Regime for Offshore Companies and Trusts*) (Moscow, Mezhdunarodnyye otnosheniya, 2015) 128.

instruments relating to some property placed in trust, should ideally be applying paragraph 2 of Article 1187 of the Russian Civil Code, which states that:

> If, in determining the applicable law, the legal concepts requiring characterisation are not known to Russian law or are known under another verbal designation or with another content and cannot be determined by interpretation in accordance with Russian law, then foreign law may be applied in their legal characterisation.

This, in turn, leads to the application of the law of the closest connection (Article 1186 of the Russian Civil Code). However, the Russian courts, when dealing with cases on property placed in trust under foreign law, mostly seem to disregard this provision of the Russian Civil Code, stating that any beneficiary rights related to trust do not qualify as 'property' under Russian law.[49]

[49] The meagre Russian court jurisprudence in such cases is mostly associated with divorce and spousal property division proceedings. See, eg the Appellate Ruling of Moscow City Court dated 22 January 2016 in case No 33-2311. Many Russian businesspersons have used foreign trusts to place assets beyond the reach of their creditors.

9

Succession (Inheritance) Law

OLGA KAMENSKAIA

A rapid development of the global economy in the past decades has significantly increased the practical importance of PIL regulation of succession. People tend to relocate to other countries, to move their funds and to invest in property in multiple jurisdictions. This inevitably brings up complex transnational succession cases along with a need for thorough cross-border estate planning.

In contrast to civil and commercial relations, whereby certain legal concepts tend toward harmonisation and unification in the interest of international trade, the substantive regulation of succession demonstrates differing legal traditions. National laws on succession display historic and cultural diversity among substantive laws. This makes the task of determining which law is applicable to deal with succession or its various aspects inherently complicated.

This chapter explores the conflict-of-laws approach to inheritance in Russia. It first outlines the basic sources of Russian conflict norms on succession, enshrined in national and international legal instruments. It further carries out a detailed analysis of intestate succession and the PIL regulation of succession of movable and immovable property. The chapter concludes by highlighting the conflict rules on testamentary disposition and the connecting factors indicating the law applicable to the legal capacity of a testator and the formal validity of a will.

I. Sources

A. National Law

Lex successionis, the law applicable to succession, covers the substantive law issues of 'opening of inheritance' (namely obtaining authority to administer the estate) and allocation of the property of the deceased among the heirs. It determines all aspects of inheritance, such as the inherited property, the term for acceptance of inheritance by beneficiaries, the allocation of assets among the legal heirs, the order of succession, the obligations imposed on the heirs by the deceased, testamentary freedom, the concept of legitimate portion and allocation of heirless property.

Academic doctrine developed two basic principles that govern the determination of the *lex successionis*. The first principle promotes the unity of the estate, ensuring that succession in its entirety and all aspects of succession are governed by one applicable law. The second principle allows for the split of the governing law, most commonly providing for separate conflict norms to apply to different parts of the estate depending on the type of inherited property. Russian law adheres to the latter principle, providing for differing conflict rules with regard to the movable or immovable nature of inherited property.

In the scholarly literature, the application of different conflict rules to a single inheritance relationship is generally recognised as a special situation of *depeçage*, or 'splitting' of conflict regulation.[1] The application of different conflict rules is criticised for fragmentation of the law of inheritance and the formation of several autonomous inheritance regimes separately for movable and immovable property.[2]

Conflict rules governing the law applicable to succession are set out in the Article 1224 of the Civil Code. Its first part envisages the conflict rules on intestate succession and provides for different connecting factors for succession of movable and immovable property. The basic connecting factor for succession is the last place of habitual residence of the deceased. It applies to all assets of the estate except for immovable property.

Succession of immovable property falls under an exception that provides for the application of the laws of the state where such property is located. Immovable property registered in Russia falls within the scope of the unilateral conflict rule that provides for application of Russian law. This special unilateral conflict norm on the succession of immovable property historically originates from the Soviet period, where the inheritance of 'buildings' located in the USSR had to be determined in all cases according to the Soviet law.[3]

Article 1224 further entails conflict rules on testamentary disposition, in particular the issues of legal capacity of the testator and the form of testamentary instrument. The general connecting factor for testamentary capacity and form of testament is the law of the state where the testator had his or her place of habitual residence at the moment of drawing up the testament.

Along with special conflict rules, cross-border succession falls under the application of general principles of private international law enshrined in Chapter 66 of the Civil Code. Among them is the concept of public policy.[4] It excludes the application of the rules of foreign law if the consequences of their application would

[1] I Karandashov, 'Prinyatie nasledstva za rubezhom i ego pravovye posledstviya na territorii Rossii' ('Acceptance of Inheritance Abroad: Legal Consequences in Russia') (2019) 8 *Zakon* 62–176.

[2] A Mashovec and I Medvedev, *Nastol'naya kniga notariusa: v 4 tomah. Tom 4: Mezhdunarodnoe chastnoe pravo, ugolovnoe pravo i process v notarial'noj deyatel'nosti* (*Handbook of a notary: in 4 volumes. Volume 4: International private law, criminal law and process in notarial activity*) (Moscow, Statut, 2015).

[3] Statya 127, Zakon SSSR ot 08.12.1961 'Ob Utverzhdenii Osnov Grazhdanskogo Zakonodatel'stva Soyuza SSR i Soyuznyh Respublik' (Article 127, Law of the USSR of 08.12.1961 'On Approval of the Fundamentals of Civil Legislation of the USSR and Union Republics').

[4] Article 1193 of the Civil Code.

clearly contradict the fundamental legal order of the Russian Federation. Instead, the relevant substantive rule of Russian law will apply. The scholars address the following examples of foreign rules which would not be applicable in Russia: (i) hereditary privileges granted by virtue of seniority, sex or religion; (ii) any grounds for 'opening an inheritance' (initiating administration of the estate) other than death; (iii) succession rights of marriage partners if the marriage is generally not recognised in Russia.[5] With regard to the latter example, Russia would not recognise the succession rights of spouses arising out of an official marriage concluded between close relatives or legally incapable persons,[6] or the rights of partners under civil partnership or same-sex marriage. At the same time, the spouses of a polygamous marriage legally concluded under the laws of a foreign state, if the marriage does not contradict Russian laws, shall not be deprived of inheritance and maintenance rights in Russia.

In the absence of a common understanding of the concepts underlying succession among the different states, legal terminology has decisive importance in cross-border issues. By determination of the applicable law, the legal terms shall be interpreted under Russian law.[7] The key substantive legal definitions on succession are codified in Part III of the Civil Code: the place of opening of the inheritance,[8] the time period for acceptance of an inheritance,[9] the actions recognised as acceptance of inheritance, the requirements as to form and validity of a testamentary instrument[10] and rules on legitimate portion.[11]

B. International Law

Russia is party to a number of international agreements entailing conflict rules with regard to succession. Among them are the 2002 Chisinau Convention on Legal Assistance and Legal Relations in Civil, Family and Criminal Matters,[12] the 1993 Minsk Convention on legal assistance and legal relations in civil, family

[5] E Petrov, RS Bezvenko, SL Budyli (eds), *Nasledstvennoe Pravo: Postatejnyj Kommentarij K Stat'yam 1110–1185, 1224 Grazhdanskogo kodeksa Rossijskoj Federacii* (*Inheritance Law: Article-by-Article Commentary on Articles 1110–1185, 1224 of the Civil Code of the Russian Federation*) (Moscow, Statut, 2018).

[6] On recognition of marriages in Russian Federation, see Articles 14 and 158 of the Family Code.

[7] Article 1187 of the Civil Code.

[8] Article 1115 of the Civil Code.

[9] Article 1154 of the Civil Code.

[10] Article 1124 of the Civil Code.

[11] Article 1149 of the Civil Code.

[12] The Chisinau Convention on Legal Assistance and Legal Relations in Civil, Family and Criminal Matters of 7 October 2002 (the 2002 Chisinau Convention). As of 2023, the Chisinau Convention is in force in Azerbaijan, Armenia, Belarus, Kazakhstan, Kyrgyzstan, Russia, Tajikistan, and Uzbekistan. The Convention entered into force for Russia on 28 June 2023. See: Federal'nyj zakon ot 30.12.2021 No 452-FZ 'O ratifikacii Konvencii o pravovoj pomoshchi i pravovyh otnosheniyah po grazhdanskim, semejnym i ugolovnym delam' (Federal Law dated 30 December 2021 No 452-FZ 'On Ratification

and criminal law matters,[13] and a wide range of bilateral treaties on mutual legal assistance in civil and family matters addressing PIL regulation of cross-border succession.

The regional multilateral conventions – the 2002 Chisinau Convention and 1993 Minsk Convention – entail conflict rules similar to those of the Civil Code, whereas some differing conflict rules are to be found in bilateral treaties. Should an international treaty provide for a conflict rule that differs from national law, the rules of such international treaty shall prevail over the conflict rules of the Civil Code.

The 'splitting' of the *lex successionis* is commonly found in international treaties that Russia is party to. All international treaties adhere to the same rule on inheritance of immovable property (*lex rei sitae*). With regard to inheritance of movables, the connecting factors may differ. For instance, the 2002 Chisinau Convention and the 1993 Minsk Convention are congruent with the Civil Code, providing for the law of the state where the deceased had his or her last place of habitual residence as a connecting factor.[14] Whereas treaties on legal assistance with Hungary,[15] Poland,[16] Bulgaria[17] and Romania[18] when determining law applicable to succession of movable property apply the law of the citizenship of the deceased.

With regard to testamentary disposition, the conflict rules of 2002 Chisinau Convention and the 1993 Minsk Convention are similar to the Civil Code. Both conventions apply the law of the place of habitual residence of the deceased at the moment of issuance of the will, to the legal capacity of the testator, and to the form of the testamentary instrument. As an additional measure of protection of the testator's will, it is ensured that a testamentary instrument cannot be recognised as invalid if its form corresponds to the laws of the state where it was made.[19] Certain bilateral treaties provide for differing approaches. In some bilateral treaties, the connecting factor of the citizenship of the deceased applies to the form of testament[20]

of the Convention on Legal Assistance and Legal Relations in Civil, Family and Criminal Matters'), https://cis.minsk.by/reestrv2/doc/1313#documentCard.

[13] Convention on legal assistance and legal relations in civil, family and criminal law matters of 22 January 1993. The Chisinau Convention supersedes the 1993 Minsk Convention among the states parties which adopted the Chisinau Convention. The 1993 Minsk Convention is in force for relations of Russian parties in inheritance matters involving Georgia and Moldova.

[14] 2002 Chisinau Convention, Article 48; 1993 Minsk Convention, Article 45.

[15] Agreement between the USSR and The Hungarian People's Republic On The Provision Of Legal Assistance In Civil, Family And Criminal Matters dated 15 July 1958, Article 37.

[16] Agreement between the Russian Federation and the Republic of Poland on Legal Assistance and Legal Relations in Civil and Criminal Matters dated 16 September 1996, Article 39.

[17] Agreement between the USSR and the People's Republic of Bulgaria on Legal Assistance in Civil, Family and Criminal Matters dated 19 February 1975, Article 32.

[18] Agreement between the USSR and the Romanian People's Republic on Legal Assistance in Civil, Family and Criminal Matters dated 3 April 1958, Article 37.

[19] 2002 Chisinau Convention, Article 50; 1993 Minsk Convention, Article 47.

[20] See, for example: Agreement between the Russian Federation and the Arab Republic of Egypt on Mutual Legal Assistance and Legal Relations in Civil, Commercial and Family Matters dated 23 September 1997, Article 31; Agreement between the Russian Federation and the Republic of Lithuania on Legal Assistance and Legal Relations in Civil, Family and Criminal Matters dated 21 July 1991, Article 44.

or to the legal capacity of the deceased.[21] Other bilateral treaties provide for further specific rules with regard to bequeathing immovable property. They require the mandatory compliance of the testamentary instrument with the laws of the state where the property is located, at the risk of invalidity of the testament.[22] If a will violates the *lex rei sitae*, it shall be deemed null and void in respect of the part that applies to immovable property. Scholars express reasonable doubts as to the necessity of these strict rules, but acknowledge that compliance with the laws of the state where the property is located is necessary, at least as long as these international treaties remain in force.[23]

Along with establishing conflict rules with regard to succession by law and by will, international treaties entail unified regulation of certain substantive aspects of cross-border succession. For instance, some treaties entail regulation of heirless property, which scholars address as an example of partial unification of PIL rules on succession.[24] Heirless property is one of the specific problems of inheritance that usually results in transfer of property of the deceased to the state. Should the cross-border succession have connections with several jurisdictions, international treaties specify the allocation of property among different states. Under the 2002 Chisinau Convention, the 1993 Minsk Convention[25] and several bilateral treaties including with Latvia,[26] Lithuania,[27] Poland,[28] Bulgaria,[29] Hungary[30] and Vietnam,[31] the movable part of the heirless estate shall be allocated to the state of

[21] See, for example: Agreement between the USSR and The Hungarian People's Republic on the Provision of Legal Assistance in Civil, Family and Criminal Matters dated 15 July 1958, Article 39; Agreement between the Russian Federation and the Republic of Poland on Legal Assistance and Legal Relations in Civil and Criminal Matters dated 16 September 1996, Article 41.

[22] Agreement between the USSR and the Republic of Greece on Legal Assistance in Civil and Criminal Matters dated 21 May 1981, Article 22; Agreement between the USSR and the Republic of Cyprus on Legal Assistance in Civil and Criminal Matters dated 19 January 1984, Article 22; Agreement between the USSR and the Republic of Finland on Legal Protection and Legal Assistance in Civil, Family and Criminal Matters dated 11 August 1978, Article 25.

[23] E Petrov, RS Bezvenko and SL Budylin (eds), *Nasledstvennoe Pravo: Postatejnyj Kommentarij K Stat'yam 1110–1185, 1224 Grazhdanskogo Kodeksa Rossijskoj Federacii* (*Inheritance Law: Article-by-Article Commentary on Articles 1110–1185, 1224 of the Civil Code of the Russian Federation*), (Moscow, Statut, 2018).

[24] A Mashovec and I Medvedev, *Nastol'naya kniga notariusa: v 4 tomah. Tom 4: Mezhdunarodnoe chastnoe pravo, ugolovnoe pravo i process v notarial'noj deyatel'nosti* (*Handbook of a notary: in 4 volumes. Volume 4: International private law, criminal law and process in notarial activity*) (Moscow, Statut, 2015).

[25] 2002 Chisinau Convention, Article 49; 1993 Minsk Convention, Article 46.

[26] Agreement between the Russian Federation and the Republic of Latvia on Legal Assistance and Legal Relations in Civil, Family and Criminal Matters dated 3 February 1993, Article 43.

[27] Agreement between the Russian Federation and the Republic of Lithuania on Legal Assistance and Legal Relations in Civil, Family and Criminal Matters dated 21 July 1991, Article 43.

[28] Agreement between the Russian Federation and the Republic of Poland on Legal Assistance and Legal Relations in Civil and Criminal Matters dated 16 September 1996, Article 40.

[29] Agreement between the USSR and the People's Republic of Bulgaria on Legal Assistance in Civil, Family and Criminal Matters dated 19 February 1975, Article 33.

[30] Agreement between the USSR and The Hungarian People's Republic on the Provision of Legal Assistance in Civil, Family and Criminal Matters dated 15 July 1958, Article 38.

[31] Agreement between the Russian Federation and the Socialist Republic of Vietnam on Legal Assistance and Legal Relations in Civil and Criminal Matters dated 25 August 1998, Article 40.

the citizenship of the deceased, whereas the immovable property shall belong to the state where it is located. Although the connecting factor of citizenship does not express the actual relationship of a person with a specific state, citizenship is a solid legal concept that does not have differing interpretations as compared to the place of habitual residence. Thus, it is a straightforward way for a state of citizenship to receive heirless property without the need to assemble additional evidence.

Some international treaties further allocate the jurisdiction of public authorities to handle inheritance cases.[32] The competence of public authorities to handle inheritance usually follows the classical 'splitting' of the applicable law. The competent authorities of the state where the immovable property is located shall handle the inheritance case with respect to such property. The movable property falls within the jurisdiction of the state of the last habitual residence or the state of the citizenship of the deceased, depending on the general connecting factor applied to determination of the *lex successionis* by the relevant international agreement.

Under some bilateral treaties, the consular institutions have the powers to represent the heirs in inheritance matters. The inherited property may be handed over to the consul of the state of the deceased in the context of absent heirs or in certain situations when the heir is not present in Russia and does not have a legal representative.[33]

II. Intestate Succession

A. Succession of Movable Property

The legal category of inheritance implies that the property of the deceased (estate property) is allocated to the heirs by way of universal succession. The concept of universal succession provides that the estate shall pass to the heirs unchanged in its entirety. Following the general conflict rule of Article 1224(1) of the Civil Code, the law applicable to inheritance – except for immovable property – shall be the law of the state of the last place of habitual residence of the deceased. This conflict rule applies to the inheritance of movable property, which includes money and securities, as well as rights and obligations arising from contracts, corporate relations and intellectual property rights.[34] For example, Russian law will apply to the rights of heirs to the bank deposit in Russia, the collection of fine arts in Switzerland, and

[32] See, for example, 2002 Chisinau Convention, Article 51.

[33] See, for example, Agreement between the Russian Federation and the Republic of Lithuania on Legal Assistance and Legal Relations in Civil, Family and Criminal Matters dated 21 July 1991, Article 49; Agreement between the Russian Federation and the Republic of Latvia on Legal Assistance and Legal Relations in Civil, Family and Criminal Matters dated 3 February 1993, Article 49.

[34] A Makovskij and E Suhanov (eds), *Kommentarij k chasti tret'ej Grazhdanskogo kodeksa Rossijskoj Federacii (postatejnyj)* (*Commentary on Part Three of the Civil Code of the Russian Federation (article-by-article)*) (Moscow, Yurist, 2002).

the corporate shares in the Cyprus-based company of the deceased, who had his last place of habitual residence in Russia.

The legal concept of the place of habitual residence is the cornerstone for determination of applicable law and the authorities empowered to administer the estate. International treaties that Russia is party to do not expressly provide for a universal definition of the place of habitual residence. The Economic Court of the Commonwealth of Independent States, while interpreting certain provisions of the 1993 Minsk Convention, has indicated two basic criteria that shall apply when determining the habitual residence of a person. First, the deceased person's habitual residence is subject to the criterion of the legality of stay, which means the compliance of the person's residential status with the administrative rules for entry and stay in the territory of the relevant state and with migration legislation. The second criterion is that the person must have had their actual permanent or predominant residence in the particular territory.[35]

The place of habitual residence, as defined by Article 20 of the Civil Code, is a place where a citizen permanently or predominantly resides. The place of residence of a Russian citizen may be evidenced by the documents on registration at their place of temporary stay or at their place of permanent residence within the Russian Federation. Russia law distinguishes between the concepts of 'the place of habitual residence' and 'the place of temporary stay'.[36] A person's stay in a particular place on a temporary basis for a specific purpose – vacation, medical treatment, business trip, military service, study – would not be regarded as permanent habitual residence even for long-term presence and therefore would be irrelevant for the purposes of determination of the applicable law. Permanent habitation has no connection with any purpose or result that the person seeks to achieve by coming to the specific place. Therefore, the place of death will not be automatically considered as the deceased's last place of habitual residence if it does not comply with permanent habitual residence criteria. For instance, the deceased who had their permanent residency in Russia, might have come to another country for medical treatment. In this case, the inheritance will be opened in Russia, the place of habitual residence of the deceased.

An important element for establishing the relationship between a person and the state would be the lawfulness of residence and the duration of stay. An illegal actual stay by the deceased in the territory of a certain state, regardless of the duration of the stay, does not affect the determination of his last place of habitual residence. If the deceased was a foreign citizen or stateless person, it would be

[35] Reshenie Ekonomicheskogo Suda SNG ot 15.01.2002 No 01-1/3-2001 'O tolkovanii punkta 1 stat'i 28 i punkta 1 stat'i 29 Konvencii o pravovoj pomoshchi i pravovyh otnosheniyah po grazhdanskim, semejnym i ugolovnym delam ot 22 yanvarya 1993 goda' (Decision of the Economic Court of the Commonwealth of the Independent States dated 15 January 2002 No 01-1/3-2001 'On interpretation of item 1 of Article 28 and item 1 of Article 29 of the Convention on legal assistance and legal relations in civil, family and criminal law matters of 22 January 1993').

[36] Article 27(1) of the Constitution.

necessary to prove the fact of his lawful residence in Russia. The permanent or predominant residence of a foreigner in the Russian territory is evidenced by their residence permit. Foreigners visiting Russia on some other basis (e.g. tourism, business trip) are considered to be temporarily residing in Russia. In this case the law of the country of their permanent habitual residence will govern the administration of the estate.

It is common that the place of residence at the time of death is difficult to determine. In this situation, the law of the country of the deceased's last known place of residence should apply. In exceptional cases the place of 'opening of the inheritance' may be established by the court.[37] According to the interpretation of the Supreme Court, when deciding on the place of opening of the inheritance, the court shall take into account the duration of the deceased's habitation at the time of opening the inheritance, the location of the estate property and other circumstances that indicate that the deceased actually predominantly resided in the particular place.[38]

If the last place of residence of the deceased who owned property in the territory of the Russian Federation is unknown or is located abroad, the place of opening of the inheritance shall be the place where the estate property is located. If the deceased owned immovable property, the place of opening of the inheritance shall be the location of that immovable property or its most valuable part. In the absence of any immovable property, the place of opening of the inheritance will be determined by the place where the movable property (or its most valuable part) is situated.[39]

The last place of habitual residence of deceased minors under 14 years old should be determined as the place of residence of their legal representatives – parents or custodians.[40] The actual place of residence of minors is irrelevant, even if it differed from the place of residence of their legal representatives.[41]

The place of habitual residence of the deceased shall be determined at the moment of opening of inheritance. The inheritance opens with a person's death or with a person being declared dead by the court. When a citizen is declared dead by the court, the day of opening the inheritance is the day when the relevant court decision enters into force or, alternatively, the day and time of death indicated in such court decision.[42]

[37] Article 264 (1) of the Civil Procedure Code of the Russian Federation.

[38] Postanovlenie Plenuma Verhovnogo Suda RF ot 29.05.2012 No 9 'O sudebnoj praktike po delam o nasledovanii' (Resolution of the Plenum of the Supreme Court of the RF dated 29 May 2012 No 9 'On Judicial Practice On Inheritance Matters').

[39] Article 1115 of the Civil Code.

[40] Article 20(2) of the Civil Code.

[41] A Makovskij and E Suhanov (eds), *Kommentarij k chasti tret'ej Grazhdanskogo kodeksa Rossijskoj Federacii (postatejnyj)* (*Commentary on Part Three of the Civil Code of the Russian Federation (article-by-article)*) (Moscow, Yurist, 2002).

[42] Articles 1113 and 1114 of the Civil Code.

B. Succession of Immovable Property

As outlined above, Russian law sets forth specific PIL regulation of succession of immovable property. Under Article 1224(1) of the Civil Code the succession of immovable property shall be governed by the law of the state where such property is located (*lex rei sitae*). This rule is supplemented by a more specific unilateral conflict norm that provides for application of Russian substantive law to the inheritance of immovable property registered in Russian state registers. The latter rule shall apply to both intestate succession and inheritance by will, unless otherwise provided in international treaties of the Russian Federation.

While the inheritance of the movable property in its entirety – wherever it is located – is governed by the law of the state where the deceased had their last place of habitual residence, the inheritance of each immovable object falls to be determined under the laws of the state of its actual location. From a private international law perspective, the movable and immovable objects are allocated to relatively independent categories of estate property.[43] As a result, each item of immovable property forms a separate estate that is governed by its own applicable law. All issues related to the inheritance as to the number of heirs and their rights, the inherited shares, order of succession, management and division of the estate, shall be attributed for each immovable object on the basis of its governing law.[44] Following this understanding, the Supreme Court clarified that all claims arising out of the succession of immovable property located abroad shall be resolved by the laws of the state where this property is located.[45]

The principle of unity of the estate means that the acceptance of only one part of inheritance shall constitute the acceptance of the inheritance as a whole, known or not, wherever it is located (in Russia or abroad). However, due to the split of applicable law, an act of acceptance of inheritance would be valid under the law that governs the part of the accepted inheritance and would not qualify as an acceptance of estate which falls under the laws of the different state. Should Russian law apply to the administration of the estate, the act of acceptance would apply to all movable property of the deceased wherever it is located and to immovable property situated in Russia. At the same time, for the acceptance of immovable property located abroad, a separate act of acceptance would be required for each

[43] M Lyubimova, 'Nekotorye problemnye aspekty vydeleniya obyazatel'noj doli i transgranichnogo nasledovaniya nedvizhimogo imushchestva' ('Some Problematic Aspects of Compulsory Share and Cross-Border Succession of Real Estate') (2022) 11 *Notarial'nyj vestnik* 48–54.

[44] E Petrov, RS Bezvenko and SL Budylin (ed), *Nasledstvennoe Pravo: Postatejnyj Kommentarij K Stat'yam 1110–1185, 1224 Grazhdanskogo Kodeksa Rossijskoj Federacii* (*Inheritance Law: Article-by-Article Commentary on Articles 1110–1185, 1224 of the Civil Code of the Russian Federation*) (Moscow, Statut, 2018).

[45] Postanovlenie Plenuma Verhovnogo Suda RF ot 29.05.2012 No 9 'O sudebnoj praktike po delam o nasledovanii' (Resolution of the Plenum of the Supreme Court of the RF dated 29 May 2012 No 9 'On Judicial Practice on Inheritance Matters').

particular jurisdiction. This approach is further complicated by intestate and testamentary regimes of the inherited estate. The heir under the will shall accept the part attributed to him by the will, and the intestate heir shall accept the property that is allocated by law. Otherwise, the act of acceptance would not have legal consequences, according to the interpretation of the Supreme Court.[46]

The consequences of splitting the applicable law are reflected in the case law. In one case, a Russian court was asked to decide on the succession of immovable property located in the United Arab Emirates.[47] The court held that the inheritance certificate issued by a Russian notary in relation to the immovable property located abroad did not have legal consequences, since the inheritance of immovable property must be carried out in accordance with the laws of the country where the property is located.

In practice, collisions may arise over legal attribution of an object to the categories of movable or immovable property. The classical approach as to the qualification of the property status is based on application of the *lex rei sitae*, and Russian PIL shares this attitude. By virtue of Article 1205.1 of the Civil Code, the attribution of property to the category of movable or immovable is determined by the law of the country where this property is located.

Under Russian law, any object which is firmly attached to the land, so that its relocation without disproportionate damage to its purpose would be impossible, counts as immovable property. Article 130 of the Civil Code expressly ranks land plots, subsoil plots, buildings and their parts, and unfinished buildings as immovable property. The law further attributes to immovable property residential and non-residential premises, parking units, enterprises as an asset complex[48] and consolidated immovable complexes.[49] The law treats as immovable aircraft, sea vessels and inland vessels, provided that they are subject to registration in Russia. Russian law shall govern the succession of such objects regardless of their actual location.

When considering the inheritance rights of foreign citizens and stateless persons, the restrictions imposed by national legislation on the ownership of certain types of property must be observed. Foreigners are not allowed to own agricultural land plots,[50] land plots in the Russian border territories[51] according to

[46] Postanovlenie Plenuma Verhovnogo Suda RF ot 29.05.2012 No 9 'O sudebnoj praktike po delam o nasledovanii' (Resolution of the Plenum of the Supreme Court of the RF dated 29 May 2012 No 9 'On Judicial Practice on Inheritance Matters').

[47] Appellate Ruling of the Moscow State Court dated 24 January 2018 case No 33-2712/2018.

[48] Article 132 of the Civil Code.

[49] Article 133.1 of the Civil Code.

[50] Article 3, Federal'nyj Zakon ot 24.07.2002 No 101-FZ 'Ob oborote zemel' sel'skohozyajstvennogo naznacheniya' (Federal Law of the Russian Federation 'On the turnover of agricultural land' dated 24 July 2002 No 101-FZ).

[51] Article 15, Zemel'nyj kodeks Rossijskoj Federacii ot 25.10.2001 No 136-FZ (Land Code of the Russian Federation dated 25 October 2001 No 136-FZ).

the list approved by the President of the Russian Federation,[52] and land plots in the seaports.[53] However, this limitation does not affect the inheritance itself: the heir shall inherit the ownership of the property under the ordinary procedure. After that, the relevant restricted assets are subject to alienation within a year from the date of passage of the right of ownership.[54]

C. Legitimate Portion

Legitimate portion ensures the right of certain categories of heirs (minor or disabled children, disabled spouses or parents) to inherit – regardless of the terms of the will – at least a half of the share that would be due under the law of intestate succession.[55] Russian PIL does not specifically address the regulation of legitimate portion. The attribution of the substantive norms on legitimate portion to the fundamental legal order or overriding mandatory rules is neither officially recognised, nor affirmed by prevailing opinion in the legal doctrine. Therefore, the right to the legitimate portion cannot be granted in cases where the inheritance is governed by the laws of a state that does not entail provisions similar to Article 1149 of the Civil Code.

If Russian law applies to the succession, it shall apply to all property wherever it is located (with the exception of the immovable property). Therefore, the notary public can include foreign assets of the deceased in the calculation of the legitimate portion. Immovable property situated outside Russia does not form part of the estate of the deceased and will not be taken into consideration for the determination of the shares of the heirs or of the legitimate portion, even if the deceased was domiciled in Russia.[56]

The definition of disability shall be determined under Russian law. An heir entitled to legitimate portion under Russian law must provide official confirmation of his/her disability. The non-uniformity of approaches as to attribution of disabled status in different states may require the heir to provide disability confirmation under Russian standards.

[52] Ukaz Prezidenta RF ot 09.01.2011 No 26 'Ob utverzhdenii perechnya prigranichnyh territorij, na kotoryh inostrannye grazhdane, lica bez grazhdanstva i inostrannye yuridicheskie lica ne mogut obladat' na prave sobstvennosti zemel'nymi uchastkami' (Decree of the President of the RF dated 9 January 2011 No 26 'On approval of the list of border territories where foreign citizens, stateless persons and foreign legal entities are not allowed to own land plots').

[53] Article 28, Federal'nyj zakon ot 08.11.2007 No 261-FZ 'O morskih portah v Rossijskoj Federacii i o vnesenii izmenenij v otdel'nye zakonodatel'nye akty Rossijskoj Federacii' (Federal Law No 261-FZ dated 8 November 2007 'On Seaports in the Russian Federation and on Amendments to Certain Legislative Acts of the Russian Federation').

[54] Article 238 of the Civil Code, see also: V Ral'ko, 'Nasledstvennye prava inostrannyh grazhdan v Rossijskoj Federacii' ('Inheritance rights of foreign citizens in the Russian Federation') (2005) 4 *Notarius*.

[55] Article 1149 of the Civil Code.

[56] E Voytovich, 'Nasledovanie obyazatel'noj doli v mezhdunarodnom chastnom prave' ('Inheritance of a Compulsory Portion in Private International Law') (2018) 3 *Nasledstvennoe pravo* 42–46.

III. Testamentary Disposition

A. Legal Capacity

Whereas inheritance by will underlies the generic conflict rules of testate inheritance and completely falls within the sphere of application of *lex successionis*, testamentary capacity and form of the testament required by the legislator are governed by special conflict rules.

The conflict rule on testamentary capacity is set out by Article 1224(2) of the Civil Code. It provides that testamentary capacity is determined under the laws of the country where the testator had his place of habitual residence at the time of compilation of such a will or testamentary act.

Testamentary capacity determines a person's capacity to make a will and to grant rights and to impose duties on third parties. According to Russian substantive rules, a will can be created only by a person having full legal capacity. Testamentary capacity is a part of the more general concept of civic capacity. Under Russian PIL rules, the civic capacity of an individual will be determined by his/her citizenship. Russian citizens have full legal capacity at the age of 18, or, in exceptional cases, at the age of 16.[57] Legal capacity of foreigners and stateless persons is determined by their personal law (Articles 1195 and 1197 of the Civil Code). Thus, if a foreigner has not reached the age of full legal capacity under the law of his citizenship, he will not be permitted to make a will in Russia.

The connecting factor of habitual residence at the time of compilation of the will, applied to determine the capacity of a person to compile a will, has practical meaning. For example, the making of a will in the testator's country of temporary residence or even outside the territory of any state (for example, on the high seas) will not affect testamentary capacity. If the testator changes his place of habitual residence after compilation of the will, his legal capacity and the succession will be governed by different laws.

Testamentary capacity refers to the person's capacity not only to create a will, but also to revoke or to change it. The right to change the will is not mentioned in the Article 1224(2) because it is not allowed to change a will other than through creation of a new one,[58] while the revocation of a will cannot be accompanied by any other testamentary arrangements of the testator.

B. Formal Validity of the Will

The law applicable to the form of a will or act of its revocation provides that the form of the will shall be governed by the laws of the state where the testator had

[57] Articles 21 and 27 of the Civil Code.
[58] Article 1130(2) of the Civil Code.

his place of habitual residence at the time of drawing up the testamentary instrument. However, following the principle of *favor testamenti*, the law provides for an additional connecting factor stating that a will (or its revocation) may not be recognised as invalid as the result of mere non-observance of form, if it satisfies the requirements of either the place of creation of the will, or Russian law. Therefore, the Civil Code provides for three alternative connecting factors to be applied to the formal validity of a will: the testator's place of habitual residence at the time of making the will, the place of creation of the will, and Russian law. In fact, if a will (or the act of its revocation) conforms to the requirements of Russian law it shall be recognised as valid in the territory of the Russian Federation, even if its form does not comply with the legislation of the state where it was created.

The will, under Russian law, must be compiled in writing and notarised.[59] In certain cases, the law allows certification of the will by persons having special authorities or in written form without notarisation or certification for extraordinary circumstances. A will violating the legal requirements as to form is null and void.

[59] Article 1124 of the Civil Code.

10

Jurisdiction of Russian Courts in Civil and Commercial Cross-border Matters

ANDREY PANOV

I. The Russian Courts System and Allocation of Jurisdiction Among Russian Courts

The purpose of this chapter is to provide a brief overview of the international jurisdiction of Russian courts.

Russia has two branches of state courts: courts of general jurisdiction and *arbitrazh* (commercial) courts.[1]

Courts of general jurisdiction adjudicate civil disputes, primarily those involving individuals, including consumer disputes, labour, family, and inheritance matters. In addition to civil disputes, courts of general jurisdiction also hear and decide criminal and other public law matters, including judicial review cases that do not concern commercial activities. The Civil Procedural Code (the CPC) largely governs the civil procedure in the courts of general jurisdiction.

Courts adjudicating commercial matters are called *arbitrazh* courts. Despite the similarity of the name '*arbitrazh*' to arbitration, these courts are not arbitral tribunals, but are instead a part of the Russian state courts. They hear and decide commercial disputes between businesses or businesses and the state. Certain cases involving individuals also fall within the jurisdiction of the *arbitrazh* courts, in particular matters of individual personal bankruptcy and corporate disputes where the shareholders are individuals. The *Arbitrazh* Procedural Code (the APC) governs the civil procedure in the *arbitrazh* courts.

In addition to subject-matter jurisdiction, where the categories of disputes are allocated between two branches of Russian judiciary, Russian law also allocates jurisdiction among various courts of the same level within a particular

[1] In addition to these two branches, there is also a Constitutional Court of the Russian Federation, which is tasked with evaluating compliance of legislative provisions with the Constitution.

branch depending on their location (so called territorial jurisdiction). Being the biggest country in the world by territory, Russia has numerous courts spread across its territory. Thus, there are over 2,000 district courts of general jurisdiction that resolve the majority of cases as courts of first instance.[2] There are also 85 *arbitrazh* courts of first instance (one per each of the regions or units of the Russian Federation, such as the *Arbitrazh* Court of the City of Moscow or the *Arbitrazh* Court of Samara Region).

As a general rule, unless another court has exclusive jurisdiction over a dispute,[3] cases must be brought in the district court (in civil cases) or *arbitrazh* court (in commercial cases) of the place of the respondent's domicile or incorporation.[4] In certain circumstances, the claimant may choose to commence proceedings in a court of the claimant's domicile.[5] If the respondent's current whereabouts are unknown, cases can only be brought in the court of the place where the respondent's assets are located.[6] In some cases, claims can also be brought in the court of a place which is closely connected with the subject-matter of the dispute.[7]

Prior to 2014, each of the two branches had its own highest court. The Russian Supreme Court was the highest court in the system of the courts of general jurisdiction, whereas the Russian Supreme *Arbitrazh* Court was the last instance court in commercial matters heard by the *arbitrazh* courts. However, as of 6 August 2014, the Russian Supreme Court became the highest instance for both branches of the Russian courts, and the Supreme *Arbitrazh* Court was abolished.

Even though Russia is a civil law system with no formal doctrine of precedent, over the past years, jurisprudence has started to play a more significant role for the day-to-day practice of Russian lawyers. This is mostly due to publication of all judgments and rulings of *arbitrazh* courts on the Internet,[8] which has allowed lawyers to rely on court practice to support their arguments. The trend is less visible in the courts of general jurisdiction, where the judgments and rulings only recently became easily accessible. Furthermore, the Russian Supreme Court (and prior to

[2] The smallest civil cases are resolved by justices of the peace, and the appeals against their rulings and judgments would be heard by the district courts. However, this is hardly relevant in the context of cross-border litigation.

[3] Examples of when the courts would have exclusive jurisdiction and hence the case can only be commenced at such a court include: actions *in rem* in relation to real estate – the *arbitrazh* or district court at the place where the real estate is located (Article 30(1) of the CPC and Article 38(1) of the APC); actions in corporate disputes – the *arbitrazh* court at the place of incorporation of the relevant entity (Article 38(4.1) of the APC); actions in bankruptcy – the *arbitrazh* court at the place of incorporation of the entity or domicile of an individual (Article 38(4) of the APC); etc.

[4] Article 28 of the CPC and Article 35 of the APC.

[5] For example, in maintenance or filiation cases, or in cases of torts arising out of causing bodily harm (Article 29(3) and (5) of the CPC).

[6] Article 29(1) of the CPC and Article 36(1) of the APC.

[7] For example, at the place where the contract was performed or ought to have been performed (Article 36(4) of the APC).

[8] All judgments and rulings of the *arbitrazh* courts in all matters (other than those which are heard in private) started being published online since 2010.

6 August 2014, also the Supreme *Arbitrazh* Court), from time to time, issues guidance in relation to various aspects of Russian procedural and substantive law, most importantly in the form of Resolutions of the Plenum of the Supreme Court. These Resolutions not only provide authoritative interpretation of legislation, but also develop law and new principles which cannot be found in statutes.

II. International Jurisdiction of Russian Courts

Both Russian courts of general jurisdiction and *arbitrazh* courts have their own rules on international jurisdiction. At the same time, jurisprudence in cross-border commercial cases is by far more developed than for civil, non-commercial cases. In addition to statutory provisions in the CPC and APC, the main document outlining principles of international jurisdiction in cross-border commercial matters is the Resolution of the Plenum of the Supreme Court No 23 dated 27 June 2017 (Resolution No 23).

For the question of international jurisdiction to arise, a dispute must have a certain foreign (non-Russian) element. Usually, it would be involvement of at least one party with a place of incorporation, nationality, or domicile outside of Russia.[9] Proper analysis to determine where a claim involving a certain foreign element should be brought includes two steps: first, one needs to determine whether the case in question could in principle be commenced in the Russian courts (ie, whether there is international jurisdiction);[10] and secondly, once international jurisdiction of the Russian courts is established, one needs to understand at which specific court in Russia the claimant should file the claim.[11]

A place of incorporation,[12] nationality, or domicile of the parties may change as the proceedings progress. However, if a Russian court has grounds to assume jurisdiction over a matter when the claim if brought, it considers the case on the merits, and any subsequent changes with respect to parties' place of incorporation, nationality, or domicile does not take away the jurisdiction from the Russian court.[13]

[9] In certain cases, the subject-matter of a dispute can also give rise to a conflict of jurisdictions. For example, where a dispute between two Russian parties concerns rights *in rem* over real estate located in a different country it is likely that the foreign court would have jurisdiction over the matter despite both litigants being Russian. The same logic may apply in the case of a contractual dispute between two Russian parties, where the place of performance is in a different country. The courts at the place of performance may have jurisdiction over the matter; however, for a Russian court there would be no conflict of jurisdictions issue, other than in the context of *lis pendens*.

[10] This is determined by Articles 402–404 of the CPC and Articles 247–249 of the APC.

[11] This question is answered by reference to the same provisions of the procedural codes which apply in the absence of any foreign element (Chapter 3 of the CPC and Chapter 4 of the APC).

[12] Russian procedural codes use the term 'location', which usually refers to the registered legal address of an entity in question.

[13] Article 405 of the CPC and Article 247(4) of the APC.

A. Statutory Jurisdiction of Russian Courts

Rules on international jurisdiction differ somewhat under the CPC and the APC.

For the courts of general jurisdiction, the starting point in the analysis is whether the respondent is domiciled (in case of an individual) or located (in case of an entity) in Russia. If this is the case, a Russian or a foreign[14] claimant can start proceedings against such a respondent in the Russian courts.[15] Jurisdiction among the various Russian courts is allocated in accordance with the rules briefly outlined above.

In addition to the general rule of jurisdiction at the respondent's location or domicile in Russia, the CPC allows the claimant to choose a Russian court in certain circumstances. The relevant factors may relate to the respondent, the cause of action, or the domicile or nationality of the claimant. Thus, non-Russian respondents can be sued in Russia, if their assets are located in Russia or they advertise products to Russian consumers on the Internet,[16] or where a foreign entity has its management body, branch, or representative office located in Russia.[17] With respect to the assets, it may be sufficient that the assets are present in Russia temporarily. For example, a maritime claim may be brought against a foreign respondent if, at the time of bringing the claim, the vessel is located in a Russian seaport.[18]

A claimant domiciled in Russia may bring the following claims against a foreign respondent in Russian courts:

- claims for maintenance or filiation;[19]
- tortious claims arising out of causing bodily harm or death;[20]
- divorce claims;[21]
- defamation claims;[22]
- claims arising out of a breach in relation to personal data handling;[23] and
- claims to be forgotten.[24]

[14] There is no definition of a 'foreign' party in the CPC. Chapter 43 of the CPC, which deals with international jurisdiction of the courts of general jurisdiction, applies to cases involving foreign citizens, apatrides, foreign companies and international organisations (Article 398(1) of the CPC).

[15] Article 402(2) of the CPC.

[16] Article 402(3)(2) of the CPC.

[17] Article 402(3)(1) of the CPC.

[18] Paragraph 2 of the Resolution of the Plenum of the Supreme Court of the Russian Federation No 18 dated 20 November 2003.

[19] Article 402(3)(3) of the CPC.

[20] Article 402(3)(4) of the CPC. Note that this type of claim can also be brought in Russia if the harm was caused in Russia.

[21] Article 402(3)(8) of the CPC. Note that a divorce claim may still be brought in Russia irrespective of the domicile of the parties, if at least one of the spouses is a Russian citizen.

[22] Article 402(3)(9) of the CPC.

[23] Article 402(3)(10) of the CPC.

[24] Article 402(3)(11) of the CPC. This right under Russian law is somewhat analogous to the right codified in Article 17 of the EU General Data Protection Regulation.

Furthermore, the claimant may bring claims in Russia, if:

- in relation to tortious claims arising out of causing bodily harm or death, the harm was caused in Russia;[25]
- in relation to tortious liability arising out of causing harm to property, the harmful act took place in Russia;[26]
- in relation to a contractual claim, the contract was or ought to have been performed in full or in part in Russia;[27] and
- in relation to restitution claims, the unjust enrichment took place in Russia.[28]

There are also a number of cases where the Russian courts of general jurisdiction would have exclusive international jurisdiction, namely:

- in cases concerning rights *in rem* over immovable property located in Russia;
- in matters arising out of carriage agreements, if the carrier is located in Russia;
- in divorce cases between a Russian and a foreign citizen (or an *apatride* (stateless person)), if both persons are domiciled it Russia.

The APC approaches the question of international jurisdiction in commercial matters slightly differently. For a Russian court to assume jurisdiction in a commercial matter, a case must have close connection to Russia (Article 247(1)(10) of the APC). The APC also provides a non-exhaustive list of factors, which would weigh in favour of a close connection with the territory of the Russian state. These factors may relate to the respondent, the subject-matter, or the claimant.

A close connection is presumed when the respondent is located or domiciled in Russia,[29] where their assets are located in Russia,[30] or where the management body, branch or representative office of a foreign entity is located in Russia.[31]

The only instance where the close connection is presumed based on the location of the claimant in Russia relates to cases concerning business reputational harm.[32] Thus, for example, if a foreign person has published damaging statements on the Internet, the Russian claimant may bring claims against such a person in the Russian courts, irrespective of whether the claimant can show any harm occurring in Russia or whether the respondent targeted a Russian audience with

[25] Article 402(3)(4) of the CPC.

[26] Article 402(3)(5) of the CPC.

[27] Article 402(3)(6) of the CPC. For example, Russian courts assumed jurisdiction over a claim by Russian citizens against Facebook Inc, because the relationships between the parties were governed by the Users' Agreement, which was to be performed in Russia (see Ruling of the Supreme Court dated 9 June 2020, No 5-КГ20-49, M-10004763/19).

[28] Article 402(3)(7) of the CPC.

[29] Article 247(1)(1) of the APC.

[30] Ibid.

[31] Article 247(1)(2) of the APC. To the extent that the claim arises out of the activities of the relevant branch or representative office.

[32] Article 247(1)(6) of the APC. Article 402(3)(9) of the CPC contains identical provision for cases concerning a person's reputation.

its statements. The fact that the claimant is in Russia is sufficient to establish jurisdiction for the Russian courts in such a matter.

A close connection is also presumed for the purposes of international jurisdiction where Russia is:

- a place where the performance under the contract took place or ought to have taken place;
- a place where the damage to a property occurred or where the harmful event occurred;
- a place where the unjust enrichment took place;
- a place of issue of securities which are the subject-matter of the dispute, etc.[33]

Even where the case has a close connection to Russia by virtue of one or more of the criteria above, it does not prevent foreign courts from assuming jurisdiction over the matter if the jurisdiction of Russian courts is non-exclusive. However, where Russian *arbitrazh* courts have exclusive jurisdiction over the matter, only Russian courts are presumed to have jurisdiction. Examples of exclusive jurisdiction include:

- disputes over state property of the Russian Federation, including privatisation or expropriation disputes;
- disputes in relation to rights *in rem* over real estate in Russia;
- disputes concerning entries in the Russian public registries;
- disputes concerning establishment, registration or liquidation of legal entities in Russia, as well as the challenges to corporate resolutions of relevant entities; etc.[34]

Any judgment of a foreign court rendered in breach of the exclusive jurisdiction of the Russian courts is unenforceable in Russia.[35]

B. Choice of Court Agreements

Instead of relying on the statutory criteria for jurisdiction, parties may choose a forum for their dispute. Article 404 of the CPC very briefly notes this possibility, and provides that such an agreement cannot alter the exclusive jurisdiction of the Russian courts of general jurisdiction. In practice, choice of court agreements seem to be rare in cross-border civil, non-commercial cases.

In contrast, forum selection clauses are rather common in commercial contexts. Russian courts' jurisprudence developed and expanded the principle of

[33] Article 247(1) APC.

[34] Article 248 of the APC.

[35] Article 244(1)(3) of the APC and paragraph 4 of Resolution of the Plenum of the Supreme Court of the RF dated 27.06.2017 No 23 'On Consideration by Arbitrazh Courts of Cases on Economic Disputes Arising from Relations With a Foreign Element'.

party autonomy. The principle also appears in the APC. Article 249(1) of the APC provides that where parties, at least one of which is a non-Russian person, have entered into a forum selection agreement in favour of the Russian *arbitrazh* courts, such courts will have exclusive jurisdiction over the matter,[36] provided that the agreement does not violate the exclusive jurisdiction of foreign courts.

Foreign parties may agree to refer their disputes to Russian courts.[37] There is no need for the case to have any Russian nexus.

No APC or CPC provision prevents Russian parties from choosing a foreign court as the forum for resolution of their disputes. Whether the selected foreign court would entertain jurisdiction in a case involving two Russian parties based on a forum selection clause is a question of the *lex fori*. However, Russian courts will disregard the clause if it purports to alter Russian rules on exclusive jurisdiction.

Even though there is no direct statutory rule to this effect, the Russian Supreme Court pointed out that any jurisdictional objection (with reference to a forum selection clause or otherwise) must be made before the party's first statement on the merits of the dispute.[38]

The only legislative requirement in relation to a choice of forum agreement is that it shall be in writing.[39] The form requirement will be met not only where the agreement is included in a single document executed by the parties, but also if it is concluded:

- through an exchange of documents or correspondence (including electronic correspondence);
- through an exchange of submissions, where one party alleges the existence of a choice of forum agreement and the other party does not raise any objection in this regard; or
- through incorporation by reference to a document containing a forum selection clause, provided that the reference clearly shows an intention to make such a clause part of the contract.[40]

Paragraph 10 of Resolution No 23 underlines that the principle of separability applies to forum selection clauses. This means that invalidity of an underlying contract does not necessarily lead to invalidity of a choice of court clause. In other words, generally, a forum selection agreement is not affected by invalidity or non-existence of the main agreement. Furthermore, a choice of court clause generally survives expiration or termination of the underlying contract, unless the parties agree otherwise.

Russian jurisprudence also developed rules applicable in case of a change of the parties to the underlying contract. In this case, the forum selection clause

[36] See also para 6 of Resolution No 23.
[37] Ibid.
[38] Paragraph 11 of Resolution No 23.
[39] Article 249(2) of the APC.
[40] Paragraph 6 of Resolution No 23.

would bind both the prior and new party to the underlying contract, unless agreed otherwise.[41]

In terms of the requirements as to the content of a forum selection clause, the Russian legislation is silent. The court practice only requires that such an agreement shows an intent of the parties to refer the despite to an *arbitrazh* court.[42] If the parties fail to specify a particular court in Russia, it will be determined according to the general rules on jurisdiction.[43]

C. Jurisdiction of Russian Courts to Issue Interim Measures

Until now, the discussion in this chapter has concerned jurisdiction to resolve a case on its merits. However, Russian courts may also have jurisdiction to issue interim measures while the case on the merits is heard elsewhere.

The applicable statutory provision is Article 250 of the APC, which states that the Russian *arbitrazh* court may grant interim relief in cases over which the court has jurisdiction under Articles 247–249 of the APC. This does not mean, however, that the proceedings on the merits must necessarily be conducted before the Russian court.[44]

There is no statutory provision allowing Russian courts to issue interim measures if the case on the merits is to be decided by a foreign court. However, jurisprudence of the *arbitrazh* courts developed the principle of 'efficient jurisdiction' with respect to interim measures.[45] This principle was later adopted by the Russian Supreme Court in paragraph 49 of the Resolution No 23, which provided that even where a Russian court has no jurisdiction to hear the case on the merits, it can still issue interim measures in support of foreign proceedings, if it would be efficient to do so. This means that its measures can be quickly and efficiently enforced. An *arbitrazh* court at the location of the applicant, or at the location of the assets with respect to which the measures are sought, or at the place where the applicant's rights were breached would have efficient jurisdiction with respect to interim measures in support of foreign proceedings.

[41] Paragraph 9 of Resolution No 23.

[42] Paragraph 8 of Resolution No 23.

[43] Chapter 3 of the CPC and Chapter 4 of the APC.

[44] Russian courts can also order interim measures in support of arbitral proceedings, irrespective of whether those proceedings are seated in Russia or abroad (Article 139(3) of the CPC and Article 90(3) of the APC). The courts at the place of arbitration, or location or domicile of the respondent or the respondent's assets have jurisdiction over such applications.

[45] The principle was first proposed in the case of *Teorema* (case No A56-95127/2009) in 2010 by a cassation court (see Resolution of the Federal *Arbitrazh* Court for the North-Western Circuit dated 29 July 2010). In this case, the courts eventually issued interim measures freezing certain Russian assets of a foreign respondent and prohibiting the respondent from undertaking certain actions in Russia. The measures effectively mirrored a freezing injunction issued by a Cyprus court, which was also considering the case on the merits.

D. Jurisdiction of Russian Courts in Matters Involving Sanctioned Persons

One rather peculiar feature of Russian procedural law is that it provides for exclusive jurisdiction of the Russian courts in cases involving persons affected by foreign sanctions. These rules were introduced in mid-2020 with a view of ensuring that the sanctioned persons who experience difficulties with access to justice outside of Russia due to the sanctions could have their cases resolved by the Russian *arbitrazh* courts.

Under Article 248.1 of the APC, the Russian *arbitrazh* courts have exclusive jurisdiction over the disputes involving sanctioned persons, unless there is a treaty or an agreement between the parties that provides otherwise. If there is an arbitration or a choice of court clause, the exclusive jurisdiction of the Russian courts only arises under Article 248.1(4) of the APC if:

- the clause provides for resolution of the dispute in a foreign court or arbitral tribunal, and
- the clause becomes inoperative due to the sanctions against a party to the proceedings, which create obstacles to access to justice for such a party.

Russian courts can also restrain the parties from issuing or continuing proceedings abroad against a Russian sanctioned person. If a Russian court has exclusive jurisdiction pursuant to Article 248.1 of the APC and there is evidence that the foreign party has commenced or is about to commence foreign court proceedings, or arbitration proceedings are pending or appear imminent, the sanctioned person can request the Russian court to issue an anti-suit injunction against the opposing party under Article 248.2 of the APC.

Initially, Russian courts tried to distinguish between asset freezes and sectoral sanctions, however, in December 2021, the Russian Supreme Court rendered a landmark decision in the case of *Ural Transport Machinery Construction Company JSC (Uraltransmash) v Pojazdy Szynowe PESA Bydgoszcz Spolka Akcyjna (PESA)*,[46] which changed the approach of Russian courts.

The *Uraltransmash* case involved a contract for supply of tram cars by PESA, a Polish producer of rolling stock, to Uraltransmash, a Russian transportation conglomerate. The contract provided for arbitration under the rules of the Arbitration Institution at the Stockholm Chamber of Commerce (the SCC). The contract was signed in 2013. From September 2014, Uraltransmash was subject to the EU sanctions.[47] The sanctions in question concerned a prohibition by which it was forbidden 'to directly or indirectly purchase, sell, provide investment services for or assistance in the issuance of, or otherwise deal with transferable securities and money-market instruments with a maturity exceeding 30 days,

[46] Ruling of the Supreme Court dated 9 December 2021 in case No A60-36897/2020.
[47] Pursuant to Article 5(2)(c) of Council Regulation (EU) No 833/2014 of 31 July 2014 (as amended).

issued [by Uraltransmash] after 12 September 2014' (Article 5(2)(c) of the Council Regulation (EU) No 833/2014 of 31 July 2014). These sanctions, however, did not affect the performance of the contract with PESA.

In 2019, PESA commenced arbitration at the SCC for unpaid price and contractual and statutory interest and penalties (over EUR 55 million in total). However, Uraltransmash commenced proceedings in the Russian courts under Articles 248.1 and 248.2 of the APC seeking an anti-suit injunction against PESA.

The lower courts were not convinced that the sanctions made the arbitration agreement inoperative or created any obstacles for Uraltransmash's participation in arbitration proceedings at the SCC. The courts found that the sanctions did not concern the contract in question. Moreover, the courts noted that Uraltransmash had made payments in Euros to PESA under the contract after the EU sanctions were introduced. Furthermore, the courts pointed out that Uraltransmash had in fact participated in the arbitration proceedings at the SCC, had paid its share of the advance on costs, appointed an arbitrator, hired legal counsel, and made submissions throughout the proceedings. Therefore, the lower courts refused to apply Article 248.1(4) of the APC.

The Russian Supreme Court initially agreed with the lower courts, but subsequently took a different approach to the interpretation of Article 248.1 of the APC. It found that Article 248.1 of the APC did not require the sanctioned person to prove the existence of obstacles to the access to justice. Instead, the very fact of introduction of sanctions against a Russian person is sufficient to conclude that there are obstacles to access to justice for such a person in a foreign state that has introduced such sanctions. The panel reasoned that the sanctions are always personal and are issued by the public authorities. Therefore, they necessarily affect the sanctioned person's rights, or at least their reputation. For this reason, they put the sanctioned person on an unequal footing with other parties to the proceedings. On this basis, the Russian Supreme Court concluded that there are serious doubts that the sanctioned person's due process rights will be observed and that it will be able to obtain justice in a state that has introduced sanctions. Accordingly, Article 248.1 of the APC only requires a unilateral declaration from a sanctioned person who can choose whether to pursue the case in a foreign court or arbitral tribunal, or avail itself of the exclusive jurisdiction of the Russian courts.

Therefore, the wording of Article 248.1(4) of the APC clearly requires that the sanctions hinder access to justice for the sanctioned party, which implies that such hindrance must be demonstrated. The Russian Supreme Court, however, introduced a *presumption* that the very existence of sanctions creates obstacles to access to justice. This presumption is for the non-sanctioned parties to rebut.

Unsurprisingly, following the *Uraltransmash* decision, Russian courts routinely assumed exclusive jurisdiction over matters if the interested party could show that it was subject to some sanctions. For example, in the case of *A1 Capital Limited (Cyprus) v Credit Suisse AG (Switzerland)*, Russian courts assumed jurisdiction by reference to Article 248.1 of the APC, on the basis of sanctions against the claimant's beneficiaries.[48] In the case of *Sberbank v Glencore Energy UK Ltd*, the court also assumed jurisdiction and disregarded the SIAC arbitration clause without even mentioning sanctions against Sberbank.[49] Article 248.1 of the APC allows Russian *arbitrazh* courts to decide underlying dispute on the merits; however, the international enforceability of judgments rendered on the basis of Articles 248.1 and 248.2 of the APC remains questionable.

[48] Judgment of the *Arbitrazh* Court of the City of Moscow dated 29 June 2023 in case No A40-191489/2022.

[49] Judgment of the *Arbitrazh* Court of the City of Moscow dated 28 February 2023 in case No A40-237252/2022.

11

Recognition and Enforcement of Foreign Judgments

OLGA KAMENSKAIA AND EGOR CHILIKOV

A foreign judgment does not have legal effect in Russia until it is lawfully recognised and enforced. The recognition and enforcement may be carried out pursuant to the terms of an international treaty to which Russia is a party, or, in the absence thereof, under the doctrine of reciprocity. Depending on the terms of an applicable treaty, a foreign judgment may or may not need an *exequatur* by a Russian court to have legal effect in Russia.

This chapter discusses the framework for recognition and enforcement of foreign judgments in Russia. It identifies the network of relevant multilateral and bilateral international treaties, and analyses the doctrine of reciprocity, which may serve as an alternative gateway to enforcement of a foreign judgment in Russia. The chapter then provides an overview of the procedure on recognition and enforcement of foreign judgments.

I. General Framework

The framework for recognition and enforcement of foreign judgments is set out in international treaties, federal laws (predominantly, procedural codes) and in case law.

A. International Treaties and Models of *Exequatur*

International treaties are the principal source of rules on recognition and enforcement of foreign judgments in Russia: Russian federal laws provide that international treaties determine the status of foreign judgments in Russia.[1] The

[1] Paragraph 2 of Article 6 of Federal'nyj konstitutsionnyj zakon ot 31.12.1996 No. 1-FKZ 'O Sudebnoy Sisteme Rossiyskoy Federatsii' (Federal Constitutional Law 'On Judiciary System of the

Russian Constitution places international treaties above federal laws in the hierarchy of sources of law.[2]

Russia is a party to a network of multilateral and bilateral treaties with certain distinct provisions on recognition and enforcement of foreign judgments, as described below.

International treaties commonly provide for one of three models pursuant to which a foreign judgment obtains legal effect in Russia. Under one model, both recognition and enforcement are carried out by an act of a Russian court permitting a foreign judgment to produce a legal effect in Russia. Such act would be formally referred in official texts as a 'ruling on (granting/refusal of) recognition and enforcement of a foreign judgment.' Such acts are also referred to as *exequatur* in this chapter, though this term is not often used in Russian legislation or judicial decisions.

Under another model, recognition of a judgment takes effect by operation of a treaty (no *exequatur* is required), while enforcement still requires an *exequatur* of a Russian court. This is a widespread model for many international treaties to which Russia is a party and a default model for the Russian Procedural Codes of the two branches of courts.

Finally, under the most liberal model, foreign judgments are considered fully equal in validity to Russian judgments, so that they are recognised and enforced as Russian judgments by operation of a treaty (no *exequatur* is required). The latter model has been used in very few regional treaties so far, such as the 2001 Treaty between Russia and Belarus.[3]

These models will be further referred to respectively as Full Exequatur Model, Half Exequatur Model and No Exequatur Model.

Boundaries between the models are not firmly observed in practice. While an *exequatur* may not be required, a party to a foreign judgment may still want to request a court to grant it, as it may facilitate further use of the foreign judgment in Russia. Some treaties were designed pursuant to the No Exequatur Model, but are construed as requiring an *exequatur* nonetheless (see, for example, comments regarding the 1992 Kiev Treaty[4]).

Russian Federation' dated 31 December 1996 No 1-FKZ); para 5 of Article 13 and Article 409 of Grazhdanskiy Protsessualniy Kodeks Rossiyskoy Federatsii ot 14.11.2002 No 138-FZ (Civil Procedural Code of the Russian Federation dated 14 November 2002 No 138-FZ); para 4 of Article 16 and Article 241 of Arbitrazhniy Protsessualniy Kodeks Rossiskoy Federatsii ot 24.07.2002 No 95-FZ (*Arbitrazh* Procedure Code of the Russian Federation dated 24 July 2002 No 95-FZ); Article 11 of Federal'nyj zakon ot 02.10.2007 No 229-FZ 'Ob Ispolnitel'nom Proizvodstve' (Federal Law of the Russian Federation 'On Enforcement Proceedings' dated 02 October 2007 No 229-FZ); Article 1 of Federal'nyj Zakon ot 26.10.2002 No 127-FZ 'O Nesostoyatel'nosti (Bankrotstve)' (Federal Law 'On insolvency (bankruptcy)' dated 06 October 2002 No 127-FZ).

[2] Article 15(4) of Konstitutsiya Rossiyskoy Federatsii (Constitution of the Russian Federation), adopted by national vote on 12 December 1993.

[3] Treaty between the Russian Federation and the Republic of Belarus dated 17 January 2001 'On the Procedure of Mutual Enforcement of Judicial Decisions of *Arbitrazh* Courts of the Russian Federation and Commercial Courts of the Republic of Belarus.'

[4] The Treaty on the Procedure of Resolution of Disputes Connected with the Performance of Commercial Activities, signed in Kiev on 20 March 1992 (the 1992 Kiev Treaty).

B. Procedural Codes, Other Federal Laws, and the Role of Courts

It follows from international treaties that, should recognition and enforcement not happen by operation of a treaty, Russian courts are tasked to consider and issue an act of recognition or enforcement of a foreign judgment (*exequatur*), pursuant to an applicable procedure.

The Russian judiciary system comprises two types of courts competent to adjudicate in civil matters: courts of general jurisdiction and *arbitrazh* (commercial) courts. In broad terms, the latter are specialised courts for 'economic' disputes, which predominantly comprise disputes involving legal entities and entrepreneurs, and the former have residual jurisdiction to adjudicate in the remainder of civil matters.

Both branches of courts are competent to carry out recognition and enforcement of foreign judgments within their jurisdiction. If a foreign judgment concerns an 'economic' matter, then an *arbitrazh* court is competent to rule on its recognition and enforcement.

Each branch of courts has its own procedural code: the courts of general jurisdiction act on the basis of the Civil Procedure Code[5] and *arbitrazh* courts hear cases under the *Arbitrazh* (Commercial) Procedure Code (the Codes are further referred to jointly as the Procedural Codes).[6]

The Codes provide for the general (and rather homogeneous) framework for recognition and enforcement of foreign judgments.[7] The approach of both Codes originates from the 1998 Decree of the Union of the Soviet and Socialist Republics (USSR) 'On recognition and enforcement of decisions of foreign courts and arbitration tribunals'.[8] Accordingly, the Codes treat foreign judgments similarly.

The opening provision of Article 409 of the Civil Procedure Code reads as follows: 'Decisions of foreign courts, including the decisions on approval of settlement agreements, are recognised and enforced in the Russian Federation, if an international agreement of the Russian Federation so provides.' It follows from this paragraph that an international treaty is not only a source of law on recognition and enforcement of foreign judgments, but also the only predicate to the recognition and enforcement of a foreign judgment by a Russian court. Article 241(1) of the *Arbitrazh* (Commercial) Procedure Code contains a similar provision.

[5] Grazhdanskiy Protsessualniy Kodeks Rossiyskoy Federatsii ot 14.11.2002 No 138-FZ (Civil Procedural Code of the Russian Federation dated 14 November 2002 No 138-FZ).

[6] Arbitrazhniy Protsessualniy Kodeks Rossiskoy Federatsii ot 24.07.2002 No 95-FZ (*Arbitrazh* Procedure Code of the Russian Federation dated 24 July 2002 No 95-FZ).

[7] Chapter 45 of the Civil Procedure Code and Chapter 31 of the *Arbitrazh* Procedure Code.

[8] Ukaz Prezidiuma Verhovnogo Soveta SSSR ot 21.06.1988 No 9131-XI 'O Priznanii i Ispolnenii v SSSR Resheniy Inostrannyh Sudov i Arbitrazhey' (Decree of the Presidium of the Supreme Soviet of the USSR dated 21 June 1988 No 9131-XI 'On Recognition and Enforcement in the USSR of Decisions of Foreign Courts and Arbitration Tribunals'). The Decree is still in force and applies in so far as it does not contradict the provisions of the Procedural Codes.

Russian courts have, however, been shown to construe these provisions broadly, such that recognition and enforcement is allowed in the absence of an international treaty, based on the doctrine of reciprocity, as outlined below. Therefore, pursuant to the Russian case law, international treaties may not be the only predicate to the recognition and enforcement of foreign judgments.

In bankruptcy matters, recognition and enforcement of foreign judgments is set forth in the Federal Law of the Russian Federation 'On insolvency (bankruptcy).'[9] Article 1(6) of this law provides for recognition of acts of foreign courts in bankruptcy matters in accordance with international treaties to which Russia is a party. It further expressly allows for recognition of decisions of foreign courts on the basis of reciprocity. This is the only reference to the principle of reciprocity as an available ground for recognition of foreign judgments in the Russian federal laws.

Actual enforcement of judgments is governed by the Federal Law 'On Enforcement Proceedings' (further referred to as the Enforcement Law) and is carried out by the Federal Bailiff Service.[10] Article 11 of the Enforcement Law provides that enforcement of foreign judgments is carried out pursuant to international treaties and federal laws. The Federal Bailiff Service would from time-to-time issue so-called 'methodological recommendations' on the enforcement of judgments with guidance to bailiffs on various enforcement issues. With regard to the enforcement of *foreign* judgments, the Federal Bailiff Service has approved the methodological recommendations 'On the fulfilment of international obligations of the Russian Federation in the course of enforcement of the judicial acts',[11] which covers a variety of procedural questions as well as providing the list of international treaties of the Russian Federation enabling recognition and enforcement of foreign judgments on a country-by-country basis.

C. Case Law

The courts in Russia have developed approaches to construction of international treaties and federal laws as to the recognition and enforcement of foreign judgments. Some of the approaches have been upheld by the highest courts and are therefore either formally binding upon lower courts or are being followed by lower courts as authoritative guidance.[12]

[9] Federal'nyj Zakon ot 26.10.2002 No 127-FZ 'O Nesostoyatel'nosti (Bankrotstve)' (Federal Law of the Russian Federation 'On insolvency (bankruptcy)' dated 6 October 2002 No 127-FZ).

[10] Federal'nyj zakon ot 02.10.2007 No 229-FZ 'Ob Ispolnitel'nom Proizvodstve' (Federal Law of the Russian Federation 'On Enforcement Proceedings' dated 2 October 2007 No 229-FZ).

[11] Pis'mo FSSP Rossii ot 29.07.2016 No 00071/16/69976-AP 'O napravlenii Metodicheskih rekomendacij' (Letter of the Federal Bailiff Service of Russia dated 29 July 2016 No 00071/16/69976-AP 'On the submission of Methodological recommendations').

[12] Postanovlenie Plenuma Verhovnogo Suda RF ot 27.06.2017 No 23 'O rassmotrenii arbitrazhnymi sudami del po ekonomicheskim sporam, voznikayushchim iz otnoshenij, oslozhnennyh inostrannym

The courts have been the principal developers of the doctrine of reciprocity, which allows for recognition and enforcement of a foreign judgment despite the absence of an international treaty.

D. Recognition and Enforcement – Meaning of the Divide

Recognition and enforcement refer to two different types of treatment of a foreign judgment in Russia.

A mere recognition of a judgment may be sufficient if the judgment, for example, declares a contract terminated or a breach to have occurred. Then, such foreign judgment, declaratory in nature, is recognised in Russia similarly to a judgment of a Russian court.

The Procedural Codes provide that foreign judgments are recognised (but not enforced) without an *exequatur*. This means that the Half Exequatur Model is currently set as a default model in the Procedural Codes. However, it remains disputed whether a gateway to recognition – a relevant international treaty or an established reciprocity – is still needed for a no *exequatur* recognition of a foreign judgment. A conservative reading views it as necessary. If an interested party disagrees with the no *exequatur* recognition of a foreign judgment, it may seek a negative *exequatur* from the competent Russian court.[13] An international treaty may provide for a different set of rules regulating this matter, which will prevail over these default rules.

Beyond mere recognition, a judgment creditor may need to enforce a foreign judgment to have it executed in Russia, through the Federal Bailiff Service or otherwise. For example, enforcement of a judgment is needed when its operative part reads that a judgment debtor should pay a sum of money, hand over an asset, or do something for the benefit of a judgment creditor. Then the judgment creditor needs to pursue the enforcement through a Russian court (*exequatur*) and, if the

elementom' (Resolution of the Plenum of the Supreme Court of the RF dated 27 June 2017 No 23 'On Consideration by Arbitrazh Courts of Cases on Economic Disputes Arising from Relations With a Foreign Element'); Informatsionnoe Pismo Presidiuma VAS RF ot 22.12.2005 No 96 'Obzor praktiki rassmotreniya arbitrazhnymi sudami del o priznanii i privedenii v ispolnenie resheniy inostrannyh sudov, ob osparivanii resheniy treteyskih sudov i o vydache ispolnitel'nyh listov na prinuditel'noe ispolnenie resheniy treteyskih sudov' (Information Letter of the Presidium of the Highest Arbitrazh Court dated 22 December 2005 No 96 'The Overview of the Practice of Consideration by Arbitrazh Courts of Cases Concerning the Recognition and Enforcement of Foreign Judgments, on Appeal of Arbitral Awards, and on Issuance of Writs on Enforcement of Arbitral Awards'); Informatsionnoe Pismo Presidiuma VAS RF ot 26.02.2013 No 156 'Obzor praktiki rassmotreniya arbitrazhnymi sudami del o primenenii ogovorki o publichnom poryadke kak osnovaniya otkaza v priznanii i privedenii v ispolnenie inostrannyh sudebnyh i arbitrazhnyh resheniy' (Information Letter of the Presidium of the Highest Arbitrazh Court dated 26 February 2013 No 156 'The Overview of the Practice of Consideration by Arbitrazh Courts of Cases Concerning the Application of Public Policy Reservation as the Ground for Refusal in Recognition and Enforcement of Foreign Judgments and Arbitral Awards').

[13] Article 413(2) of the Civil Procedure Code and Article 245.1(3) of the *Arbitrazh* Procedure Code.

judgment is not voluntarily complied with, approach the Federal Bailiffs Service to carry out the execution.

Enforcement of a judgment entails its recognition as well. However, recognition of a judgment does not automatically entail its enforcement.

II. Two Gateways to Recognition and Enforcement: Treaties and Reciprocity

There are two predicates for recognition and enforcement of a foreign judgment: an international treaty or the doctrine of reciprocity.

A. International Treaties

Russia is a party to several multilateral and many bilateral treaties enabling recognition and enforcement of foreign judicial acts. In many cases, treaties pre-date the dissolution of the USSR, and Russia became a party to such treaties as the legal successor of the USSR.[14] The full list of international treaties to which Russia is a party and their status is published on the official website of the Ministry of Foreign Affairs of the Russian Federation.[15]

(i) Regional Multilateral Treaties

The main regional treaties among former USSR states are the 1992 Kiev Treaty on settling disputes related to commercial activities,[16] the 1993 Minsk Convention

[14] Article 67.1(1) of Konstitutsiya Rossiyskoy Federatsii (Constitution of the Russian Federation); Article 1(3) of Federal'niy Zakon ot 15.07.1995 No 101-FZ 'O Mezhdunarodnykh Dogovorakh Rossiyskoy Federatssii' (Federal Law of the Russian Federation 'On the International Treaties of the Russian Federation' dated 15 July 1995 No 101-FZ); Nota Ministerstva Inostrannykh Del RF of 13.01.1992 No 11/Ugp 'O Prodolzhenii Osuschestvleniya Prav i Vypolnenii Obyazatel'stv Vytekauschikh iz Mezhdunarodnykh Dogovorov i Soglasheniy Zakluchennykh SSSR' (Diplomatic Note of Foreign Affairs Ministry of the Russian Federation dated 13 January 1992 No 11/Ugp 'On Continuation of Exercising Rights and Performing Obligations Arising out of International Treaties and Agreements Signed by USSR') (1992) 2 *Diplomaticheskiy Vestnik* 34.

[15] For multilateral treaties, see: https://www.mid.ru/ru/foreign_policy/international_contracts/international_contracts/multilateral_contract/; for bilateral treaties, see: https://www.mid.ru/ru/foreign_policy/international_contracts/international_contracts/2_contract/. An alternative unofficial list is commonly attached to the methodological recommendations of the Federal Bailiffs Services (see reference to the latest version above).

[16] The Treaty on the Procedure for Resolution of Disputes Connected with the Performance of Commercial Activities, signed in Kiev on 20 March 1992 (the 1992 Kiev Treaty). As of 2023, the Kiev Treaty is in force in the following states: Azerbaijan, Armenia, Belarus, Kazakhstan, Kyrgyzstan, Russia, Tajikistan, Turkmenistan and Uzbekistan. Ukraine was a party to the Treaty before 5 February 2023, after that a national law on denunciation of the Treaty entered into force. However, by mid-2023 no official information on Ukraine's withdrawal from the Treaty has been published by the depository, see: https://cis.minsk.by/reestrv2/doc/57#documentCard.

on legal assistance and legal relations in civil, family, and criminal law matters[17] and the 2002 Chisinau Convention on Legal Assistance and Legal Relations in Civil, Family and Criminal Matters.[18] The 2002 Chisinau Convention supersedes the 1993 Minsk Convention for the states that are the parties to both conventions.

The 2002 Chisinau Convention applies to recognition and enforcement of judgments related to civil, family, and certain criminal matters. The Convention provides that judgments are recognised without an *exequatur* provided certain conditions are met, while enforcement requires an *exequatur* issued by a competent court of the recipient state party pursuant to its procedure (Articles 54, 55 and 57). Accordingly, the Convention adheres to the Half Exequatur Model. The Convention then provides a list of documents for an application for enforcement and a list of grounds upon which to refuse enforcement (Articles 56 and 59).

The 1993 Minsk Convention governs matters of recognition and enforcement similarly to the Chisinau Convention. The 2002 Chisinau Convention supersedes the 1993 Minsk Convention among the states parties which adopted the Chisinau Convention. Hence, scope of application of the 1993 Minsk Convention is limited to the states which have not signed the 2002 Chisinau Convention. It applies to relations with Moldova and Georgia only.

The 1992 Kiev Treaty governs matters arising from contractual and civil relations between commercial parties: legal entities, entrepreneurs and business organisations in any legal form (Articles 1 and 2). Article 7 of the Treaty declares that judgments issued by competent courts of one state party shall be recognised and enforced in another state party. The Treaty does not refer to any recognition or enforcement procedure in the enforcing state party to be followed to give legal effect to a judgment of an issuing state party. Articles 7 and 8 of the Treaty further provide that judgments ordering recovery of property may be executed by competent enforcement authorities of the enforcing state party. Based on these provisions, it appears that the Treaty intends the recognition and enforcement to bypass the *exequatur* stage. The Economic Court of the Commonwealth of Independent States confirmed this reading in a decision of 21 February 2007.[19]

[17] The Minsk Convention on Legal Assistance and Legal Relations in Civil, Family and Criminal Law Matters of 22 January 1993 (the 1993 Minsk Convention). As of 2023, the Minsk Convention is in force in the following states: Azerbaijan, Armenia, Belarus, Georgia, Kazakhstan, Kyrgyzstan, Moldova, Russia, Tajikistan, Turkmenistan and Uzbekistan. Ukraine has been a party to the Convention before 29 December 2022, see: https://cis.minsk.by/reestrv2/doc/192#documentCard.

[18] The Chisinau Convention on Legal Assistance and Legal Relations in Civil, Family and Criminal Matters of 7 October 2002 (the 2002 Chisinau Convention). As of 2023, the Chisinau Convention is in force in Azerbaijan, Armenia, Belarus, Kazakhstan, Kyrgyzstan, Russia, Tajikistan, and Uzbekistan. Russia has signed the Chisinau Convention in 2002, but the Convention has entered into force for Russia only in 2023. See: Federal'nyj zakon ot 30.12.2021 No 452-FZ 'O ratifikacii Konvencii o pravovoj pomoshchi i pravovyh otnosheniyah po grazhdanskim, semejnym i ugolovnym delam' (Federal Law dated 30 December 2021 No 452-FZ 'On Ratification of the Convention on Legal Assistance and Legal Relations in Civil, Family and Criminal Matters'), https://cis.minsk.by/reestrv2/doc/1313#documentCard.

[19] Decision of the Economic Court of the Commonwealth of Independent States No 01-1/2-06 dated 21 February 2007 'On Interpretation of Articles 5, 7 of the Agreement on the Procedure of Resolution of Disputes Connected with the Performance of Commercial Activities of 20 March 1992, Articles 5,

In practice, however, applications for recognition and enforcement of judgments originating from states parties to the Treaty are common in Russian courts;[20] and Russian bailiffs do not commonly accept judgments originating from states parties to the Treaty for execution without an *exequatur* by a Russian court.[21] Therefore, in practice, the Treaty is construed as either of the Full Exequatur Model or of the Half Exequatur Model.

The 1992 Kiev Treaty provides for a list of documents required for an application for execution of a judgment (Article 8) and a list of grounds allowing competent authorities of the recipient state party to refuse execution (Article 9). Both lists generally match the respective provisions of the Procedural Codes.

Russia is a party to the 1997 Convention on Mutual Recognition and Enforcement of Judgments in Cases of Administrative Violations of Traffic Regulations.[22] It enables direct enforcement of decisions rendered by the public authorities of the Member States on certain categories of traffic violations listed in the Convention. The Convention is an example of No Exequatur Model. Should the enforcement of an administrative fine in the state of commission of the tort be impossible, the Member State of the Convention is entitled to submit a request for enforcement to another Member State. The government authority administering such requests in Russia is the Ministry of Internal Affairs.

(ii) International Multilateral Treaties

In 2019, a text of a multilateral treaty for recognition and enforcement of foreign judgments was adopted under the auspices of the Hague Conference on Private International Law – the 2019 Hague Convention on the Recognition and Enforcement of Foreign Judgments in Civil or Commercial Matters (HCCH 2019 Judgments Convention). Should a meaningful number of states adhere to this Convention, it may ensure a global and unimpeded circulation of judgments. As of 2023, the Convention has been adopted by 29 states and it remains to be

17, 51, 54 of the Convention on Legal Assistance and Legal Relations in Civil, Family and Criminal Law Matters of 22 January 1993 and Articles 5, 17, 54, 57 of the Convention on Legal Assistance and Legal Relations in Civil, Family and Criminal Matters of 7 October 2002'.

[20] Para 1, Informatsionnoe Pismo Presidiuma VAS RF ot 22.12.2005 No 96 'Obzor Praktiki Rassmotreniya Arbitrazhnymi Sudami Del o Priznanii i Privedenii v Ispolnenie Resheniy Treteiskikh Sudov i o Vudache Ispolnitel'nykh Listov na Prinuditel'noe Ispolnenie Resheniy Treteyskikh Sudov' (the Information Letter of the Presidium of the Highest Arbitrazh Court dated 22 December 2005 No 96 'The Overview of the Practice of Consideration by Arbitrazh Courts of Cases Concerning the Recognition and Enforcement of Foreign Court Judgments, Appeal of Arbitral Awards, and Enforcement of Arbitral Awards').

[21] Pis'mo FSSP Rossii ot 29.07.2016 No. 00071/16/69976-AP 'O napravlenii Metodicheskih rekomendacij' (Letter of the Federal Bailiff Service of Russia dated 29.07.2016 No. 00071/16/69976-AP 'On the submission of Methodological recommendations').

[22] As of 2023, the parties to the Convention are: Armenia, Belarus, Kazakhstan, Kyrgyzstan, Russia and Tajikistan.

seen whether the Convention will indeed play a global role.[23] Russia signed the Convention in 2021 but has not yet ratified it (a step which is required under Russian law for Russia to become a party to an international treaty).[24] The Convention has entered into force for states acceded to it on 1 September 2023, but not for Russia yet.

In addition to the HCCH 2019 Judgments Convention, there are several multilateral treaties to which Russia is a party that govern recognition and enforcement of judgments in relation to certain limited subject-matters. Examples are discussed below.

Russia is a party to the 1954 Hague Convention on Civil Procedure.[25] Article 18 of the Convention provides for the enforcement of orders for costs and expenses of the proceedings in the states signatory to the Convention. Enforcement shall be granted upon request via diplomatic channels, unless two party states agree that applications for enforcement may also be made directly by an interested party. The diplomatic procedure includes a request for legal assistance from competent authorities of a foreign state to the Ministry of Foreign Affairs of the Russian Federation, which forwards the request through the Russian Ministry of Justice to the competent Russian courts for consideration. Notwithstanding the Convention, practice of Russian courts remains diverse regarding enforcement of judgments pursuant to the Convention.[26]

The 1956 Convention on contracts for the international carriage of goods by road (CMR Convention),[27] to which Russia is a party, provides for recognition and enforcement of foreign judgments related to such contracts. Article 31 of the Convention provides that a judgment enforceable in the origin state party shall be enforceable in each state party, if certain requirements are met. In the case of Russia, the latter refers to an *exequatur* granted by a competent Russian court.

Russia is a party to the 1996 Hague Convention on Jurisdiction, Applicable Law, Recognition, Enforcement and Co-operation in Respect of Parental Responsibility and Measures for the Protection of Children.[28] The Convention covers measures

[23] As of 2023, 27 EU Member States and Ukraine are parties to the 2019 Hague Convention. Costa Rica, Israel, Montenegro, Russia, USA and Uruguay have signed the Convention but have not completed the process of accession.

[24] Rasporyazhenie Prezidenta RF ot 08.04.2021 No 83-rp 'O Podpisanii Konventsii o Priznanii i Privedenii v Ispolnenie Inostrannyh Sudebnyh Resheniy po Grazhdanskim ili Torgovym Delam' (President's Decree dated 8 April 2021 No 83-rp 'On Signing of the Convention on Recognition and Enforcement of Foreign Judicial Decisions on Civil or Commercial Matters').

[25] 49 states are parties to the 1954 Hague Convention, including a majority of EU Member States, Argentina, China, Israel, Japan, Switzerland, and Türkiye.

[26] Denying enforcement: Postanovlenie Arbitrazhnogo suda Moskovskogo okruga ot 01.11.2021 po delu No A40-55426/2021 (Judgment of *Arbitrazh* Court of Moscow District dated 1 November 2021 case No A40-55426/2021). Upholding enforcement: Opredelenie Moskovskogo gorodskogo suda ot 08.05.2019 No. 3m-206/2019 (Ruling of Moscow City Court dated 8 May 2019 No 3m-206/2019).

[27] 58 states are parties to the 1956 CMR Convention, with most European and CIS states as well as the UK among them.

[28] HCCH Convention of 19 October 1996 on Jurisdiction, Applicable Law, Recognition, Enforcement and Co-operation in Respect of Parental Responsibility and Measures for the Protection of Children.

on parental responsibility, rights of custody, guardianship, adoption of children, and management of children's property. Articles 23–28 of the Convention provide for the recognition and enforcement of measures in states parties to the Convention. Whereas recognition will be granted by operation of law (should the decision of the authorities meet certain criteria), the enforcement procedure underlies the *exequatur* procedure. Thus, the 1996 Hague Convention provides for the Half Exequatur Model.

(iii) Bilateral Treaties

Russia is a party to over 30 bilateral international treaties, which commonly regulate legal assistance in various fields, including reciprocal recognition and enforcement of judgments of the states parties. Parties to such treaties include, inter alia, certain EU Member States (Bulgaria, Croatia, Czech Republic, Cyprus, Estonia, Hungary, Greece, Italy, Latvia, Lithuania, Poland, Romania, Slovakia, Slovenia and Spain), certain other European states (Albania, Bosnia and Herzegovina, Macedonia, Montenegro and Serbia), certain Commonwealth of Independent States countries (Azerbaijan, Belarus, Kyrgyzstan, and Moldova), and certain states from various other regions of the globe (Algeria, Argentina, Vietnam, Egypt, Iraq, Iran, India, China, Yemen, Cuba, Mongolia, North Korea, and Tunisia). Some examples are discussed below.

Russia and Belarus have signed the bilateral 2001 Treaty on the procedure of mutual enforcement of judicial decisions by *arbitrazh* courts of the Russian Federation and commercial courts of the Republic of Belarus.[29] Article 1 of the Treaty provides that the judgments on commercial matters by Russian *arbitrazh* (commercial) courts and Belarusian commercial courts are mutually recognised and enforced by operation of the Treaty; and no *exequatur* is required. Judgments ordering transfer of property are executed in the same way as local judgments.

In 2015, Russia and Belarus signed the Treaty on Mutual Enforcement of Judicial Decisions on Recovery of Alimony[30] that sets forth a No Exequatur Model for judicial acts on alimony rendered in Russia and Belarus. The enforcement orders of the courts of Belarus on recovery of maintenance have the same legal force as the enforcement documents of competent Russian authorities.

In 1984, the USSR and Cyprus signed a Treaty on Legal Assistance in Civil and Criminal Matters. Article 26 of the Treaty reads: 'For the purposes of enforcing the judgments … the courts of the Contracting Party in whose territory the judgment

As of 2023, the Convention is in force in 54 states, including Australia, Cuba, EU Member States, Serbia, Switzerland, Türkiye and the UK.

[29] Treaty between the Russian Federation and the Republic of Belarus dated 17 January 2001 'On the Procedure of Mutual Enforcement of Judicial Decisions of *Arbitrazh* Courts of the Russian Federation and Commercial Courts of the Republic of Belarus'.

[30] Treaty between the Russian Federation and the Republic of Belarus dated 3 March 2015 'On the Procedure of Mutual Enforcement of Judicial Decisions on Matters Recovery of Alimony'.

is to be enforced shall render a decision authorising the enforcement.' The Treaty provides that an application for enforcement must be submitted to the court at the place of the judgment, and the latter must then transmit the application to the competent court of the Contracting Party. Notwithstanding the above procedure, both *arbitrazh* courts and courts of general jurisdiction in Russia accept direct applications by private parties on recognition and enforcement of decisions of Cypriot courts and decide on their enforcement.[31] In this regard, the courts commonly refer to Article 1(2) of the Treaty, which provides for the right of the citizens of the Contracting Parties to free and unimpeded access to the courts and other authorities in civil and criminal matters. The courts may refuse enforcement of the judgment if the conditions of Article 24 are not met, the most common ground for refusal being the failure to notify the debtor in the judicial proceedings in Cyprus.[32]

Russia does not have bilateral treaties expressly governing recognition and enforcement of foreign judgments with a significant number of states. It has no such agreement, for example, with Brazil, Canada, Republic of Chile, Germany, Israel, Republic of Korea, Republic of South Africa, the United Kingdom, the United States and other states. It will be discussed below that courts may fill in these gaps by relying either on international treaties which have no express provisions on recognition and enforcement of judgments or on the doctrine of reciprocity.

Bilateral treaties may overlap with multilateral treaties governing recognition and enforcement of judgment. It is a matter of interpretation which treaty prevails in each case. However, according to the general guidance of the Highest *Arbitrazh* Court, a multilateral treaty will apply only to those aspects which are not regulated by the bilateral treaty.[33]

[31] See judgments of *arbitrazh* courts: Judgment of *Arbitrazh* Court of Povolzhskiy District of 22.04.2019 case No A06-7837/2018; Judgment of *Arbitrazh* Court of Povolzhskiy District of 23.12.2019 case No A12-20691/2019; Judgment of Federal *Arbitrazh* Court of North-Western District of 02.04.2012 case No A56-52034/2011; Judgment of Federal *Arbitrazh* Court of North-Western District of 22.12.2012 case No A56-49591/2011; judgments of the courts of general jurisdiction: Ruling of the Second Cassation court of general jurisdiction of 01.03.2022 No 88-4921/2022; Ruling of the Eighth Cassation court of general jurisdiction of 13.12.2022 No 88-23172/2022; Appellate Ruling of the First Appellate Court of general jurisdiction of 03.02.2021 case No 66-548/2021; Ruling of Moscow City Court of 05.07.2021 case No 3m-197/2021; Ruling of Moscow City Court of 23.10.2020 case No 3m-99/2020. But compare with: Appellate Ruling of Court for Moscow Region of 17.02.2016 case No 33-1895/2016.

[32] See judgments of *arbitrazh* courts: Judgment of *Arbitrazh* Court of Moscow District of 23.03.2016 case No A40-59983/2015; Judgment of *Arbitrazh* Court of North-Western District of 16.08.2016 case No A56-13465/2016; Judgment of *Arbitrazh* Court of North-Western District of 11.08.2016 case No. A56-13051/2016; Judgment of *Arbitrazh* Court of North-Western District of 27.07.2016 case No A56-13477/2016.

[33] Informatsionnoe Pismo Presidiuma VAS RF ot 22.12.2005 No 96 'Obzor praktiki rassmotreniya arbitrazhnymi sudami del o priznanii i privedenii v ispolnenie resheniy inostrannyh sudov, ob osparivanii resheniy treteyskih sudov i o vydache ispolnitel'nyh listov na prinuditel'noe ispolnenie resheniy treteyskih sudov' (Information Letter of the Presidium of the Highest Arbitrazh Court dated 22 December 2005 No 96 'The Overview of the Practice of Consideration by Arbitrazh Courts of Cases Concerning the Recognition and Enforcement of Foreign Judgments, on Appeal of Arbitral Awards, and on Issuance of Writs on Enforcement of Arbitral Awards').

(iv) Other Treaties

The Russian federal laws do not expressly say which 'international treaties' may serve as a basis for recognition and enforcement of foreign judgments. Accordingly, those treaties which expressly govern this issue fit the term. However, there is a grey area as to whether other treaties may fit this term as well. There are treaties that do not expressly govern mutual recognition of judgments, but nevertheless indicate the spirit of good economic or political relations between the states parties. On several occasions, Russian courts have treated such treaties as providing a basis for recognition and enforcement of judgments originating from such states parties. Some scholars disagree with this approach.[34]

In 2002, the Russian Supreme Court recognised and enforced a judgment of an English court with reference to the 1994 Treaty on Partnership and Cooperation Establishing a Partnership between the Russian Federation and the European Communities and their Member States, and the 1992 Treaty between the Government of the United Kingdom of Great Britain and Northern Ireland and the Government of the Russian Federation on Economic Co-operation.[35] These treaties do not contain express provisions allowing for mutual recognition and enforcement of judgments; however the Supreme Court considered that cooperative spirit of these treaties was sufficient to allow such recognition. This approach was later reflected in rulings of the Highest *Arbitrazh* Court that enforced judgments of English courts based on the aforementioned treaties and the 2003 United Nations Convention Against Corruption.[36] The Russian Supreme Court once referred to the 1950 Convention for the Protection of Human Rights and Fundamental Freedoms, interpreting Article 6 of the Convention as Russia's undertaking to ensure a fair trial along with effective enforcement of judgments when enforcing a South Korean judgment.[37]

In the bankruptcy context, there have been diverse approaches as to which international treaties are sufficient for recognition and enforcement of foreign bankruptcy judgments. Initially, the courts considered that such judgments may be enforced based on general treaties governing recognition and enforcement of judgments.[38] However, in the past decade, a trend has emerged that the courts

[34] See, eg, N Shebanova, 'Priznanie i Privedenie v Ispolnenie Inostrannyh Sudebnyh Resheniy v Praktike Rossiyskih Sudov' ('Recognition and Enforcement of Foreign Courts' Decisions in Russian Judicial Practice') (2017) 1 *Trudy Instituta gosudarstva i prava Rossiyskoy akademii nauk* 40.

[35] Opredelenie Verhovnogo Suda RF ot 07.06.2002 N 5-G02-64 (Ruling of the Supreme Court of the Russian Federation dated 7 June 2002 N 5-G02-64).

[36] Postanovlenie Prezidiuma VAS RF ot 08.10.2013 N 6004/13 po delu N A40-56571/12-141-521 (Resolution of the Presidium of the Highest Arbitrazh Court of the Russian Federation dated 8 October 2013 N 6004/13 on the matter N A40-56571/12-141-521).

[37] Opredelenie Verhovnogo Suda RF ot 15.02.2019 No 303-ES18-25322 (Ruling of the Supreme Court of Russia of 15 February 2019 No 303-EC18-25322).

[38] Ruling of *Arbitrazh* Court of Moscow City of 15.10.2012 case No A40-108389/2012 (*BTA Bank* case); E Mokhova, 'Globalizaciya transgranichnyh bankrotstv v Rossii: opyt dvizheniya na zapad i perspektivy razvitiya v evrazijskom napravlenii' (Globalisation of cross-border insolvencies in Russia: westward practices and Eurasian prospects) (2017) 5 *Zakon* 130–32.

expect a specialised treaty on recognition and enforcement of judgments in the bankruptcy context to grant *exequatur* in respect of bankruptcy judgments.[39]

B. The Doctrine of Reciprocity

The other basis for recognition and enforcement of foreign judgments is the doctrine of reciprocity. The doctrine provides that, in the absence of an international treaty, recognition and enforcement of a judgment of a foreign state is still possible if it is shown that Russian courts' decisions are recognised and enforced by the courts of such foreign state. The doctrine is often referred to as 'the doctrine of reciprocity and international comity'.

The doctrine is not present in the Procedural Codes or other Russian federal laws, except for the Federal Law of the Russian Federation 'On insolvency (bankruptcy)',[40] which expressly allows for recognition and enforcement of foreign judgments on bankruptcy cases based on reciprocity.[41]

Nevertheless, Russian courts uphold and apply this doctrine. The Russian Supreme Court first applied it in 2002 in respect of a judgment rendered by the High Court of Justice of England and Wales.[42] The Russian Supreme Court ruled that a foreign judgment could be recognised and enforced in the absence of an international agreement with the state of its origin, provided that judgments of the Russian courts are recognised and enforced by the courts of such state.

Since the 2002 judgment, other courts in the Russian Federation have upheld the doctrine.[43] In 2009, the Highest *Arbitrazh* Court referred to the doctrine of reciprocity as a recognised principle of international law.[44]

[39] Judgment of *Arbitrazh* Court of North-Western District of 14.11.2016 case No A56-27115/2016 (*Kekhman* case); Ruling of the Chamber for Commercial Disputes of the Supreme Court of Russian Federation of 08.10.2020 case No A83-6324/2018 (*Vitmet* case); E Mokhova, 'Priznanie inostrannyh bankrotstv v Rossii: vopros o primenenii mezhdunarodnyh dogovorov o pravovoj pomoshchi' (Recognition of Foreign Bankruptcies in Russia: The Question of the Application of International Treaties on Legal Assistance) (2022) 10 *Zakon* 112–38.

[40] Federal'nyj Zakon ot 26.10.2002 No 127-FZ 'O Nesostoyatel'nosti (Bankrotstve)' (Federal Law of the Russian Federation 'On insolvency (bankruptcy)' dated 26 October 2002 No 127-FZ).

[41] By way of comparison, the doctrine is expressly embodied in the legislation of several states of the former USSR: Belarus, Kazakhstan and the Kyrgyz Republic. In Russia, the doctrine has been expressly mentioned in a concept of the unified code of civil procedure – a legislative initiative aimed at merging the two Procedural Codes into one; however, this legislative initiative has not resulted in adoption of the code yet and perspectives are unclear. See Decision No 124(1) of the Committee on Civil, Criminal, Commercial and Procedural Legislation of the State Duma of the Federal Assembly of 12 December 2014.

[42] Opredelenie Verhovnogo Suda RF ot 07.06.2002 No 5-G02-64 (Ruling of the Supreme Court of the Russian Federation dated 7 July2002 No 5-G02-64).

[43] See judgments of *arbitrazh* courts: Ruling of *Arbitrazh* Court of Moscow of 19.12.2022 case No A40-237638/22 (on the judgment rendered in Switzerland); Judgment of *Arbitrazh* Court of Dalnevostochniy District of 08.10.2018 No F03-4115/2018 case No A24-2543/2018 (on the judgment rendered in the Republic of Korea); Judgment of *Arbitrazh* Court of the Republic of Bashkortostan dated 17.03.2014 on the matter No A07-16859/2013 (on the judgment rendered by the High Court of Justice of England and Wales); Resolution of the Cassation *Arbitrazh* Court of Moscow District dated

The existing court practice of reciprocity in Russia was recognised in 2010 by the European Court of Human Rights. In *Korolev v Russia*, the ECtHR referred to the 2002 Ruling of the Russian Supreme Court as allowing for enforcement 'in the event that the courts of the relevant foreign State recognize the judgments of the Russian courts on the basis of reciprocity',[45] and then stated that

> in view of the decision of the Supreme Court of Russia of 7 June 2002 …, it is cognisant that the Russian legal system does not exclude enforcement of the judgments adopted by the courts of the State with which Russia has no pertinent agreement and authorizes the courts of general jurisdiction to consider other relevant factors when examining the case.[46]

When determining whether reciprocity exists, Russian courts look to ascertain whether courts of the relevant foreign state have enforced judgments of Russian courts in the past or may enforce them in the future. In practice, the courts may rely either on precedents of enforcement by the foreign courts, an expert opinion of a lawyer practising in the relevant jurisdiction, or other materials confirming that a foreign court would enforce a Russian judgment. The courts may also rely on previous Russian judgments where reciprocity with the relevant jurisdiction has already been established.[47]

As of the date of this publication, the Russian courts have determined that reciprocity exists with respect to enforcement of foreign judgments with the following states: the United Kingdom, Northern Ireland, British Virgin Islands, the Netherlands, and the Republic of Korea. Reciprocity has been denied in relation to the following states: Israel, New Zealand, and Bangladesh. There is mixed

19.04.2012 No F05-3243/2012 on the matter No A40-119397/2011 (on the judgment rendered by the Patents Court of the High Court of Justice of England and Wales); Ruling of the Highest *Arbitrazh* Court of the Russian Federation dated 07.12.2009 No VAS-13688/09 on the matter No A41-9613/09; judgments of the courts of general jurisdiction: Ruling of the Eighth Cassation court of general jurisdiction dated 23.04.2020 No 88-4957/2020 on the matter No 8G-3029/2020 (on the judgment rendered in Austria).

[44] Opredelenie VAS RF ot 07.12.2009 No. VAS-13688/09 (Ruling of the Highest *Arbitrazh* Court of 7 December 2009 No VAS-13688/09). When doing so, the Highest *Arbitrazh* Court tried to fill in the absence of a reference to the doctrine in the *Arbitrazh* Procedure Code and hence justify a formal ground for referral to the doctrine absent reference in the federal laws. This approach has been questioned by scholars: K Branovitskij, 'Printsip vzaimnosti v mezhdunarodnom grazhdanskom protsesse' ('The Reciprocity Principle in International Civil Procedure') (2005) 8 *Arbitrazhnyj i grazhdanskiy protsess*; D Kaysin, 'Doktrina mezhdunarodnoy vezhlivosti i privedenie v ispolnenie inostrannyh sudebnyh resheniy v Rossii' ('Doctrine of International Comity and Enforcement of Foreign Judicial Decision in Russia') (2014) 6 *Zakon* 152–60; N Shebanova, 'Priznanie i Privedenie v Ispolnenie Inostrannyh Sudebnyh Resheniy v Praktike Rossiyskih Sudov' ('Recognition And Enforcement Of Foreign Courts' Decisions In Russian Judicial Practice') (2017) 1 *Trudy Instituta gosudarstva i prava Rossiyskoy akademii nauk* 40.

[45] *Korolev v Russia*, no 38112/04, §41, ECtHR 21 October 2010.

[46] *Korolev v Russia*, no 38112/04, §52, ECtHR 21 October 2010.

[47] Judgment of *Arbitrazh* Court of the Republic of Bashkortostan dated 17.03.2014 case No A07-16859/2013 (on the judgment rendered by the High Court of Justice of England and Wales); Judgment of the Cassation *Arbitrazh* Court of Moscow District dated 19.06.2019 case No A40-68312/2018 (on the judgment rendered in the Netherlands).

practice as to the following states: the United States, Germany (prevailing case law is that there is no reciprocity), Belgium, and France.

Nevertheless, in recent years, Russian courts – the courts of general jurisdiction in Russia in particular – have been less receptive to the doctrine of reciprocity, especially given the current geopolitical climate.[48] Russian legislation currently provides for the list of 'unfriendly' states, which have implemented sanctions against Russia and its nationals.[49] The list includes, for example, Canada, the EU Member States, Singapore, Switzerland, the United Kingdom, and the United States. There have been judgments stating that evidence of reciprocity prior to 24 February 2022 is irrelevant, as the geopolitical landscape has changed thereafter.[50] The Russian courts have referred to the 'unfriendly' status of a state that rendered a judgment when deciding on the existence of reciprocity.[51] It remains to be seen how this tendency alters the doctrine of reciprocity in Russia.

III. Procedure for Granting an *Exequatur*

Acts of recognition and enforcement of foreign judgments are issued by courts of general jurisdiction and *arbitrazh* (commercial) courts through a special procedure generally governed by the Procedural Codes. Rules of the Codes may overlap with that of an applicable international treaty, in which case an international treaty prevails.[52]

Under the Procedural Codes, the fundamental principle is that the court must not review the case on the merits, but only determine whether grounds and criteria for its recognition and enforcement – as defined in the applicable international treaty or a Procedural Code – are met.[53] Even if a court disagrees with the reasoning or operative part of a foreign judgment, it will still enforce it, should the grounds and criteria for enforcement be satisfied. However, arguably, the no-review-on-merits principle appears to have been eroded by the fact that the courts check foreign judgments for compliance with public policy (see below on public policy (*ordre public*) as a ground for refusal of recognition and enforcement).

[48] Judgments of courts of general jurisdiction: Ruling of the Ninth Cassation Court of General Jurisdiction of 31.03.2020 case No 88-2141/2020; Appellate Ruling of the First Appellate Court of General Jurisdiction of 28.09.2022 case No 66-3165/2022. Judgments of *arbitrazh* courts: Judgment of *Arbitrazh* Court of Moscow District of 01.04.2019 case No A40-188140/2018; Judgment of *Arbitrazh* Court of Moscow District of 25.03.2019 case No A40-232485/2018.

[49] See: Rasporyazhenie Pravitel'stva RF 'Ob utverzhdenii perechnya inostrannyh gosudarstv i territorij, sovershayushchih nedruzhestvennye dejstviya v otnoshenii Rossijskoj Federacii, rossijskih yuridicheskih i fizicheskih lic' (Government Executive Order 'On Approval of the List of Countries and Territories that Perform Unfriendly Actions toward the Russian Federation, Russian Legal Entities and Individuals') dated 05.03.2022 No 430-r.

[50] Ruling of *Arbitrazh* Court of Moscow City of 28.04.2023 case No A40-242631/2022.

[51] Appellate Ruling of the First Appellate Court of General Jurisdiction of 11.01.2023 case No 66-81/2023.

[52] Article 15(4) of Konstitutsiya Rossiyskoy Federatsii (Constitution of the Russian Federation).

[53] Article 411(4) of the Civil Procedure Code; Article 243(4) of the *Arbitrazh* Procedure Code.

Russian courts will have jurisdiction to issue an *exequatur* if the judgment debtor has its place of residence or has property in Russia.[54] The said criteria serve to determine the so-called 'efficient jurisdiction', where the judgment has the best chance of being enforced. Absent these jurisdictional links, Russian courts are unlikely to grant an *exequatur*. However, an applicant may seek judicial assistance in proving the location of the debtor's property in Russia.[55]

There is a three-year statute of limitation from the date of issuance of a foreign judgment with respect to applications for *exequatur*. A court may still accept an application for *exequatur* if the applicant demonstrates a justifiable reason for missing the deadline.[56]

To enforce a foreign judgment, an applicant applies directly to a competent Russian court. Certain international treaties – commonly the older ones – envisage such applications either through diplomatic channels or a foreign court. These procedures are generally considered outdated, and direct applications are normally allowed. However, it remains at the court's discretion as to which procedure shall apply in each case.[57]

The following documents should usually accompany an application for enforcement of a foreign judgment: a certified copy of the foreign judgment; a document that confirms the entry of the judgment into legal force; a certificate of due notice to the debtor about the judicial procedure in the foreign court that rendered the judgment; and confirmation of sending the copy of the application for enforcement to the debtor.[58] The documents must be translated into Russian by a certified translator. International treaties may require other documents to be attached.

Adjudication of applications for enforcement of foreign judgments happens at hearings to which the applicant and the judgment debtor are summonsed. At such hearings, the court checks whether the basis for enforcement is met, whether existence of a foreign judgment is proven, and whether grounds to refuse recognition or enforcement are absent.

Acts of *exequatur* enter into force immediately. Acts of *exequatur* cannot be appealed to the courts of appeal (second-tier courts) but may be subject to a cassation appeal in the cassation courts (third-tier courts) and, thereafter, review by the Russian Supreme Court.[59]

[54] Article 410 of the Civil Procedure Code; Article 242(1) of the *Arbitrazh* Procedure Code.

[55] Judgment of *Arbitrazh* Court of North-Western District of 18.05.2023 case No A46-14313/2022; Judgment of *Arbitrazh* Court of North-Western District of 18 May 2023 case No A46-14311/2022.

[56] Article 412 of the Civil Procedure Code; Article 244 of the *Arbitrazh* Procedure Code.

[57] For instance, denying the enforcement due to mandatory diplomatic procedure: Opredelenie Vos'mogo kassatsionnogo suda obshchey yurisdiktsii ot 24.08.2021 No 88-14665/2021 (Ruling of the Eighth Cassation Court of General Jurisdiction dated 24 August 2021 No 88-14665/2021). Upholding the enforcement: Opredelenie Moskovskogo gorodskogo suda ot 08.05.2019 No 3m-206/2019 (Ruling of Moscow City Court dated 8 May 2019 No 3m-206/2019). See also above regarding application of the Russia-Cyprus bilateral treaty.

[58] Article 411 of the Civil Procedure Code; Article 242 of the *Arbitrazh* Procedure Code.

[59] Postanovlenie Plenuma Verhovnogo Suda RF ot 30.06.2020 No 13 'O primenenii Arbitrazhnogo processual'nogo kodeksa Rossijskoj Federacii pri rassmotrenii del v arbitrazhnom sude kassacionnoj

IV. Grounds for Granting an *Exequatur*

The Procedural Codes set out the following grounds on which a court may refuse recognition or enforcement of a foreign judgment:[60]

(a) No final foreign judgment
Russian courts commonly expect that a foreign judgment is 'final' and would not enforce an interim judgment (even if it has formally entered into force in the country of origin).[61] The entry into force of a foreign judgment may follow from the judgment itself or, alternatively, be confirmed by a certificate issued by an authority of the state of origin.

(b) Lack of proper notification
Lack of proper notification is a common reason to deny recognition or enforcement in Russian courts. A notification is commonly recognised as appropriate if carried out pursuant to an international treaty (for example, the 1965 Hague Convention), or if there is evidence of other effective notification of the party about proceedings in a foreign court.[62] If the debtor was not duly notified of the foreign court proceedings, the debtor could not defend himself/herself, and therefore the fundamental principle of access to justice would be violated.

(c) Breach of the three-year statute of limitation (see discussion in section III above).

(d) Exclusive jurisdiction of a Russian court.
Russian courts will not enforce a foreign judgment if the subject-matter of the foreign judgment is subject to the exclusive jurisdiction of a Russian court. Under the Procedural Codes, Russian courts are vested with exclusive jurisdiction regarding the following: disputes concerning immovable property located in the territory of Russia; disputes arising out of contracts of carriage, if the carriers are located in Russia; divorce cases between citizens of the Russian Federation, if both spouses are domiciled in Russia; disputes regarding intellectual property rights (patents, trademarks, utility models) if

instancii' (Resolution of the Plenum of the Supreme Court of the RF dated 30 June 2020 No 13 'On the Application of the Arbitrazh Procedure Code of the Russian Federation when Considering Cases in an Arbitrazh Cassation Court').

[60] Article 412 of the Civil Procedure Code; Article 244 of the *Arbitrazh* Procedure Code.

[61] Informatsionnoe Pismo Presidiuma VAS RF ot 07.07.2004 No 78 'Obzor praktiki primeneniya arbitrazhnymi sudami predvaritel'nyh obespechitel'nyh mer' (Information Letter of the Presidium of the Highest *Arbitrazh* Court dated 7 July 2004 No 78 'The Overview of the Practice of Application by *Arbitrazh* Courts of Preliminary Interim Measures').

[62] Opredelenie Sudebnoj kollegii po ekonomicheskim sporam Verhovnogo Suda RF ot 30.04.2019 po delu No A35-2592/2018 (Ruling of Chamber for Commercial Disputes of the Supreme Court of Russian Federation of 30.04.2019 case No A35-2592/2018); Opredelenie Verhovnogo Suda RF ot 03.12.2021 No 305-ES21-14991 (Ruling of the Supreme Court of 3 December 2021 No 305-ES21-14991; Punkt 55, Obzor Sudebnoj Praktiki Verhovnogo Suda Rossijskoj Federacii No 3 (2019) (utv. Prezidiumom Verhovnogo Suda RF 27.11.2019) (Item 55, Overview of the Court Practice of the Supreme Court of the Russian Federation No 3 (2019) (approved by the Presidium of the Supreme Court on 27 November 2019).

they are registered in Russia; disputes concerning records in the official state registers of Russia; and disputes concerning registration and liquidation of legal entities in Russia.[63]

(e) Prior or concurrent Russian court proceedings on the same subject-matter and grounds.
Russian courts will refuse enforcement if a Russian court issued a judgment in a dispute between the same parties, on the same subject-matter and on the same grounds, or such case is being decided by a Russian court.

(f) *Ordre public*
Russian courts will refuse enforcement of a foreign judgment if doing so contradicts the public policy of the Russian Federation. Russian courts have a wide discretion to determine what matters constitute matters of public policy and whether a public policy interest has been infringed or will be infringed if a foreign judgment is recognised or enforced. The highest courts commonly advise restrictive application of the public policy exception; however, practice of Russian courts continues to diverge in this respect.[64] At various times the following matters have been recognised as matters of public policy and recognition and enforcement of judgments have been refused on this basis: prohibition of evasion of laws, including money laundering control;[65] the principle of the binding nature of judicial decisions of Russian courts and inadmissibility of a foreign court's decision contradicting a national judgment;[66] the principle of proportionality of civil liability and prohibition of bad faith actions;[67] and the jurisdictional immunity of the Russian Federation.[68]

[63] Article 248 of *Arbitrazh* Procedure Code; Article 403 of the Civil Procedure Code.

[64] Informatsionnoe Pismo Presidiuma VAS RF ot 26.02.2013 No 156 'Obzor praktiki rassmotreniya arbitrazhnymi sudami del o primenenii ogovorki o publichnom poryadke kak osnovaniya otkaza v priznanii i privedenii v ispolnenie inostrannyh sudebnyh i arbitrazhnyh resheniy' (Information Letter of the Presidium of the Highest *Arbitrazh* Court dated 26 February 2013 No 156 'The Overview of the Practice of Consideration by Arbitrazh Courts of Cases Concerning the Application of Public Policy Reservation as the Ground for Refusal in Recognition and Enforcement of Foreign Judgments and Arbitral Awards').

[65] Obzor po otdel'nym voprosam sudebnoj praktiki, svyazannym s prinyatiem sudami mer protivodejstviya nezakonnym finansovym operaciyam (utv. Prezidiumom Verhovnogo Suda RF 08.07.2020) (The Overview on Certain Issues of Judicial Practice Related to the Adoption by the Courts of Countermeasures to Illegal Financial Transactions (approved by the Presidium of the Supreme Court of the Russian Federation on 08 July2020)).

[66] Postanovlenie FAS Moskovskogo okruga ot 27.08.2012 po delu No. A40-56571/12-141-521 (Judgment of Federal *Arbitrazh* Court of Moscow District of 27 August 2012 case No A40-56571/12); Postanovlenie Arbitrazhnogo suda Moskovskogo okruga ot 18.03.2022 No A40-105856/2021 (Judgment of *Arbitrazh* Court of Moscow District of 18 March 2022 case No A40-105856/2021).

[67] Opredelenie Sudebnoj kollegii po ekonomicheskim sporam Verhovnogo Suda RF ot 22.01.2018 po delu No A07-27391/2016 (Ruling of Chamber for Commercial Disputes of the Supreme Court of Russian Federation of 22 January 2018 case No A07-27391/2016).

[68] Opredelenie Sudebnoj kollegii po ekonomicheskim sporam Verhovnogo Suda RF ot 01.02.2017 po delu No. A41-22518/2014 (Ruling of Chamber for Commercial Disputes of the Supreme Court of Russian Federation of 1 February2017 case No A41-22518/2014); Opredelenie Verhovnogo Suda RF ot 13.06.2017 po delu No. A41-22518/2014 (Ruling of the Supremet Court of the RF of 13 June 2017 case No A41-22518/2014).

12

International Commercial Arbitration

IVAN CHUPRUNOV

I. Applicable Legal Instruments and Fundamental Concepts

On the one hand, Russian laws applicable to international commercial arbitration (ICA) are modern ones and, in many important respects, are in line with internationally recognised principles, as reflected in the UN Convention on the Recognition and Enforcement of Foreign Arbitral Awards of 1958 (NY Convention) and the UNCITRAL Model Law on International Commercial Arbitration of 1985 (Model Law). On the other hand, ICA in Russia is often subject to a significantly higher level of state control, as a matter of both law and practice, than in many other jurisdictions, especially any of the major arbitration forums. In particular, while Russia is a party to the NY Convention as well as the European Convention on International Commercial Arbitration of 1961, application by Russian courts of some of the concepts enshrined therein (eg arbitrability, public policy), as will be demonstrated below, is not always fully in line with the international standards.

Russia has traditionally had two separate sets of rules for (i) purely domestic arbitration – the Arbitration Law (AL); and (ii) ICA – the International Commercial Arbitration Law (ICAL). The ICAL is based on the UNCITRAL Model Law (including some of the 2006 amendments), but, as will be shown, deviates from it in a few respects. The other key legislative acts relevant to the ICA sphere are the *Arbitrazh* Procedure Code (APC) and the Civil Procedure Code (CPC).

In 2016 both domestic arbitration and ICA underwent a major legislative reform (2016 Reform), which fundamentally reshaped the arbitration landscape in Russia, although it kept the dualism of legal instruments applicable to domestic and international commercial arbitration. Perhaps the most important feature of this controversial 2016 Reform was that it required any Russian arbitral institution to obtain a licence from the Russian Ministry of Justice and restricted the reference of certain categories of disputes to arbitration not administered by such a licensed 'permanent arbitral institution' (PAI).[1] This, coupled with significant difficulties with obtaining a PAI licence,[2] led to what is sometimes called 'oligopolisation' of the ICA sphere in Russia and put ICA under additional control by the Russian state. Although Russian legislation expressly permits the parties to refer their disputes to an ad hoc arbitration, such arbitration is subject to more restrictive rules than arbitration administered by a PAI.[3]

As a general rule, the ICAL only applies to an ICA when its seat is in Russia. The 'seat' in this context is generally understood to mean 'legal' seat as opposed to the place where arbitration hearings may take place. However, in line with the Model Law, Articles 8, 9, 35 and 36 – ie provisions regarding the principle of *Kompetenz-Kompetenz* and recognition of arbitration agreements by state courts, injunctive relief in support of arbitration, and recognition and enforcement of an arbitral award – apply irrespective of where the arbitration seat is.

It is important to note that Article 1(3) of the ICAL deviates from the UNCITRAL Model Law approach in that it provides that a civil law dispute may be referred to ICA only if (i) one of the parties' place of business is located outside of Russia, (ii) a substantial part of the relevant obligation is to be performed outside of Russia, (iii) the subject-matter of the dispute is most closely connected with a foreign jurisdiction, or (iv) the dispute relates to foreign investments into Russia or outbound investments from Russia. A dispute that does not satisfy any of these conditions and is arbitrable may be referred to arbitration in Russia, but will be subject to the rules on domestic arbitration.[4]

However, there are significant controversies as to whether such a 'domestic' dispute may be referred to arbitration with a seat outside of Russia. One of the authoritative scholarly views in this respect is that arbitration of such disputes should remain subject to the mandatory Russian rules on domestic arbitration and, therefore, they may only be referred to arbitral institutions having a PAI licence.[5] While this approach is the product of, and in line with, the 2016 Reform, it is hard to see why the ICAL definition of *international* arbitration is (or should be) relevant for an arbitral tribunal with a seat outside of Russia – therefore, the arbitrators should have full discretion to ignore it, especially to the extent that the future arbitral award may be enforced outside of Russia.

[1] For more details on the 2016 Reform see eg BR Karabelnikov, 'National Report for Russian Federation (2020 through 2022)' in L Bosman (ed), *ICCA International Handbook on Commercial Arbitration* (Alphen aan den Rijn, Kluwer Law International, 2022) 1–5.

[2] As of the time of this writing, only five Russian and four non-Russian arbitral institutions have obtained PAI licences. Two Russian arbitral institutions (the International Commercial Arbitration Court and Maritime Arbitration Commission at the Russian Chamber of Commerce and Industry) were exempted from the licensing requirements.

[3] In particular, see section III.C of this chapter.

[4] See para 8 of Decree of the Plenum of the Russian Supreme Court No 53 'On Fulfilment by Courts of the Russian Federation of the Functions of Assistance and Oversight in Respect of Arbitral Proceedings and International Commercial Arbitration'.

[5] See eg AV Asoskov, 'Dopustimo li peredavat' chisto vnutrennie spory bez inostrannogo elementa na razreshenie inostrannogo arbitrazha?' ('Is It Permissible to Refer to Foreign Arbitration Purely Domestic Disputes without a Foreign Element?') (2017) 8 *Zakon* 115, 115–23.

Finally, it is worth mentioning that in Russian scholarship, as well as court practice, the predominant view is that ICA is localised strictly within the *lex loci arbitri*, and that the arbitral tribunal's competence stems from the legal order of the arbitral forum (legal seat). Although European theories of autonomous or de-localised (detached) arbitration are well-known to Russian academics, they generally do not find any substantial support and are certainly alien to Russian courts. It is not surprising, therefore, that the parties' right to limit the scope of Russian courts' intervention in arbitration (eg the right to exclude the set-aside procedure under Article 34(1) of the ICAL)[6] is viewed as merely being granted to them by the *lex loci arbitri*.

II. Arbitration Agreement

A. General Remarks

The ICAL provides the definition of an arbitration agreement (Article 7(1)) – which mirrors almost *verbatim* the equivalent provisions of the Model Law – and sets out the general requirement that the arbitration agreement shall be in written form (Article 7(2)) as well as detailed rules as to what exactly constitutes 'written form' for these purposes (Article 7(3)–(6)). These rules are largely based on Option I of Article 7 from the 2006 amendments to the Model Law; in particular, the written form requirement may be met by means of electronic communications, exchange of a statement of claim and statement of defence, etc.[7] In addition, in some cases, the ICAL allows for an arbitration agreement in respect of corporate disputes[8] to be included in a legal entity's charter (subject to unanimous approval by its participants) (Article 7(8)).

On the face of it, the ICAL goes even further than the Model Law to promote the effectiveness of arbitration agreements. Article 7(9) of the ICAL expressly sets out the *in favorem validatis* principle – an arbitration agreement should be interpreted in a manner that favours its validity and capability of being performed. Furthermore, the ICAL provides for an expansive default scope of an arbitration clause: unless the parties agree otherwise, such a clause contained in a contract will cover any disputes relating to its execution and entering into force, any changes thereto, the termination and validity thereof, including disputes regarding restitution in case the contract is declared invalid or non-existent (Articles 7(10) and 7(12)). The Supreme Court extends the default scope of arbitration clause even further: unless the parties agree otherwise, it will cover

[6] See section VII of this chapter regarding exclusion of the set-aside procedure in respect of an arbitral award.

[7] For more details see A Kotelnikov, S Kurochkin and O Skvortsov, *Arbitration in Russia* (Alphen aan den Rijn, Kluwer Law International, 2019) para 3.03.

[8] See section III.C of this chapter.

disputes in relation to tort or unjust enrichment to the extent that those are connected with the underlying contract.[9]

However, this pro-arbitration agreement approach, crystallised in the ICAL, has not prevented the Russian courts in one of the cases from declaring model ICC arbitration clauses to be incapable of being performed.[10] Hopefully, this problem should have now been resolved with the adoption of the 2018 Supreme Court Review of Cases (2018 SC Review)[11] (paragraph 5) and Plenum Resolution No 53 (paragraph 30), which both reiterate the need to adopt the *in favorem validatis* approach when interpreting arbitration agreements and expressly confirm that a model arbitration clause recommended by an arbitral institution is certainly capable of being performed. However, this is a very good example of a sharp contrast that is sometimes there between pro-arbitration statutory provisions and their application by Russian courts.

It is sometimes argued in Russian scholarship that an arbitration agreement has not only procedural, but also substantive law effects – it imposes binding obligations upon parties to refer their disputes to arbitration, and their breach may thus result in a damages claim.[12] Nevertheless, at the moment these views do not find wide support among Russian scholars or courts.[13]

B. Separability. Applicable Law

The ICAL (Article 16(1)) expressly recognises the principle of separability (autonomy) of an arbitration agreement according to which an arbitration clause in a contract is seen as a separate agreement, the legal effect of which does not necessarily depend on the validity or effectiveness of the underlying contract. This fundamental ICA concept is also widely recognised in Russian court practice.[14]

Due to the principle of separability, the law governing an arbitration agreement may be different from the governing law of the underlying contract. As in many other countries, there is no full consensus in Russian scholarship regarding which law should govern an arbitration agreement. An express choice of law applicable to the arbitration agreement still remains relatively rare, especially outside of high- or mid-market mergers and acquisitions transactions. The prevailing view seems

[9] See para 21 of Plenum Resolution No 53.

[10] See Postanovlenie Arbitrazhnogo Suda Moskovskogo Okruga (Resolution of the *Arbitrazh* Court of the Moscow District) of 25 April 2018 Case No A40-176466/17.

[11] Review of Cases Related to the Functions of Assistance and Control in Relation to Arbitration and International Commercial Arbitration (Adopted by the Presidium of the Supreme Court of the Russian Federation on 26 December 2018).

[12] In support see IS Chuprunov, 'Dopustimost' vzyskaniya ubytkov iz narusheniya arbitrazhnogo ili prorogatsionnogo soglasheniy' ('Availability of Damages Claim for a Breach of Arbitration or Forum Selection Agreements') (2011) 6 *Civil Law Review* 62, 62–101.

[13] See Opredelenie Sudebnoi Kollegii po Ekonomicheskim Sporam Verkhovnogo Suda RF (Resolution of the Commercial Chamber of the Supreme Court) of 2 November 2016 No 306-ЭС16-4741.

[14] See eg paras 20–21 of Plenum Resolution No 53; para 3 of 2018 SC Review.

to be that, in the absence of such express choice, the proper law of the arbitration agreement shall be the *lex loci arbitri* as the seat of arbitration represents the closest connection with the arbitration agreement.[15] On the face of it, this approach is further supported by Article V(1)(a) of the NY Convention and Articles 34(2)(1) and 36(1)(1) of the ICAL. Furthermore, paragraph 27 of Plenum Resolution No 53 in line with these provisions suggests that, in the absence of the parties' choice of law applicable to the arbitration agreement, it shall indeed be governed by the *lex loci arbitri*.

In reality, this approach mistakenly overemphasises the autonomy of the arbitration clause – the fact that its governing law *may be* different from the governing law of the underlying contract does not mean that it *needs* to be different. If the parties have chosen the law applicable to the main contract, it does feel unnatural (and hardly in line with the parties' expectations) to limit the scope of such choice exclusively to all provisions of the contract save for the arbitration clause and then single out the latter as the only clause that is subject to a completely different set of rules. We need to be mindful that the law of the arbitration agreement governs, inter alia, the issues of its validity eg due to duress or forgery; it is very hard to conceive why these matters could be governed by a law different from the law chosen by the parties in respect of the underlying contract, especially where the same circumstances would be affecting the validity of both the contract and the arbitration clause included therein. Therefore, we believe that a much better view is that the principle of separability should be interpreted functionally and should not overstep its original realm of application – as a consequence, the parties' choice of applicable law in respect of the underlying contract should be presumed to cover the arbitration clause as well.[16]

Since the principle of autonomy of an arbitration agreement is not a purely theoretical concept, but rather a very pragmatic instrument to promote effectiveness of the agreement, there are also other natural limits to application of this concept. In particular, to put an end to scholarly disputes as to whether an arbitration clause is autonomous in the context of assignment of rights or obligations from the main contract, Article 7(11) of the ICAL now expressly says that the arbitration clause is binding for any assignee, irrespective of its prior knowledge of such clause. Plenum Resolution No 53 goes further and expressly indicates that (i) a purchaser of an equity interest in a legal entity is bound by an arbitration clause contained in the charter of the relevant entity (paragraph 23), and (ii) an arbitration clause binds any universal successor of an original party to such clause, including as a result of re-organisation of legal entities (paragraph 25).

[15] See eg AA Kostin and DL Davydenko, 'Russia' in K Hobér and Y Kryvoi (eds), *Law and Practice of International Arbitration in the CIS Region* (Alphen aan den Rijn, Kluwer Law International, 2017) para 1.60.

[16] In support see eg E Gaillard and J Savage (eds), *Phillipe Fouchard, Emmanuel Gaillard, Berthold Goldman on International Commercial Arbitration* (Alphen aan den Rijn, Kluwer Law International BV, 1999) para 712.

While there is no clarity on which law should govern the impact that assignment of rights and/or duties from the underlying contract has on an arbitration clause, the better view is that this should be the *lex causae* governing such assignment.[17]

C. Defects of the Arbitration Agreement

Since, according to the prevailing view in Russian scholarship, an arbitration agreement is a substantive law contract that has procedural effects, such agreement may be null or declared invalid on the basis of the general civil law provisions applicable to other contracts and, more generally, civil law transactions. However, in addition to that, there are some other grounds for invalidity of arbitration agreements as a matter of Russian law.

There is no absolute clarity on whether a party to an arbitration agreement may avoid it on the basis that that party does not have substantial funds to finance participation in arbitration proceedings. Although the Supreme Court in a specific case expressly disagreed with a party's claim that its difficult financial position might automatically lead to the arbitration agreement becoming incapable of being performed, it did not rule out such a possibility in its entirety (especially for natural persons), but rather emphasised the high burden of proof associated with making such a claim.[18] It is yet to be seen how this concept develops in the practice of Russian lower courts.

Russian courts have traditionally been hostile towards so-called asymmetric or unilateral dispute resolution agreements, ie such agreements which enable only one of the parties to choose one of the several forums (arbitration or court). In 2012, the Highest *Arbitrazh* Court declared that asymmetric agreements are invalid, as they violate the principle of equality of the parties,[19] but it has been unclear whether they are invalid in their entirety or whether asymmetric elements alone are not effective as a matter of Russian law. The current position of the Supreme Court is that an asymmetric agreement is automatically transformed into a symmetric one, which means that a party who has been discriminated against may choose between the same forum options as are available to its counterparty.[20] At the same time, Russian courts do not see any issues with symmetric alternative

[17] See eg IS Chuprunov, 'The Arbitration Agreement and Arbitrability: Effects of Contractual Assignment on an Arbitration Clause – Substantive and Private International Law Perspectives' in C Klausegger, P Klein et al (eds), *Austrian Yearbook on International Arbitration 2012* (Munich CH Beck, Vienna MANZ Verlag, Bern Stämpfli Verlag, 2012).

[18] See Opredelenie Sudebnoi Kollegii po Ekonomicheskim Sporam Verkhovnogo Suda RF (Resolution of the Commercial Chamber of the Supreme Court) of 12 July 2017 No 307-ЭС17-640.

[19] See eg Postanovlenie Prezidiuma Vysshego Arbitrazhnogo Suda (Resolution of the Presidium of the Supreme *Arbitrazh* Court) of 19 June 2012 No 1831/12. See a commentary eg in AV Asoskov, 'Unilateral Optional Dispute Resolution Clauses – From Russia with Prejudice', in G Affaki and H Grigera Naón (eds), *Jurisdictional Choices in Times of Trouble* (Alphen aan den Rijn, Wolters Kluwer Law & Business, 2015).

[20] See para 24 of Plenum Resolution No 53; para 7 of 2018 SC Review.

dispute resolution agreements where each of the parties has the same right to elect the forum.[21]

In respect of certain categories of disputes, Russian law allows for an arbitration agreement to be entered into only after the dispute has arisen. The most common example relates to consumer loan agreements – any pre-dispute arbitration agreement in respect of matters relating to such an agreement is invalid as a matter of Russian law.[22]

In 2020, new Articles 248.1 and 248.2 were introduced into the APC providing Russian courts with exclusive jurisdiction over disputes covered by an agreement for arbitration with a seat outside of Russia, provided that (i) such disputes involve sanctioned Russian persons (whether legal entities or individuals) (Sanctioned Person) and (ii) the arbitration agreement is incapable of being performed due to sanctions that limit the Sanctioned Person's 'access to justice'.[23] According to the Supreme Court's interpretation of these rules, the introduction of sanctions (even non-blocking) against a Sanctioned Person shall be per se viewed as creating limits to its 'access to justice'.[24] Therefore, these rules open a door for a Sanctioned Person to ignore the arbitration clause and initiate proceedings in the Russian courts, including in respect of obtaining anti-arbitration injunctions,[25] as well as resist enforcement of any future foreign award in Russia.[26]

III. Arbitrability

A. General Remarks

One of the key features of the Russian ICA framework has always been a predominantly restrictive approach by the Russian courts (and some scholars alike) towards arbitrability of certain categories of disputes.

Historically, the most vulnerable category was in relation to real estate: Russian courts widely believed that, due to the state registration requirements, these disputes involved public policy elements and, as such and whether arising out of contract or not, were not arbitrable.[27] Although this approach has been disavowed by the Constitutional Court[28] and is no longer followed in practice,

[21] See eg para 6 of 2018 SC Review.

[22] See para 19 of Plenum Resolution No 53.

[23] It is worth mentioning that drafting of Art 248.1 is extremely imprecise and there could be an argument that it needs to be interpreted so that Russian courts would not have exclusive jurisdiction over a dispute if arbitration proceedings have already been started in respect of the same dispute.

[24] Opredelenie Sudebnoi Kollegii po Ekonomicheskim Sporam Verkhovnogo Suda RF (Resolution of the Commercial Chamber of the Supreme Court) of 9 December 2021 No 309-ЭС21-6955(1-3).

[25] See section IV.B of this chapter.

[26] See section VIII of this chapter.

[27] See eg para 26 of Informatsionnoe pis'mo Prezidiuma Vysshego Arbitrazhnogo Suda (Review of the Presidium of the Supreme *Arbitrazh* Court) of 22 December 2006 No 96.

[28] Postanovlenie Konstitutsionnogo Suda RF (Resolution of the Constitutional Court) of 26 May 2011 No 10-П.

Russian courts still tend to interpret the statutory provisions on arbitrability in quite a restrictive manner.

While Article 1(3) of the ICAL declares that, unless the law provides otherwise, any civil law dispute may be referred to ICA, in fact, various statutes provide for exceptions from this general principle. Most importantly, Article 33(2) of the APC expressly provides a list of non-arbitrable disputes, which includes eg insolvency matters; registration of legal entities; disputes concerning public or administrative relations; group claims; (subject to a few conditions discussed below) corporate disputes; privatisation disputes; and public procurement matters.

Though an opposing view is still widely supported among Russian ICA scholars and even in court practice,[29] non-arbitrability of a dispute does not *invalidate* the relevant arbitration agreement. Instead, the arbitration agreement becomes unenforceable, but solely to the extent that the particular relevant disputes are not arbitrable (and, therefore, its effect in respect of arbitrable disputes remains intact). This distinction is important, inter alia, from the governing law perspective – the law applicable to arbitrability must be determined independently from the law governing the arbitration agreement.

B. Applicable Law

While it is still often argued in Russian scholarship that arbitrability is governed by the *lex loci arbitri* at any stage of proceedings, it is hard to completely agree with these views. The arbitrability rules in the sphere of ICA are a functional equivalent of the overriding mandatory provisions in the PIL sphere: their applicability is not determined by choice of law, but rather depends primarily on their interpretation and the determination of their sphere of application (ie this is not a choice of law question). Therefore, it is a better and more consistent view that the rules governing arbitrability should be determined based on the same principles as are used in respect of overriding mandatory provisions.[30] This means that, as a general rule, Russian courts may apply *lex fori* rules on arbitrability even at the pre-award stage (provided that the relevant matter falls within their scope). On the other hand, an arbitral tribunal, even with a seat in Russia, is not strictly required to apply the *lex loci arbitri* or any other rules on arbitrability, though it may still want to consider those to the extent required to ensure enforceability of the future arbitral award. Therefore, an arbitral tribunal is free to ignore Russian rules on non-arbitrability of eg corporate disputes to the extent that (i) they are idiosyncratic and not in line

[29] See eg Kostin and Davydenko, 'Russia' (n 15 above) para 1.29; Opredelenie Sudebnoi Kollegii po Ekonomicheskim Sporam Verkhovnogo Suda RF (Resolution of the Commercial Chamber of the Supreme Court) of 2 November 2016 No 306-ЭС16-4741.

[30] See IS Chuprunov, 'Problematika opredeleniya prava, primenimogo k voprosam arbitrabel'nosti' ('Issues Relating to Determination of Law Applicable to Arbitrability') (2011) 5 *Civil Law Review* 92, 92–127.

with international standards, and (ii) there are reasonable prospects of enforcing any future award outside of Russia.

C. Arbitrability of Corporate Disputes

Russian rules regarding arbitrability of corporate disputes are quite complicated and not always clear. The notion of a 'corporate dispute' is defined very vaguely and, while the APC expressly mentions a few categories of disputes that are by definition 'corporate' (eg disputes relating to re-organisation or liquidation of a legal entity, invalidation of corporate resolutions, claims against the management, etc), this list is not exhaustive. Some of the listed categories are described in a perhaps deliberately imprecise manner. As a result, Russian courts sometimes follow a very broad interpretation of the 'corporate dispute' category and may deem that almost any dispute somehow linked to corporate matters is a 'corporate' one.[31]

As far as arbitrability is concerned, corporate disputes are often divided into two categories:

(1) non-arbitrable disputes. This category covers corporate disputes which arguably involve some kind of interests of public policy[32] – eg most disputes in relation to a legal entity which, as of the date when the proceedings start, is a 'strategic' one under the Russian foreign investment legislation;
(2) conditionally arbitrable disputes. These disputes may be referred to arbitration, but only if administered by a PAI, and fall into the following two sub-categories.
   - The first sub-category covers corporate disputes that may be heard by a PAI under regular arbitration rules; in particular, they include corporate disputes regarding ownership, and enforcement of a pledge over, shares (inter alia, disputes from share purchase agreements and pledge agreements).
   - The second sub-category of arbitrable corporate disputes may also be referred to arbitration administered by a PAI, but only if (i) the legal entity itself, all of its participants and all of the relevant other parties have entered into an arbitration agreement (which may be included in the charter of the relevant entity), (ii) the seat of arbitration is in Russia, and (iii) the PAI administering the dispute has adopted special rules for resolution of corporate disputes. This sub-category covers, for instance, disputes in relation to appointment (or early termination of authority) of the members of corporate bodies of a legal entity.

[31] The most notorious example is perhaps Postanovlenie Arbitrazhnogo Suda Moskovskogo Okruga (Resolution of the *Arbitrazh* Court of the Moscow District) of 10 October 2011 Case No A40-35844/11-69-311 – the court (before the 2016 Reform) declared that a dispute in respect of payment of the purchase price for shares is a corporate one and, as such, is not arbitrable.

[32] See OY Skvortsov, MY Savranskiy and GV Sevastyanov (eds), *Mezhdunarodnyi Kommercheskiy Arbitrazh* (*International Commercial Arbitration*), 2nd edn (Treteyskiy sud, Statut, 2018) para 6.3.1.

D. Arbitrability of Other Categories of Disputes

Russian courts have historically taken a restrictive approach to the arbitrability of disputes relating to contracts entered into as a result of public procurement procedures.[33] In particular, in 2015 the Supreme Court declared that a contractual claim regarding payment due under a contract entered into as a result of procurement is not arbitrable due to the significant public element enrooted therein.[34] Following the 2016 Reform, disputes arising out of public procurement contracts were recognised as non-arbitrable until the enactment of a special federal law on this issue.[35] However, a more liberal view is taken in respect of procurement contracts entered into by state-controlled commercial companies. Disputes arising out of such contracts are conditionally arbitrable – they may be referred to arbitration, provided they are administered by a PAI and the seat of arbitration is in Russia.[36]

The same restrictive approach is also relevant for 'privatisation' disputes – Russian courts interpret this category broadly to potentially cover any transfer of public property to a private person, including, eg, as a result of enforcement of a pledge.[37]

IV. Court Intervention and Assistance

A. *Kompetenz-Kompetenz*

The Russian legislation expressly recognises the principle of *Kompetenz-Kompetenz*, whereby questions of the arbitral tribunal's jurisdiction are to be decided by the tribunal itself (Article 16(1) of the ICAL). Furthermore, Article 8(1) of the ICAL follows the pattern of Article II(3) of the NY Convention and Article 8(1) of the Model Law – a Russian court seized of an action in a matter covered by an arbitration agreement shall refer the parties to arbitration at the request of a party, unless this agreement is invalid, inoperative or incapable of being performed. Although Russian law refers to the arbitration agreement being 'not valid' here (and not 'void'), the Supreme Court, in paragraph 16 of its Plenum Resolution No 53, indicates that at this pre-award stage the court review of the arbitration agreement shall be based solely on a prima facie standard (any invalidity, inoperativeness or incapability of being performed needs to be clearly apparent), which makes the mentioned distinction much less significant.

[33] See eg Postanovlenie Prezidiuma Vysshego Arbitrazhnogo Suda (Resolution of the Supreme *Arbitrazh* Court) of 28 January 2014 No 11535/13.

[34] See eg para 15 of 2018 SC Review; Opredelenie Sudebnoi Kollegii po Ekonomicheskim Sporam Verkhovnogo Suda RF (Resolution of the Commercial Chamber of the Supreme Court) of 3 March 2015 No 305-ЭС14-4115.

[35] Article 33(2)(6) of the APC. Such a special federal law has not been enacted as of June 2023.

[36] Article 45(10) of ICAL.

[37] See para 14 of SC Review 2018.

However, it is yet to be seen to what extent the Supreme Court's 'prima facie' approach will be followed by the lower courts.

Notwithstanding the above, Russian court practice admits the bringing of claims directly challenging the validity of the arbitration agreement itself[38] (although this approach is widely condemned in Russian scholarship).

B. Court Intervention

In line with the provisions of the Model Law, Article 5 of the ICAL expressly prohibits any form of court intervention into ICA matters, unless permitted by law.

The following forms of court intervention are permitted under the ICAL:

(1) prima facie review of the arbitration agreement if the court is seized of an action in respect of the matter covered thereby at the pre-award stage;[39]
(2) adoption of anti-arbitration injunctions in support of Sanctioned Persons to prevent arbitration abroad (Article 248.2 of the APC);[40]
(3) taking decisions on a party's challenge to or termination of powers of an arbitrator;
(4) setting aside an arbitral award, including an interim award recognising jurisdiction of the tribunal; and
(5) recognition and enforcement of an arbitral award.

C. Court Assistance

Article 9 of the ICAL expressly enables Russian courts to adopt interim measures in support of ICA (whether the arbitration has its seat in Russia or abroad), unless such measures are incompatible with the arbitration agreement. Although Russian law is generally silent on whether courts may adopt an anti-suit injunction in support of arbitration, whether with a seat in Russia or abroad, there are also no restrictions that could formally prevent that, especially given the broad discretion enjoyed by the Russian courts when granting an interim measure (Article 91(1) of the APC). Nevertheless, so far there have been no instances of Russian courts issuing anti-suit injunctions in support of arbitration.

In certain situations, Russian courts are also authorised to appoint a member of an arbitral tribunal (eg if one of the parties fails to choose its arbitrator or the parties fail to agree on who should be the sole arbitrator) (Article 11(3)–(6) of the ICAL).

[38] See eg Opredelenie Sudebnoi Kollegii po Ekonomicheskim Sporam Verkhovnogo Suda RF (Resolution of the Commercial Chamber of the Supreme Court) of 2 December 2015 No 308-ЭС15-10232.

[39] See section IV.A of this chapter.

[40] Also see section II.C of this chapter.

Russian courts are also empowered to provide support to an ICA in relation to obtaining evidence, but only where such arbitration is administered by a PAI (Article 27 of the ICAL).

D. Exclusion by 'Direct Agreement'

An interesting feature of the ICAL is that parties, by their 'direct agreement' – ie express agreement in an arbitral clause rather than an agreement by reference to the rules of an arbitral institution – may exclude court intervention / support in respect of: (i) appointment or substitution of, and challenges against, arbitrators; and (ii) setting aside awards, including interim ones.[41]

V. Arbitral Procedure

The ICAL expressly allows the parties to an arbitration to agree upon any aspects of the arbitral procedure (Article 19(1)) as well as the place for the hearings (Article 20(1)) subject to mandatory principles of parties' equality and the right of a party to present its case (Article 18). In the absence of such agreement, the procedure (including in respect of production of evidence) shall be determined by the arbitral tribunal. The parties' freedom to agree upon the arbitral procedure may be further subject to the mandatory provisions of the relevant arbitral rules, including in respect of corporate disputes.[42]

An arbitral tribunal and – in case of a dispute managed by a PAI where an arbitral tribunal has not been formed – the PAI itself (if so empowered by the arbitration clause) (Article 17 of the ICAL) may adopt interim relief directed against a party to arbitration. However, given that Russian courts do not enforce arbitral awards on interim measures,[43] the effectiveness of any such relief may be very limited. In practice, if a party is looking for interim measures enforceable in Russia, it would normally seek assistance from a Russian court in the first place.[44]

VI. Law Applicable to the Merits

An arbitral tribunal is required to resolve a dispute in accordance with such rules of law as have been chosen by the parties (Article 28(1) of the ICAL). The reference to 'rules of law' here also includes non-state codifications such as the UNIDROIT Principles.

[41] See section VII of this chapter.
[42] See section III.C of this chapter.
[43] See section VIII of this chapter.
[44] See section IV.C of this chapter.

In case the parties fail to choose an applicable law, an arbitral tribunal may determine it on the basis of such conflict-of-laws rules as it deems appropriate (Article 28(2) of the ICAL). Interestingly enough, the ICAL does not envisage any direct choice of applicable law (*voie directe*) by an arbitral tribunal. Empirical studies demonstrate that, in most cases, an arbitral tribunal with a seat in Russia will be either using solely Russian conflict-of-laws rules or demonstrating that there is no real conflict of laws since application of any potentially relevant conflict-of-laws rules would lead to the same result.[45]

Although, formally, an arbitral tribunal is not required to take into account overriding mandatory provisions, rules regarding arbitrability or public policy considerations of any legal order, including the *lex loci arbitri*, the arbitrators may still wish to consider those in view of their widely recognised duty to render an enforceable award. That said, in the case of an arbitration with a legal seat in Russia, in practice, an arbitral tribunal may be very much inclined to apply, eg, Russian overriding mandatory provisions to avoid their award being set aside by Russian courts.

VII. Setting Aside Arbitral Awards

The ICAL and APC are based on the same principles relating to setting aside an arbitral award (including an interim award recognising the arbitral tribunal's jurisdiction) as the UNCITRAL Model Law: (i) only an award issued by an arbitration with a legal seat in Russia may be set aside by the Russian courts; (ii) Russian courts may not review the substance of an arbitral award; and (iii) applicable legislation provides for an exhaustive list of grounds for setting aside an award that is largely similar to the list set out in Article 34(2) of the UNCITRAL Model Law:

(1) a party to the arbitration agreement is under some incapacity, or this arbitration agreement is not valid[46] under the law chosen by the parties or, in the absence of such choice, under Russian law;
(2) the party was not given proper notice of the appointment of an arbitrator or of the arbitral proceedings, including the time and place of hearings, or was otherwise unable to present its case;
(3) the arbitral award was issued in respect of a dispute not covered by the arbitration agreement;
(4) the composition of an arbitral tribunal or the arbitral procedure was not in accordance with the parties' agreement or the provisions of a federal law;
(5) the subject-matter of the relevant dispute was not arbitrable; or
(6) the arbitral award is in conflict with Russian public policy.

[45] See eg AN Zhiltsov, 'Obzor praktiki MKAS pri TPP RF za 2019 god: obschaya kharakteristika i kollizionnye voprosy' ('Review of the Practice of ICAC at the CCI of the RF for 2019: General Characteristics and Choice of Law Questions') (2021) 8 *Arbitrazh and Civil Procedure* 18, 18–25.

[46] On difference between 'void' and 'not valid' see section IV.A of this chapter.

Grounds (5) and (6) may be raised by a Russian court *ex officio*, while the others, only by the applicant requesting the setting aside of an award.

As demonstrated above, the 2016 Reform made arbitrability of certain categories of disputes conditional upon them being referred to arbitration administered by a PAI with a legal seat in Russia. The purpose of this was most likely to make sure that Russian courts would have jurisdiction over setting aside any award rendered in such arbitration. Given that enforcement of annulled awards has by no means become a general global trend in ICA, Russian courts' control over awards at the set-aside stage became very important, if not critical, for the purposes of their enforceability abroad. That said, in view of the well-known cases where national courts have enforced arbitral awards annulled at the place of arbitration (including due to idiosyncrasies of the local legislation or court practice), there is always a chance that a decision of a Russian court to set aside an arbitral award, eg due to peculiar municipal rules on arbitrability, will nevertheless be ignored by a foreign court at the place of enforcement on the basis of Article V(1)(e) of the NY Convention.

A very interesting and unusual feature of the ICAL – which is not entirely easy to reconcile with the otherwise not very pro-arbitration bias of the Russian courts – is that the parties may, by a so-called 'direct agreement' (ie not by a mere reference to arbitration rules), exclude any set-aside procedures (including in respect of interim awards recognising jurisdiction) if an arbitration is administered by a PAI (Articles 16(3) and 34(1) of ICAL). In contrast to some other examples of national ICA legislation, the parties are free to exclude proceedings to set-aside an arbitral award even if the relevant dispute has a direct connection with the arbitration forum, eg where one of the parties is Russian, dispute relates to performance of a contract in the territory of Russia etc. This arguably puts Russia on the list of the most pro-arbitration jurisdictions (though this is perhaps one of the very few reasons for this). Notwithstanding the law being silent on this, Russian courts would be ready to ignore the exclusion of the set-aside procedure if an award violated public policy or the relevant matter was not arbitrable.[47]

VIII. Recognition and Enforcement of Awards

The Russian legislation (Article 36(1) of the ICAL and equivalent provisions of the APC and CPC) provides an exhaustive list of grounds when recognition or enforcement of an award may be refused. This list is in line with Articles V(1) and V(2) of the NY Convention and largely follows the same pattern as the grounds for setting aside an award described above, ie there are the same five grounds upon which enforcement may be refused at the request of a party (eg incapacity of a party, invalidity of the arbitration agreement, etc) and two grounds on which enforcement may be refused by the Russian court *ex officio* (non-arbitrability and public policy).

[47] See para 21 of 2018 SC Review.

While the Russian enforcement rules themselves closely follow international standards, their interpretation by Russian courts (similarly to courts of some other not entirely arbitration-friendly parties to the NY Convention) is much less in line with the prevailing international approaches. First of all, as already indicated above, Russian courts have taken a restrictive approach regarding the arbitrability of a few significant categories of commercial disputes.

Furthermore, there are a few recent notorious examples of unduly broad interpretation of the public policy exception by Russian courts. For instance, the Moscow District Court quoted the public policy exception as the reason for non-enforcement of a foreign award where the claimant had failed to provide original or duly certified copies of the underlying contracts containing the arbitration clause.[48] The same court also decided that enforcement of an award against a strategically important legal entity whose ultimate beneficiary was the Russian Federation would violate Russian public policy, as this would have resulted in losses to the Russian budget,[49] while the North-Western District Court decided that enforcement of a foreign award may be refused on public policy grounds if it would otherwise result in a breach of Russian currency control restrictions.[50] In addition, a court may refuse to enforce an award if the respondent is able to demonstrate that the awarded amount of liquidated damages or contractual penalty was punitive in nature.[51]

Finally, where a foreign arbitral award has been issued against a Sanctioned Person, they may also resist its enforcement in Russia, unless they have accepted jurisdiction of the arbitral tribunal (Article 248.1(5) of the APC). It is not clear yet what exact legal grounds Russian courts may use to justify non-enforcement of such awards, but they will most likely cite either Article V(2)(a) (non-arbitrability) or Article V(2)(b) (public policy) of the NY Convention.

Russian courts are likely to resist enforcement of an award issued in an arbitration with a legal seat outside of Russia in respect of a 'domestic' matter. So far, the legal basis for this has been mainly the public policy exception, on the basis that (i) the real legal seat of the tribunal was in Russia (including because all of the hearings have taken place there) and (ii) the relevant arbitration was administered by a foreign institution that did not have a PAI licence.[52] It remains to be seen which variation of these arguments will be used going forward, eg in cases where the relevant arbitral institution has a PAI licence.

[48] Postanovlenie Arbitrazhnogo Suda Moskovskogo Okruga (Resolution of the *Arbitrazh* Court of the Moscow District) of 15 March 2018 Case No A40-60583/2016.

[49] Postanovlenie Arbitrazhnogo Suda Moskovskogo Okruga (Resolution of the *Arbitrazh* Court of the Moscow District) of 29 August 2019 Case No A40-117326/2018.

[50] Postanovlenie Arbitrazhnogo Suda Severo-Zapadnogo Okruga (Resolution of the *Arbitrazh* Court of the North-Western District) of 9 November 2021 Case No A56-131886/2019.

[51] See para 6 of Informatsionnoe pis'mo Prezidiuma Vysshego Arbitrazhnogo Suda (Review of the Presidium of the Supreme *Arbitrazh* Court) of 26 February 2013 No 156.

[52] See eg Opredelenie Sudebnoi Kollegii po Ekonomicheskim Sporam Verkhovnogo Suda RF (Resolution of the Commercial Chamber of the Supreme Court) of 12 March 2020 No 304-ЭС19-20506; Postanovlenie Arbitrazhnogo Suda Moskovskogo Okruga (Resolution of the *Arbitrazh* Court of the Moscow District) of 19 July 2017 Case No A40-219464/16.

It is also worth mentioning that Russian courts have historically adopted a very conservative approach towards enforcement of any interim awards, including in respect of any interim measures, on the basis that only 'final' arbitral awards are subject to enforcement in accordance with the NY Convention regime.[53] The 2016 Reform failed to deal with this problem, as none of the relevant provisions from the 2006 version of the Model Law (Articles 17(H) and 17(I)) have been incorporated into the ICAL.

The ICAL (in deviation from the Model Law) provides for the right of a party to object against recognition of an arbitral award where such award does not require enforcement (eg an award on prospective termination of a contract) (Article 35(3)).

We are not aware of any instances where Russian courts have relied on their discretionary powers in Article V(1)(e) of the NY Convention and enforced a foreign award that was set aside at the place of its issue.[54]

[53] See eg Postanovlenie Prezidiuma Vysshego Arbitrazhnogo Suda (Resolution of the Presidium of the Supreme *Arbitrazh* Court) of 5 October 2010 No 6547/10.

[54] See Skvortsov, Savranskiy and Sevastyanov (eds), *International Commercial Arbitration* (n 32 above) para 20.4.

BIBLIOGRAPHY

A

Abashidze, A, Gasanova, K, and Strigunova, D (eds), *Mezhdunarodnoe Chastnoe Pravo: Uchebnik dlya Studentov Vuzov, Obuchayoushikhsya po Napravleniyu Podgotovki Yourisprudentsiya (Private International Law: Coursebook for University Students Pursuing Legal Studies)*, 2nd edn (Moscow, UNITY-DANA: Zakon i Pravo, 2022).

Abdullin, A, *Ocherki Istorii Nauki Mezhdunarodnogo Chastnogo Prava v Rossii: Problemy Ponimaniya Prirody Mezhdunarodnogo Chastnogo Prava v Trudah Otechestvennykh Pravovedov XIX–Nachala XX Vekov (Essays on the History of Science of Private International Law in Russia: Problems of Understanding of the Nature of Private International Law in the Works of Russian Legal Scholars of the Nineteenth–the beginning of the Twentieth Century)* (Kazan, Kazansky Gosudarstvennyi Universitet, 2004).

Abova, TE, Boguslavskiy, MM, and Svetlanov AG (eds), *Kommentariy k Grazhdanskomu Kodeksu Rossiyskoy Federatsii, chasti tret'ei (postateynyi) (Commentary to the Civil Code of the Russian Federation, Part Three (Article-by-Article)* (Moscow, Urait, 2004).

Ageshkina, N, *Nauchno-Praktichenskyi Kommentariy k Federal'nomu Zakonu ot 15 iula 1995 g. No 101-FZ 'O Mezhdunarodnykh Dogovorakh Rossiyskoy Federatsii' (Scientific Practical Commentary to the Federal Law of the Russian Federation 'On the International Treaties of the Russian Federation' dated 15 July 1995 No. 101-FZ)* (ConsultantPlus, 2013).

Ananyeva, K and Ananyev, A, 'Obychaj i Iego Znacheniye kak Istochnika Grazhdanskogo Prava' ('Customary Rule and its Meaning as a Source of Civil Law') (2015) 15 *Yurist* 35.

Asoskov, AV, 'Dopustimo li peredavat' chisto vnutrennie spory bez inostrannogo elementa na razreshenie inostrannogo arbitrazha?' ('Is It Permissible to Refer to Foreign Arbitration Purely Domestic Disputes without a Foreign Element?') (2017) 8 *Zakon* 115.

—— *Kollizionnoe regulirovanie dogovornyh objazatel'stv* (*Contractual Obligations in the Conflict of Laws*) (Moscow, Infotropik Media, 2012).

—— 'Kollizionnoe regulirovanie voprosov pravosposobnosti yuridicheskogo litsa i polnomochiy ego organov: kak naiti balans mezhdu interesami uchastnikov yuridicheskogo litsa i potrebnostyami grazhdanskogo oborota?' ('Conflict of Law Regulation of the Capacity Matters of a Legal Entity and of the Authorities of Its Organs: How to Find Balance between the Interests of the Participants of the Legal Entity and the Needs of the Civil Commerce') (2014) 4 *Civil Law Review* 7.

—— 'Novoe Postanovlenie Plenuma Verhovnogo Suda RF o primenenii norm mezhdunarodnogo chastnogo prava: kljuchevye raz'jasnenija' (New Resolution of the Plenum of the Supreme Court of the Russian Federation on the Application of Rules of Private International Law: Key Explanations) (2019) 11 *Sud'ja* 12.

—— 'Unilateral Optional Dispute Resolution Clauses – From Russia with Prejudice' in G Affaki and H Grigera Naón (eds), *Jurisdictional Choices in Times of Trouble* (Wolters Kluwer Law & Business, 2015) 55.

—— 'National Report on Russian Federation' in J Basedow, G Rühl, F Ferrari and P De Miguel Asensio (eds), *Encyclopedia of Private International Law* (Cheltenham, Edward Elgar Publishing, 2017) 2459.

Asoskov, AV and Zhiltsov, AV (eds), *Kommentariy k Razdelu VI 'Mezhdunarodnoe Chastnoe Pravo' Grazhdanskogo Kodeksa Rossiyskoy Federatsii (postateynyi) (Commentary to Section VI 'Private International Law' of the Civil Code of the Russian Federation (Article-by-Article)* (Moscow, Statut, 2021).

B

Badykov, M, 'The Russian Civil Code and the Rome Convention: Applicable Law in the Absence of Choice by the Parties' (2005) 1(2) *Journal of Private International Law* 270.

—— 'The Characteristic Performance Test in the Russian Civil Code and 1980 European Convention on the Law Applicable to Contractual Obligations' in I Erpyleva, ME Gashi-Butler and JE Henderson (eds), *Forging A Common Legal Destiny* (London, Wildy, Simmonds & Hill Publishers, 2005) 727.

Bakhin, S, 'Mezhdunarodnaya Sostavlayschaya Pravovoi Sistemy Rossii' ('International Element of Russian Legal System') (2007) 6 *Pravovedenie* 126.

—— 'K Voprosu ob Istokhakh Izucheniya Mezhdunarodnogo Chastnogo Prava Rossii' ('On the Origins of the Study of Private International Law in Russia') (2022) 4 *Russian Law Journal* 56.

Bakhin, S and Ignatiev, A, 'Pravovaya pomoshch' i pravovye otnosheniya po grazhdanskim i semeynym delam: korrektirovka reglamentatsii v ramkah SNG (Kishinyovskaya konventsiya 2002)' ('Legal Assistance and Legal Relations in Civil and Family Matters: Amendments to the Regulation within the CIS (2002 Kishinev Convention)') (2005) 4 *Zhurnal mezhdunarodnogo chastnogo prava* 3.

Bardina, MP, 'The Russian Civil Code on the Law Applicable to Contractual Obligations: Comparison with the 1980 Rome Convention' in I Erpyleva, ME Gashi-Butler and JE Henderson (eds), *Forging A Common Legal Destiny* (London, Wildy, Simmonds & Hill Publishers, 2005) 747.

Behrens, P, 'Connecting Factors for the Determination of the Proper Law of Companies' in P Mankowski and W Wurmnest (eds), *Festschrift für Ulrich Magnus zum 70. Geburtstag* (Berlin, Otto Schmidt/De Gruyter, 2014) 353.

Belov, V, 'Chto takoe predvidimost?' ('What is Foreseeability?') (2019) 3 *Zakon*.

Bernitt, C, *Die Anknuepfung von Vorfragen im europaischen Kollisionsrecht* (Tübingen, Mohr Siebeck, 2010).

Bogdanova-Pataud, N, '*Emergence d'un nouveau droit international privé en Russie et en CEI*' (Doctor of Law thesis, Université Paris 1 Panthéon Sorbonne, 2005).

Boguslavskiy, M, *Mezhdunarodnoe Chastnoe Pravo: Uchebnik* (*International Private Law: Textbook*), 6th edn (Moscow, Norma: INFRA-M, 2009).

—— *Mezhdunarodnoe Chastnoe Pravo: Uchebnik* (*Private international law: Coursebook*), 7th edn (Moscow, Norma: INFRA-M, 2016).

—— (ed), *Sovremennoye Mezhdunarodnoye Chastnoye Pravo v Rossii i Evrosoyuze (Modern Private International Law in Russia and European Union)* (Moscow, Norma, 2013).

Bonomi, A, 'Incidental (Preliminary) Question' in J Basedow, G Ruehl, F Ferrari and PM Asensio (eds), *Encyclopedia of Private International Law* Vol 2 (Cheltenham, Edward Elgar Publishing, 2017) 912.

Borodkin, S, 'Novyj podhod k klassifikacii ob'ektov veshchnyh prav' ('A new approach to the classification of objects of property rights') (2018) 2 *Zhurnal rossijskogo prava* (*Journal of Russian Law*) 53.

Brun, M, 'Mezhdunarodnoe Chastnoe Pravo, Lektsii, Chitannye v Moskovskom Kommercheskom Institute v 1908–09 Akadmicheskom Godu' ('Private International Law, Courses Given at the Moscow Commercial Institute in 1908–09 Academic Year') in A Kolodkin and V Ershov (eds), *Zolotoy Fond Rossiiskoy Nauki Mezhdunarodnogo Prava* (*Golden Heritage of the Russian Science of Private International Law*) (Moscow, Mezhdunarodnye otnosheniya, 2009) 107 (translation from Russian).

—— *Mezhdunarodnoe Chastnoe Pravo, Kurs, Chitannyi v Moskovskom Kommercheskom Institute 1910–11 (Private International Law, Course Given at the Moscow Commercial Institute 1910–11)* (Moscow, Publishing House of Prokhorov and Yashkin, 1911).

Budilin, S, 'Process o dvadcati dvuh milliardah, ili Neverojatnye prikljuchenija RIKO v Rossii' ('Case on Twenty Two Billions, or the Incredible Adventures of RICO in Russia') (2008) 10 *Corporate Lawyer*.

Bykova, E, 'O Ratifikatsii Konventsii o Pravovoi Pomoschi i Pravovykh Otnosheniyakh po Grazhdankim, Semeinym i Ugolovnym Delam' ('On Ratification of the Convention on Legal Assistance and Legal Relationship in Civil, Family and Criminal Matters') (2013) 9 *Rossijskij Sud'ya* 39.

C

Carruthers, J, *The Transfer of Property in the Conflict of Laws* (Oxford, Oxford University Press, 2005).

Chigrinova, KS and Getselevich, LI (eds), *Zolotoy Fond Rossiiskoy Nauki Mezhdunarodnogo Prava* (*Golden Heritage of the Russian Science of Private International Law*) (Moscow, Mezhdunarodnye otnosheniya, 2009).

Chuprunov, IS, 'Dopustimost' vzyskaniya ubytkov iz narusheniya arbitrazhnogo ili prorogatsionnogo soglasheniy' ('Availability of Damages Claim for a Breach of Arbitration or Forum Selection Agreements') (2011) 6 *Civil Law Review* 62.

—— 'Problematika opredeleniya prava, primenimogo k voprosam arbitrabel'nosti' ('Issues Relating to Determination of Law Applicable to Arbitrability') (2011) 5 *Civil Law Review* 92.

—— 'The Arbitration Agreement and Arbitrability: Effects of Contractual Assignment on an Arbitration Clause – Substantive and Private International Law Perspectives' in C Klausegger, P Klein et al (eds), *Austrian Yearbook on International Arbitration 2012* (Munich C.H. Beck, Vienna MANZ Verlag, Bern Stämpfli Verlag, 2012) 32.

Collins, L, Harris, J et al (eds), Dicey, *Morris and Collins on the Conflict of Laws*, 16th edn (London, Sweet & Maxwell, 2022).

Csach, K, 'Cross-border Shareholders' Agreements and Private International Law' in S Mock, K Csach and B Havel (eds), *International Handbook on Shareholders' Agreements* (Berlin, De Gruyter, 2018) 83.

D

Dmitrieva, GK (ed), *Mezhdunarodnoe Chastnoe Pravo: Uchebnik* (*Private international law: Coursebook*), 4th edn (Moscow, Prospekt, 2016).

E

Egeler, E, *Konsensprobleme im internationalen Schuldvertragsrecht* (St Gallen, Dike 1994).

Erpyleva, N, *Mezhdunarodnoe Chastnoe Pravo: Uchebnik dlya Vuzov* (*Private International Law: Coursebook for Universities*) (Moscow, Higher School of Economics Publishing House, 2015).

Esakov, G, 'The Russian Criminal Jury: Recent Developments, Practice, and Current Problems' (2012) 60 *The American Journal of Comparative Law* 665.

F

Fawcett, J and Carruthers, J, *Cheshire, North & Fawcett, Private International Law*, 14th edn (Oxford, Oxford University Press, 2008).

Fonotova, O, 'Printsypy UNIDROIT Kak "Primenimoe Pravo" (Prakticheskiy Aspekt)' ('UNIDROIT Principles as "Applicable Law" (Practical Aspect)' (2017) 10 *Pravo i Ekonomika*.

G

Gaillard, E and Savage, J (eds), *Phillipe Fouchard, Emmanuel Gaillard, Berthold Goldman on International Commercial Arbitration* (Alphen aan den Rijn, Kluwer Law International BV, 1999).

Getman-Pavlova, I, *Mezhdunarodnoe Chastnoe Pravo: Uchebnik (Private International Law: Coursebook)*, 3rd edn (Moscow, Eksmo, 2011).

Getman-Pavlova, I and Yerpyleva, N, 'Rossiiskoye Zakonodatel'stvo po Mezhdunarodnomu Chastnomu Pravu: Problemy Sovershenstvovaniya' ('Russian Legislation on Private International Law: Improvement Problems') (2009) 1 *Mezhdunarodnoye Publichnoye i Chastnoye Pravo*.

Gongalo, B (ed), *Grazhdanskoe pravo: Uchebnik. V 2-h tomah. Tom 1* (*Civil Law: Textbook in 2 volumes Vol 1*), 2nd edn (Moscow, Statut, 2017) 201.

Grigoryeva, O, 'Razvitiye Pravovykh Osnov Mezhdunarodnoi Pomoschi po Grazhdanskim Delam v Ramkakh Souyza Nezavisimykh Gosudarstv' ('Development of Legal Grounds of International Assistance on Civil Matters Within the Commonwealth of Independent States') (2011) 1 *Pravo i Ekonomika* 72.

H

Haudek, W, *Die Bedeutung des Parteiwillens im internationalen Privatrecht* (Berlin, Julius Springer, 1931).

Hay, P, Weintraub, R and Borchers, P, *Conflict of Laws. Cases and Materials*, 14th edn (Galeta, Foundation Press, 2013)

Hodykin, R, 'Commentary to Article 1220.1 of the Civil Code' in I Zykin, A Asoskov and A Zhiltsov (eds), *Kommentarij k razdelu VI 'Mezhdunarodnoe chastnoe pravo' chasti tret'ej Grazhdanskogo kodeksa Rossijskoj Federacii (postatejnyj)* (*Commentary on Section VI 'Private International Law' of Part Three of the Civil Code of the Russian Federation (Article-by-Article)*) (Moscow, Statut, 2021).

Honsell, H, Vogt, NP, Schnyder, A, and Berti, S, *Basler Kommentar Internationales Privatrecht*, 2nd edn (Basel, Helbing & Lichtenhahn, 2007).

I

Ivanov, G and Makovskiy, A, *Mezhdunarodnoe chastnoe morskoe parvo* (*International Private Maritime Law*) (Leningrad, 'Sudostroenie', 1984).

J

Jaspers, MB, *Nachträgliche Rechtswahl im internationalen Schuldvertragsrecht: unter besonderer Berücksichtigung der Rechtspraxis in England, Frankreich, Dänemark und Deutschland – Saarbrücker Studien zum Privat- und Wirtschaftsrecht*, Band 30 (Frankfurt, Peter Lang, 2002).

K

Kabatova, E, 'Commentary to Article 1210 of the Civil Code' in T Abova, M Boguslavskiy and A Svetlanova (eds), *Kommentariy k Grazhdanskomy Kodeksy Rossiyskoy Federatsii, Chasti Tretiey, Tom 3* (*Commentary to the Civil Code of the Russian Federation, Part III*) (Moscow, Urait-Izdatelstvo, 2004).

—— 'The Latest Amendments in the Russian International Private Law' (2014) 4(86) *Zhurnal mezhdunarodnogo chastnogo prava.*

—— *Delikty v mezhdunarodnom chastnom prave (Torts in Private International Law)* (1992) 9 *Gosudarstvo i pravo.*

Kanashevsky, V, *Mezhdunarodnoe Chastnoe Pravo: Uchebnik* (*Private International Law: Coursebook*) (Moscow, Mezhdunarodnye Otnosheniya, 2019).

—— 'O Neposredstvonnom Deystvii Mezhdunarodnykh Dogovorov v RF' ('On Direct Application of International Treaties in RF') (2002) 4 *Rossijskij Yuridicheskiy Zhurnal.*

—— *Vneshneekonomicheskie sdelki: material'no-pravovoe i kollizionnoe regulirovanie* (*Foreign Economic Transactions: Substrative and Conflict of Law Regulation)* (Alphen aan den Rijn, Wolters Kluwer, 2008).

—— *Pravovoy rezhim ofshornykh kompaniy i trastov* (*Legal Regime for Offshore Companies and Trusts*) (Moscow, Mezhdunarodnyye otnosheniya, 2015).

—— 'Kollizionnye voprosy razdela mezhdu suprugami sovmestno nazhitogo imushchestva, nahodyashchegosya za rubezhom' ('Collision Issues of Division between Spouses of Jointly Acquired Property Located Abroad') (2020) 2 *Zakon* (*The Law*) 181.

Karabelnikov, BR, 'National Report for Russian Federation (2020 through 2022)' in L Bosman (ed), *ICCA International Handbook on Commercial Arbitration* (Alphen aan den Rijn, Kluwer Law International, 2020).

Karandashov, I, 'Prinyatie nasledstva za rubezhom i ego pravovye posledstviya na territorii Rossii' ('Acceptance of Inheritance Abroad: Legal Consequences in Russia') (2019) 8 *Zakon* 162.

Kashkin, S, *Integratsionniye Pravo v Sovremennom Mire: Sravnitel'no-Pravovoye Issledovaniye* (*Integrated Law in the Modern World: a Comparative Legal Study*) (Moscow, Prospekt, 2015).

Karayanidi, M, 'Adjudicative Jurisdiction in Civil and Commercial Matters in Russia: Analysis and Commentary' (2016) 64 *The American Journal of Comparative Law* 981.

—— 'Russian Perspectives on the Hague Principles' in D Girsberger, T Kadner Graziano and JL Neels (eds), *Choice of Law in International Commercial Contracts* (Oxford, Oxford University Press, 2021).

Khuzhokova, I, *Doktrina Dobrykh Nravov i Publichnogo Poryadka v Dogovornom Prave: Sravnitel'noye Issledovaniye* (*The Doctrine of Bona Fides and Public Policy in the Contract Law: a Comparative Study*) (Moscow, Norma, 2011).

Kolesnikova, S, 'O doveritel'noy sobstvennosti (traste), ili 15 let spustya' ('On trusts, or 15 years later') (2007) 10 *Zakon* (*The Law*) 188.

Komarov, A, *Printsypy Mezhdunarodnykh Kommercheskikh Dogovorov UNIDROIT 2010* (*UNIDROIT Principles 2010 in International Commercial Contracts*) (2013) VIII.

—— 'Reference to the UNIDROIT Principles in International Commercial Arbitration practice in the Russian Federation' (2011) 16(3) *Uniform Law Review* 657.

—— 'Commentary to Article 1210 of the Civil Code' in N Marysheva and K Yaroshenko (eds), *Kommentariy k Grazhdanskomy Kodeksy Rossiyskoy Federatsii, Chasti Tretiey* (*Postateyniy*) (*Article-by-Article Commentary to the Civil Code of the Russian Federation, Part III*) (Moscow, Kontrakt, 2009) 479.

Kostin, AA and Davydenko, DL, 'Russia' in K Hobér and Y Kryvoi (eds), *Law and Practice of International Arbitration in the CIS Region* (Alphen aan den Rijn, Kluwer Law International, 2017).

Kotelnikov, A, Kurochkin, S and Skvortsov, O, *Arbitration in Russia* (Alphen aan den Rijn, Kluwer Law International, 2019).

Koval, V, 'Primenenie negosudarstvennyh svodov chastnogo prava rossijskimi sudami' ('Application of Non-State Restatements of Private Law by Russian Courts') in A Shirvindt and N Scherbakov (eds), *Opyty civilisticheskogo issledovanija* (*Essays in Civil Law*), 5th edn (Moscow, Statut, 2023).

Krivenky, A, *Zarozhdenie i Razvitie Mezhdunarodnogo Chastnogo Prava (XII–XX veka)* (*Emergence and Development of Private International Law (Twelfth–Twentieth centuries)*) (Moscow, INFRA-M, 2022).

Kutashevskaia, I, 'Princip avtonomii voli kak sposob nivelirovaniya problemy konkurencii vnedogovornyh trebovanij v mezhdunarodnom chastnom prave' ('The Principle of Autonomy of Will as a Way of Levelling the Problem of Concurrence of Non-contractual Claims in Private International Law') (2022) 4 *Vestnik grazhdanskogo prava*.

L

Lando, O, 'Party Autonomy in the EC Convention on the Law Applicable to Contractual Obligations' in F Rigaux and P Bourrel (eds), *The Influence of the European Communities upon Private International Law of the Member States* (Bruxelles, Larcier, 1981).

Laptev, V, 'Lokal'niy Pravovoy Obychay kak Istochnik Regulirovaniya Pradprinimatel'skikh Otnosheniy' ('A Local Custom as a Source of Regulation of Business Relations') (2017) 4 *Lex russica* 110.

Lebedev, S, 'On the Nature of Private International Law' (1980) *Soviet Yearbook of International Law* 61.

Lebedev, S, and Kabatova, E (eds), *Mezhdunarodnoe Chastnoe Pravo: Uchebnik v Dvuh Tomah, Tom 1: Obchshaya Chast* (*Private international law: Coursebook, in 2 volumes, Volume 1: General Part*) (Moscow, Statut, 2011).

—— *Mezhdunarodnoe Chastnoe Pravo: Uchebnik* (*Private International Law: Textbook*) Volume 2 (Moscow, Statut, 2015).

Lebedev, S, Muranov, A, Khodykin, R and Rabatov, E, 'New Russian Legislation on Private International Law' (2002) 4 *Yearbook of Private International Law* 117.

Lipstein, K, 'Introduction: The Preliminary Draft Convention on the Law Applicable to Contractual and Non-Contractual Obligations' in K Lipstein (ed), *Harmonization of Private International Law by the E.E.C* (London, Institute of Advanced Legal Studies, 1978).

Lorents, DV, and Shott, EK, 'Pravosposobnost' nastsiturusa: nasledstvenno-pravovoi aspect' ('Legal Capacity of the Nasciturus: Succession Law Aspect') (2015) 3 *Law of Succession* 24.

Lorenzen, E, '*The Theory of Qualifications and the Conflict of Laws*' (1920) 20(3) *Columbia Law Review* 247.

Lukashuk, I, *Sovremennoye Pravo Mezhdunarodnykh Dogovorov* (*Modern Law of International Treaties*) Vol 1, (Moscow, Wolters Kluwer Russia, 2004).

Lunts, L, *Kurs Mezhdunarodnogo Chastnogo Prava: v 3 t.* (*Course of Private International Law in 3 Volumes*) (Moscow, Spark, 2002).

—— *Voprosy Mezhdunarodnogo Chastnogo Prava* (*Private International Law Issues*) (Moscow, Gosudarstvennoe Izdatelstvo Youridicheskoy Literatury, 1956).

Lyubarskaya, T and Lashkov, N, '*Problemy kollizionnogo regulirovaniya zaloga v Rossii i za rubezhom*' (Contemporary Issues in the Law Applicable to the Security Interests in Movable Property in Russia and Abroad) (2018) 8 *Zakon* (*The Law*) 156.

Lyubimova, M, 'Nekotorye problemnye aspekty vydeleniya obyazatel'noj doli i transgranichnogo nasledovaniya nedvizhimogo imushchestva' (Some Problematic Aspects of Compulsory Share and Cross-Border Succession of Real Estate) (2022) 11 *Notarial'nyj vestnik* 48.

M

Makovskiy, A, *O Kodifikatsii Grazhdanskogo Prava (1922–2006)* (*On Codification of Civil Law (1922–2006)*) (Moscow, Statut, 2010).

Makovskiy, A and Sukhanov, E (eds), *Kommentarij k chasti tret'ej Grazhdanskogo kodeksa Rossijskoj Federacii (postatejnyj)* (*Commentary on Part Three of the Civil Code of the Russian Federation (article-by-article)*) (Moscow, Yurist, 2002).

Maleshin, D, 'The Russian Style of Civil Procedure' (2007) 21 *Emory International Law Review* 543.

Malkin, O, Domrachev, V, 'Primenenie principov mezhdunarodnyh kommercheskih kontraktov UNIDRUA dlja tolkovanija i vospolnenija nacional'nogo zakonodatel'stva' (The Use of the UNIDROIT Principles of International Commercial Contracts to Interpret and Supplement Domestic Law) 2016 *Zhurnal mezhdunarodnogo chastnogo prava* 3.

—— 'Vybor principov UNIDRUA v kachestve primenimogo prava: ispol'zovanie gosudarstvennymi sudami podhodov MKAS pri TPP RF' ('Choice of the UNIDROIT Principles as Applicable Law: the Use by State Courts of the Approaches of the International Commercial Arbitration Court at the Chamber of Commerce and Industry of the Russian Federation') (2022) 1 *Tretejskij sud* (*The Arbitral Tribunal*) 79.

Malyushin, A, *Konstitutsionno-sudenboye Pravotvorchestvo v Rossiiskoy Federatsii: Problemy Teorii i Praktiki* (*Lawmaking of Constitutional Court in the Russian Federation: Theoretical and Practical Problems*) (Moscow, Yurist, 2013).

Marysheva, N, 'K Voprosy Kodifikatsii Norm Mezhdunarodnogo Grazhdanskogo Protsessa v Rossii' ('On Codification of International Civil Procedure Norms in Russia') (2004) 6 *Zhurnal Rossijskogo Prava*.

—— (ed), *Mezhdunarodnoe Chastnoe Pravo: Uchebnik* (*International Private Law: Textbook*), 3rd edn (Moscow, Kontrakt, 2011).

—— *Mezhdunarodnoye Chastnoye Pravo: Uchebnik* (*Private International Law: Textbook*), 4th edn (Moscow, IZiSP Kontrakt, 2018).

Marysheva, N and Zvekov, V, 'Novaya Kodifikatsiya Norm Mezhdunarodnogo Chastnogo Prava' ('New Codification of Private International Law Norms') (2002) 4 *Khozyaistvo i Pravo* 3.

Mashovec, A and Medvedev, I, *Nastol'naya kniga notariusa: v 4 tomah. Tom 4: Mezhdunarodnoe chastnoe pravo, ugolovnoe pravo i process v notarial'noj deyatel'nosti* (*Handbook of a notary: in 4 volumes. Volume 4: International private law, criminal law and process in notarial activity*) (Moscow, Statut, 2015).

Max Planck Institute for Comparative and International Private Law: 'Comments on the European Commission's Green Paper on the Conversion of the Rome Convention of 1980 on the Law Applicable to Contractual Obligations into a Community Instrument and its Modernization' (2004) 68(1) *The Rabel Journal of Comparative and International Private Law*.

Mazhorina, M, 'Primenime Pravo v Mezhdunarodnykh Kommercheskikh Kontraktakh: Sovremennoe Tolkovanie i Prognoziruemaya Praktika Mezhdunarovnykh Kommercheskikh Arbitrazhei i Natsionalnukh Sudov' ('Applicable Law in International Commercial Contracts: Contemporary Interpretation and Prognosed Practice of International Commercial Arbitral Tribunals') (2015) 6 *Zakonodatel'svo* 79.

Mistelis, L, *Charakterisierungen und Qualifikation im internationalen Privatrecht: zur Lehre einer parteispezifischen Qualifikation im Kollisionsrecht der privaten Wirtschaft* (Tübingen, Mohr Siebeck, 1999).

Muranov, A (ed), *Mezhdunarodnuy Kommercheskiy Arbitrazh: Oput Otechestvennogo Regulirovaniya/Samoregulirovaniya* (*International Commercial Arbitration: Experience of Domestic Regulation/Self-Regulation*) vol I (2012).

N

Neshataeva, T, 'K Voprosy ob Istochnikakh Prava – Sudebnom Pretsedente i Doktrine' ('On the Sources of Law – Court Precedent and Doctrinal Writings') (2000) 5 *Vestnik VAS RF* 105.

Novitskiy, I, *Obychaj Grazhdanskogo Oborota v Projekte Obyazatel'stvennogo Prava* (*Customary Rule in Civil Commerce in the Draft Law of Obligations*) Vol 1 (Moscow, Statut, 2006).

Nygh, P, *Autonomy in International Contracts* (Oxford, Oxford University Press, 1999).

O

'Obobscheniya Diskussij Rabochei Gruppy po Podgotovke Izmenenyi i Dopolnenyi v Razdel VI "Mezhdunarodnoye Chastnoye Pravo" GK RF' ('Overviews of the Discussions of the Working Group on the Preparation of Amendments to the Division VI "Private International Law" of the Civil Code of the Russian Federation') (2019) 19(2) *Vestnik Grazhdanskogo Prava*.

Osminin, B, *Prinyatie i Pealizatsiya Gosudarstvami Mezdunarodnykh Dogovornykh Obyazatelstv* (*Undertaking and Performance of International Contractual Obligations by the States*) (Moscow, Wolters Kluwer, 2006).

—— *Zaklucheniye i Implementatsiya Mezhdunarodnykh Dogovorov i Vnutrigosudarstvennoye Pravo* (*Conclusion and Implementation of International Treaties and Internal Legislation*) (Moscow, Infotropik, 2010).

Ostapovich, I, 'Osobennosti Zakonotvorcheskikh Polnomochiy Konstitutsionnogo Suda Rossiyskoy Federatsii' (Features of Legislative Powers of the Constitutional Court of the Russian Federation) (2014) 4 *Vestnik Omskogo Universiteta* 100.

Overbeck, A, 'Contracts: the Swiss Draft Statute Compared with the E.E.C. Convention' in P North (ed), *Contract Conflicts: The E.E.C. Convention on the Law Applicable to Contractual Obligations: a Comparative Study* (Amsterdam, North-Holland Publishers, 1982) 271.

P

Panarina, M, 'Rol' Pravovykh Obychaev v Sovremennoi Sudebnoi Praktike: Pravovoye Issledovaniye' ('The Role of Customary Rules in the Modern Judicial Practice: Legal Review') (2018) 3 *Advokatskaya Praktika* 18.

Petrov, E, Bezvenko, RS and Budylin, SL (eds), *Nasledstvennoe Pravo: Postatejnyj Kommentarij K Stat'yam 1110–1185, 1224 Grazhdanskogo kodeksa Rossijskoj Federacii* (*Inheritance Law: Article-by-Article Commentary On Articles 1110–1185, 1224 of the Civil Code of the Russian Federation*) (Moscow, Statut, 2018).

Plekhanov, V, *Perekhod prava sobstvennosti po dogovoru mezhdunarodnoj kupli-prodazhi tovarov* (*Transfer of Ownership under a Cross-Border Contract for the Sale of Goods*) (Dissertation for the PhD degree / degree of candidate of legal sciences, Moscow 2008).

Podkopalov, I, 'Nekotoryye aspekty pravovogo regulirovaniya transgranichnogo oborota tsennykh bumag, uchityvayemykh cherez posrednika' ('Some Aspects of the Legal Regulation of Cross-Border Transactions with Securities through an Intermediary') (2021) 12 *Vestnik ekonomicheskogo pravosudiia Rossiiskoi Federatsii* (*Bulletin of Economic Justice of the Russian Federation*) 73.

Pokrovskaya, A, *Soglashenie o prave, primenimom k chastnopravovym otnosheniyam, oslozhnennym inostrannym elementom* (*Agreement on Law Applicable to Private Relations with Foreign Element*) (Dissertation for the obtainment of a degree of candidate of legal sciences, Moscow, 2006).

Polak, M, 'Recognition, Enforcement and Transformation of Foreign Proprietary Rights' in U Drobnig, H Snijders and E Zippro (eds), *Divergences of Property Law, an Obstacle to the Internal Market* (Munich, Sellier European Law Publishers, 2006) 126.

Popondopulo, V, 'Mezhdunarodnoe Chastnoe Pravo: Priroda i Tendentsii Razvitiya' ('Private International Law: Its Nature and Trends of Development') (2018) 2 *Russian Law Journal* 91.

R

Ral'ko, V, 'Nasledstvennye prava inostrannyh grazhdan v Rossijskoj Federacii' (Inheritance rights of foreign citizens in the Russian Federation) (2005) 4 *Notarius*.

Reithmann, C and Martiny, D (eds), *Internationales Vertragsrecht. Das internationale Privatrecht der Schuldverträge* (OttoSchmidt, 2010).

Rozenberg, M (ed), *Praktika Mezhdunarodnogo Kommercheskogo Arbitrazhnogo Suda pri TPP RF za 2001–2002 gg* (*Practice of the International Commercial Arbitration Court of the Russian Chamber of Industry and Commerce for 2001–2002*) (Moscow, Statut, 2004).

—— *Praktika Mezhdunarodnogo Kommercheskogo Arbitrazhnogo Suda pri TPP RF za 1999–2000 gg* (*Practice of the International Commercial Arbitration Court of the Russian Chamber of Industry and Commerce for 1999–2000*) (Moscow, Statut, 2002).

—— *Praktika Mezhdunarodnogo Kommercheskogo Arbitrazhnogo Suda pri TPP RF za 1996–1997 gg* (*Practice of the International Commercial Arbitration Court of the Russian Chamber of Industry and Commerce for 1996–1997*) (Moscow, International Center of Financial-Economic Development, 1998).

Rozhdestvensky, A, *Dva Etyuda* (*Two Sketches*) (Moscow, Snegireva Publishing House, 1916).

Rubanov, A, '"Avtonomia Voli" v Mezhdunarodnom Chastnom Prave Kak Teoretichestkaya Problema' ('"Party Autonomy" in International Private Law as a Theoretical Problem') (1986) *Sovetskiy Ezhegodnik Mezhdunarodnogo Prava* (*Soviet Yearbook of International Law*) 214.

S

Sadikov, O, 'Die Kodifikation des Internationalen Privatrechts Rußlands' (2003) 67(2) *Rabels Zeitschrift für Ausländisches und Internationales Privatrecht* 318.

Samsonov, N, 'K Voprosy o Sudebnykh Obychayakh i Obyknoveniyakh' ('On Judicial Customs and Usages') (2020) 3 *Vestnik Grazhdanskogo Protsessa* 261.

Shakhnazarov, B, 'Neposredstvennoye Primenenie Pravil Mezhdunarodnykh Dogovorov pri Osyschestvlenii Zaschity Prav Subjektov Vnutrigosudarstvennykh i Transgranichnykh Otnoshenii' ('Direct Application of the Rules of International Agreements in the Implementation of the Protection of the Rights of Subjects of Domestic and Cross-Border Relations') (2020) 8 *Aktualnye Problemy Rossiiskogo Prava* 174.

Shirvindt, A, 'Reforming the Russian Civil Code – A Search for Better Law-Making' in J Basedow, H Fleischer and R Zimmermann (eds), *Legislators, Judges, and Professors* (Tübingen, Mohr Siebeck, 2016).

—— 'The Effectiveness of International Legal Harmonization through Soft Law (with a Focus on the UCP 600): Russian Report' in A Brandão, L Gama, G Saumier (eds), *The effectiveness of international legal harmonization through soft law (with a focus on the UCP 600)* General Report presented at the XXI Congress of the International Academy of Comparative Law (Intersentia, forthcoming 2024).

—— 'The UNIDROIT Principles as Reference for the Uniform Interpretation of National Laws: National Report for Russian Federation' in AM Garro and JA Moreno Rodríguez (eds), *Use of the UNIDROIT Principles to Interpret and Supplement Domestic Contract Law* (Cham, Springer, 2021).

Shtykova, N, 'Pravovaya Priroda Obychaev Delovogo Oborota v Grazhdanskom Oborote Rossii' ('Legal Nature of Business Customary Rules in Russian Civil Commerce') (2013) 4 *Rossijskaya Yustitsiya* 7.

Shugurova, I, 'Mezhdunarodnoye Chastnoye Pravo: Vzaimodeystviye Nauki i Praktiki' ('Private International Law: Interaction of Science and Practice') (2008) 5 *Mezhdunarodnoye Publichnoye i Chastnoye Pravo*.

Sinitsyn, S, 'Mezhdunarodnye Dogovory i Rossiiskoye Grazhdanskoe Zakonodatel'stvo: k Structure i Sisteme Sovremennogo Prava (chast' 1)' ('International Agreements and Russian Civil Laws: on the Modern Law Structure and System (Part 1)') (2021) 2 *Mezhdunarodnoe Publichnoe i Chastsnoye Pravo* 23.

Skoryukin, A, '*Yuridicheskie riski zaloga s inostrannym elementom*' ('Legal Risks of Pledge with a Foreign Element') (2016) 1 *Yuridicheskaya rabota v kreditnoj kooperacii* (*Legal Work in Credit Institutions*), http://futurebanking.ru/reglamentbank/article/3510.

Skvortsov, OY, Savranskiy, MY and Sevastyanov, GV (eds), *Mezhdunarodnyi Kommercheskiy Arbitrazh (International Commercial Arbitration)*, 2nd edn (Treteyskiy sud, Statut, 2018).

Solomon, D, 'The Private International Law of Contracts in Europe: Advances and Retreats' (2008) 82 *Tulane Law review* 1709.

Sonnentag, M, 'Renvoi' in J Basedow, G. Ruehl, F Ferrari and PM Asensio (eds), *Encyclopedia of Private International Law* Vol 2 (Cheltenham, Edward Elgar Publishing, 2017) 1537.

—— *Der Renvoi im Internationalen Privatrecht* (Tübingen, Mohr Siebeck, 2001).

Sukhanov, EA, *Veshchnoe pravo: Nauchno-poznavatel'nyj ocherk* (*Property Law: A Scientific and Educational Essay*) (Moscow, Statut, 2017).

—— (ed), *Rossiyskoe Grazhdanskoe Pravo: Uchebnik* (*Russian Civil Law: Textbook*), Vol I (Moscow, Statut, 2011).

Symeonides, S, 'Party Autonomy and Private-Law Making in Private International Law: The Lex Mercatoria that Isn't' in *Festschrift für Konstantinos D. Kerameus 1397–1423* (Athens/Brussels, Ant. N Sakkoulas & Bruylant Publishers, 2009).

T

Taribo, E, *Sudebnyj Konstitutsionnyi Normokontrol': Osmysleniye Rossiiskogo Opyta* (*Normative Control of Constitutional Court: Understanding of Russian Experience*) (Moscow, Norma, 2018).

Thoma, I, 'Public Policy (Ordre Public)' in J Basedow, G. Ruehl, F Ferrari and PM Asensio (eds), *Encyclopedia of Private International Law* Vol 2 (Cheltenham, Edward Elgar Publishing, 2017) 1453.

Tolstykh, V, *Mezhdunarodnoe chastnoe parvo: kollizionnoe regulirovanie* (*Private International Law: Conflict of Laws Regulation*) (Izd-vo R. Aslanova IU͡ridicheskiĭ ts͡entr Press, 2004).

Tretyakov, S, *Yuridicheskaya Priroda Avtonomii Voli v Mezhdunarodnom Chastnom Prave* (*Legal Nature of Party Autonomy in International Private Law*) (Dissertation for the obtainment of a degree of candidate of legal sciences, Moscow, 2003).

Trigubovich, N, *Avtonomia voli v mexhfunarodnom chastnom prave* (*Party Autonomy in Private International Law*) (Dissertation for the obtainment of a degree of Candidate of Legal Sciences, Saratov, 1999).

U

Usacheva, K, *Vozvrashchenie poluchennogo kak posledstvie rastorzheniya narushennogo dogovora: normoobrazuyushchie faktory i ih sootnoshenie pri reshenii konkretnyh voprosov (Unwinding as a Consequence of the Termination of the Violated Contract: Norm-Forming Factors and Their Correlation in Solving Specific Issues)* (Moscow, Infotropik, 2020).

V

Vereschagin, A, 'O Proiskhozdenii Rossiiskoi Sudebnoi Sistemy i ee Persepktivakh' ('Russian Judicial System: Roots and Prospects') (2019) 4 *Zakon* 54.

Vilkova, N, *Dogovornoe pravo v mezhdunarodnom oborote (Contract Law in International Context)* (Moscow, Statut, 2004).

—— 'Rol' MKAS pri TPP RF v Stanovlenii I razvitii sovremennogo kollizionnogo regulirovaniya dogovornykh otnosheniy s inostrannym elementom' ('The Role of MKAS of the Russian Chamber of Commerce and Industry in the Creation and Development of Modern Conflict of Law Regulation of Contractual Relations with Foreign Element') in A Komarov (ed), *Mezhdunarodniy Kommercheskiy Arbitrazh: Sovremennie Problemy i Resheniya: Sbornik Statey k 75-letiyu Mezhdunarodnogo Kommercheskogo Arbitrazhnogo Suda pri Torgovo-Promyshlennoy Palate Rossiyskoy Federatsii Federatsii* (*International Commercial Arbitration: Contemporary Problems and Solutions: Collection of Articles for the 75th Anniversary of MKAS of the Russian Chamber of Commerce and Industry of the Russian Federation*) (Moscow, Statut, 2007).

Vischer, F, Huber, L, Oser, D, *Internationales Vertragsrecht*, 2nd edn (Bern, Vischer, 2000).

Vogenauer, S (ed), *Commentary on the UNIDROIT Principles of International Commercial Contracts (PICC)*, 2nd edn (Oxford, Oxford University Press, 2015).

Vorobieva, O, *Private International Law in Russia* (Alphen aan den Rijn, Kluwer Law International BV, 2012).

Voytovich, E, 'Nasledovanie obyazatel'noj doli v mezhdunarodnom chastnom prave' ('Inheritance of a Compulsory Portion in Private International Law') (2018) 3 *Nasledstvennoe pravo* 42.

W

Wedemann, F, 'Der Begriff der Gesellschaft im Internationalen Privatrecht. Neue Herausforderungen durch den entrepreneur individual à responsabilité limitée' (2011) 75 *The Rabel Journal of Comparative and International Private Law* 541.

Wolff, M, *Private International Law*, 2nd edn (Oxford, Clarendon Press, 1950).

Y

Yurova, N, *Mezhdunarodnoye Grazhdanskoye Protsessual'noye Pravo: Teoreticheskiye Osnovy Implementatsii Norm v Pravovoy Sisteme Rossiiskoy Federatsii* (*International Civil Procedure Law: Theoretical Grounds of Implementation of Norms in the Legal System of the Russian Federation*) (Moscow, Wolters Kluwer, 2008).

Z

Zaphiriou, G, *The Transfer of Chattels in Private International Law: A Comparative Study* (University of London, The Athlone Press, 1956).

Zasemkova O, 'Mezhdunarodnoe Chastnoe Pravo v XXI Veke: Sovremennye Vyzovy I Perspektivy Razvitiya' ('Private International Law in the 21st Century: Contemporary Challenges and Development Prospects') (2019) 11 *Lex Russica* 30.

Zhiltsov, A, 'Primenenie Razdela VI Chasti Tretiey GK RF v Praktike MKAS pri TPP RF' ('Application of Section VI of Part III of the Civil Code of the Russian Federation in Practice of the ICAC at the Chamber of Commerce and Industry of the Russian Federation') (2014) 2 *Vestnik Mezhdunarodnogo Kommercheskogo Arbitrazha* 13.

—— 'Obzor praktiki MKAS pri TPP RF za 2019 god: obschaya kharakteristika i kollizionnye voprosy' ('Review of the Practice of ICAC at the CCI of the RF for 2019: General Characteristics and Choice of Law Questions') (2021) 8 *Arbitrazh and Civil Procedure* 18.

—— 'K Voprosy o Tselesoobraznosti Ratifikatsii Konventsii o Pravovoi Pomoschi i Pravovykh Otnosheniyakh po Grazhdankim, Semeinym i Ugolovnym Delam of 7 October 2002 (Kishinevskoi Konventsii)' ('On the Issue of Practicability of Ratification of the Convention on Legal Assistance and Legal Relations in Civil, Family and Criminal Matters of 7 October 2002 (the Kishinev Convention)') (2021) 8 *Jurist* 52.

Zhuikov, V, 'Rossiyskoe Zakonodatel'stvo i Mezhdunarodnoe Pravo: Problemy Vzaimodeystviya na Osnove Konstitutsii Rossiyskoy Federatsii' ('Russian Legislation and International Law: Interaction on the Basis of the Russian Constitution') (2020) 3 *Zakon* 115.

Zhuikov, V, Alekseeva, LB and Lukashuk, II (eds), *Mezhdunarodnye Normy o Pravakh Cheloveka i Primenenie ikh Sudami Rossiyskoy Federatsii* (*International Norms on Human Rights and their Application by Russian Courts*) (Moscow, Prava cheloveka, 1996).

Zor'kyn, V (ed), *Kommentarij k Konstitutsii Rossiyskoy Federatsii* (*Commentary to the Constitution of the Russian Federation*), 2nd edn (Moscow, Norma, 2011).

Zvekov, V, *Obyazatel'stva vsledstvie prichineniya vreda v kollizionnom prave* (*Conflict of Laws of Torts*) (Moscow, Wolters Kluwer Russia, 2007).

Zykin, IS, 'Commentary to Article 1210 of the Civil Code' in A Makovsky and EA Sukhanov (eds), *Kommentariy k Chasti Tretiey Grazhdanskogo Kodeksa Rossiyskoy Federatsii* (*Commentary to Part III of the Civil Code of the Russian Federation*) (Moscow, Yurist, 2002) 429.

—— *Vneshneekonomicheskie Operatsii: Pravo i Praktika* (*Foreign Economic Operation: Law and Practice*) (Moscow, International Relations Publishers, 1994).

Zykin, IS, Asoskov, A, and Zhiltsov, A (eds), *Kommentarij k razdelu VI 'Mezhdunarodnoe chastnoe pravo' chasti tret'ej Grazhdanskogo kodeksa Rossijskoj Federacii (postatejnyj)* (*Article-by-Article Commentary on Division VI 'Private International Law' of Part Three of the Civil Code of the Russian Federation*) (Moscow, Statut, 2021).

INDEX

www.ingramcontent.com/pod-product-compliance
Ingram Content Group UK Ltd.
Pitfield, Milton Keynes, MK11 3LW, UK
UKHW020811290926
15470UKWH00003B/1095

9 781509 964314